Kurt Weill
The Threepenny Opera

Edited by
STEPHEN HINTON

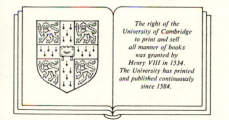

The right of the
University of Cambridge
to print and sell
all manner of books
was granted by
Henry VIII in 1534.
The University has printed
and published continuously
since 1584.

CAMBRIDGE UNIVERSITY PRESS

Cambridge
New York   Port Chester
Melbourne   Sydney

Published by the Press Syndicate of the University of Cambridge
The Pitt Building, Trumpington Street, Cambridge CB2 1RP
40 West 20th Street, New York NY 10011, USA
10 Stamford Road, Oakleigh, Melbourne 3166, Australia

First published 1990

Printed in Great Britain at the University Press, Cambridge

This Handbook is written and published with the assistance of the
Kurt Weill Foundation for Music

British Library cataloguing in publication data
Kurt Weill: The Threepenny Opera. – (Cambridge opera
handbooks).
1. German music. Weill, Kurt, 1900–1950
I. Hinton, Stephen
780'.92'4

Library of Congress cataloguing in publication data applied for

ISBN 0 521 33026 2 hard covers
ISBN 0 521 33888 3 paperback

In memory of Carl Dahlhaus (1928–1989)

Contents

Illustrations

ix

General preface

This is a series of studies of individual operas, written for the serious opera-goer or record-collector as well as the student or scholar. Each volume has three main concerns. The first is historical: to describe the genesis of the work, its sources or its relation to literary prototypes, the collaboration between librettist and composer, and the first performance and subsequent stage history. This history is itself a record of changing attitudes towards the work, and an index of general changes of taste. The second is analytical and it is grounded in a very full synopsis which considers the opera as a structure of musical and dramatic effects. In most volumes there is also a musical analysis of a section of the score, showing how the music serves or makes the drama. The analysis, like the history, naturally raises questions of interpretation, and the third concern of each volume is to show how critical writing about an opera, like production and performance, can direct or distort appreciation of its structural elements. Some conflict of interpretation is an inevitable part of this account; editors of the handbooks reflect this – by citing classic statements, by commissioning new essays, by taking up their own critical position. A final section gives a select bibliography, a discography and guides to other sources.

Preface

If popularity breeds myths, then the enduringly popular *Threepenny Opera* has surely engendered its fair share. The following quotation, with its blend of truth, half-truth and fond fabrication, is a typical example. It is taken from an article published in British Airways' in-flight magazine, *High Life*, in celebration of the city of Berlin's 750th anniversary. In the 1920s, it says,

> Prussian discipline was replaced by the exuberance of the 'Mad Twenties'. Berlin emerged as the country's first truly cosmopolitan centre, and a permissive air pervaded the city. These were the 'divinely decadent days' of Christopher Isherwood's Sally Bowles. Theatre and cabarets flourished; jazz was imported from America; modern painters and poets attracted attention with radical ideas; film directors produced classics like the *Blue Angel*; composer-writers like Bertold [sic] Brecht gave the world exciting works like *The Threepenny Opera*. For an all-too-brief period Berlin became the most creative city in Europe. (*High Life*, May 1987, p. 12)

For better or for worse, *The Threepenny Opera* has become synonymous with the nostalgic, clichéd image of the 'Mad Twenties'. As for Brecht being the work's composer, Brecht himself was partly responsible for that myth when he remarked that he 'dictated to Weill, bar by bar, by whistling and above all performing'. Yet it is not just Brecht and popular imagination that leave his other collaborators out of the reckoning. In 1960, Siegfried Unseld, director of the West German publishers Suhrkamp, edited a volume entitled *Brechts Dreigroschenbuch*, in which he reprinted the various incarnations of the 'Threepenny' theme (opera libretto, film scenario, 'trial' and, in subsequent editions, the novel) as well as some of the more substantial critical writings on the opera. Twenty-five years later the same publishers brought out *Brechts Dreigroschenoper* (ed. Werner Hecht, Frankfurt/Main, 1985). Why only Brecht? In one respect the latter volume was only conforming with publishing formalities: Hecht's is one of a series of books which present source materials and other writings relating to Brecht's major theatrical works. Yet the title also reflects a bias: the section 'concerning the music' constitutes only a tenth of that particular book's contents.

In going to the other extreme and naming just Weill on the cover, it could also be argued that the present volume is similarly conforming with formalities dictated by the series in which it appears. If it nonetheless reflects a bias, it is also at pains to correct one. By concentrating on Brecht's contribution, much of the previous literature on *The Threepenny Opera* has tended to make light of Weill's side of the collaboration, thereby passing up an opportunity, which the Cambridge Opera Handbook series now affords, to consider the work in its generic context, as 'opera'.

Of course *The Threepenny Opera*'s claim to being a 'real' opera is scarcely greater than that of the work on which it is based, *The Beggar's Opera*. Each is *sui generis*. Each stands at a remove from the traditional opera of its age while, at the same time, anticipating future developments in the genre. *The Beggar's Opera* was at once a send-up of the 'outlandish' *opera seria* and an adumbration of the later *Singspiel*. By the same token, *The Threepenny Opera* can be seen as 'the most consistent reaction to Wagner', to quote Weill's own description, as well as an important model for later innovations in twentieth-century music theatre, not least the American musical (see chapter 4 on '*The Threepenny Opera* in America'). In fact, the generic question could be said to form the very substance of the piece. As Weill wrote, it 'presented us with the opportunity to make "opera" the subject matter for an evening in the theatre'.

In covering 'history, analysis and criticism', the present volume largely follows the guidelines for the series laid down in the general preface. Partly because of *The Threepenny Opera*'s hybrid nature, however, it did not always prove either possible or desirable to make neat distinctions between these three concerns. They frequently overlap. In dealing with the genesis, for example, chapter 2 traces a gradual transformation of borrowed and original material which continued from the time of the work's inception in the winter of 1927/28 until shortly before Brecht's death in 1956. The nature of the sources and the revisions – as well as ignorance of them – has had a direct bearing on the critical postures discussed in later chapters.

The work's structure also necessitated an analytical approach different from other volumes in the series. Chapter 1, a hitherto unpublished synopsis of the plot written by Brecht himself, is intended among other things as a quick reference guide to the sequence of

a

individual numbers. Rather than analyse these numbers individually, however, the chapter on 'Motifs, tags and related matters' by David Drew draws attention to the way in which the work as a whole is unified by long-range thematic connections. Analytical issues of a more local kind are addressed in several of the other chapters. Of the previously published material reprinted here, the essays by Theodor W. Adorno, Ernst Bloch and Walter Benjamin appear for the first time in English translation.

I should like to thank all the contributors to this book, not least for their patience during its protracted genesis. Thanks are also due to the following institutions and their staff: the Bertolt Brecht Archive, Berlin (GDR) ; the Nationalbibliothek, Universal Edition and the Stadtbibliothek, Vienna; the Weill-Lenya Research Center, New York; and the Weill/Lenya Archive at Yale University. Research expenses were funded in part with a grant from the Kurt Weill Foundation for Music. I gratefully acknowledge the generous support and encouragement of the Foundation's director and archivist, David Farneth, and its president, Kim Kowalke. Steve Giles and Jürgen Schebera helped with the collation of primary sources. Michael Zimmermann critically scrutinized large portions of the manuscript. I am indebted, above all, to Linda Holt, who collaborated in research and made countless editorial suggestions.

Stephen Hinton
Berlin–Schöneberg

Acknowledgements

The publishers gratefully acknowledge permission to reprint the following: Chapter 1 by permission of Barbara Brecht-Schall (© Stefan Brecht 1989. All rights reserved by Suhrkamp Verlag Frankfurt/Main). Chapter 5: Bertolt Brecht, 'Die Dreigroschenoper', © Suhrkamp Verlag Frankfurt/Main (1984); chapter 8: Theodor W. Adorno, 'Zur "Dreigroschenoper"', © Suhrkamp Verlag Frankfurt/Main (1984); chapter 9: Ernst Bloch, 'Zur "Drei-groschenoper"', © Suhrkamp Verlag Frankfurt/Main (1962); chapter 11: Walter Benjamin, 'L'Opéra de Quat'Sous' © Suhrkamp Verlag Frankfurt/Main (1989). Chapter 6 (*The Times* © *Times* Newspaper Ltd., 1928. *The Times*' Berlin Correspondent, Mr. A. Ebbutt); chapter 12 (*Music Review*); chapter 13 ('Motifs, tags, and related matters' © David Drew 1989). Figure 3 by permission of the Kurt Weill Foundation of Music; figure 8 by permission of the Nationalbibliothek Vienna; figure 9 by permission of the Bertolt Brecht Archive; figures 13–17 by permission of the Weill-Lenya Research Center, New York; figure 18 courtesy of Jürgen Schebera, Berlin (GDR); figure 19 by permission of the Theatermuseum der Universität zu Köln.

Music examples in chapters 2 and 13 reproduced from Weill, *Die Dreigroschenoper*, copyright 1928 by Universal Edition A. G., Wien. Copyright renewed.
Copyright assigned to European American Music Corporation, all rights reserved. Used by permission of European American Music Corporation.

SYNOPSIS

1 *Brecht's narration for a concert version of 'Die Dreigroschenoper'*

EDITED AND TRANSLATED BY STEPHEN HINTON

You are about to hear an opera for beggars. Since this opera was intended to be as splendid as only beggars can imagine, and yet cheap enough for beggars to be able to watch, it is called the THREEPENNY OPERA.

No.1 OVERTURE

London 1730: A fair in Soho. The beggars are begging, the thieves thieving, the whores whoring. A ballad singer sings the Ballad of Mac the Knife, the notorious bandit, who commits his countless misdeeds without ever being caught.

No.2 THE BALLAD OF MAC THE KNIFE
(DIE MORITAT VON MACKIE MESSER)

[Act I]

To combat the increasing callousness of mankind Jonathan Jeremiah Peachum, a man of business, has opened a shop where the poorest of the poor could acquire the sort of appearance that could still touch the hardest of hearts. For this reason he is called the king of the massed beggars of London. Hear now his Morning Hymn.

No.3 PEACHUM'S MORNING HYMN
(MORGENCHORAL DES PEACHUM)

Jonathan Peachum learns from his wife that his daughter Polly is having a curious relationship with a young man. Having gathered that his daughter's beloved is the notorious gang leader Mac the Knife in person, he tells his outraged wife.

No.4 INSTEAD-OF SONG
(ANSTATT DASS-SONG)

Five o'clock the next afternoon. Deep in the heart of Soho the bandit Mac the Knife is celebrating his marriage to Polly Peachum,

1

daughter of the beggar king. We are in a stable fitted out with exclusive furnishings, which Mac the Knife's gang have stolen.

No. 5 WEDDING SONG
(HOCHZEITSLIED)

But Mac is not happy with the work of his gang. It's the work of apprentices, not of grown men. To clear the air and liven things up a little, Polly volunteers to sing a song.

No. 6 PIRATE JENNY
(SEERÄUBERJENNY)

At this point there appears London's most senior police commissioner, Brown. The bandits call him Tiger Brown. He is a good friend of Mac the Knife, whose evil deeds he neither sees nor hears. Tiger Brown has come to congratulate Mac the Knife on his wedding.

No. 7 CANNON SONG
(KANONEN-SONG)

Tiger Brown quickly takes his leave. He still has preparations to make for the coronation celebrations which are to take place the following day. Once the bandits have also left, the wedding night begins. Hear now Polly and Mac's *Liebeslied*.

No. 8 LOVE SONG
(LIEBESLIED)

Back in Peachum's outfitting shop for beggars. For Peachum, who knows how hard the world can be, the loss of his daughter spells utter ruin. Polly is received by her parents.

No. 9 BARBARA SONG

No. 10 FIRST THREEPENNY FINALE
(ERSTES DREIGROSCHENFINALE)

[Act II]

Jonathan Peachum has hit on a good idea. He wants to hand Mackie over to the sheriff. Mrs Peachum suspects that he is hiding out in Turnbridge with his whores. She wants to bribe the girls so that they give the bandit away. Polly, however, springs to Mac's defence and points out that the police commissioner is his best friend.

Polly informs Macheath of the danger, and advises him to flee.

During his absence she will continue to run the business as captain of the gang. They take leave of each other.

No. 11a MELODRAMA
(MELODRAM)

No. 11b POLLY'S SONG
(POLLYS LIED)

[No. 12 THE BALLAD OF SEXUAL DEPENDENCY]
(DIE BALLADE VON DER SEXUELLEN HÖRIGKEIT)

The coronation bells had not yet died down. Instead of fleeing to Highgate Moor as intended, Mac the Knife is sitting with the whores of Turnbridge. It is Thursday evening. Mackie and the whore Jenny remember in a song the pleasant hours they have spent together.

No. 13 PIMPS' BALLAD
(ZUHÄLTERBALLADE)

While Mac was singing, Jenny stood at the window and gave a signal to the constable. Thus the famous Mac the Knife, betrayed by the whores, fell into the hands of the police and was put behind bars in the Old Bailey. Tiger Brown is very unhappy at the fact that he could have spared his friend the trouble.

MAC: Judge for yourselves, Gentlemen, if you will,
My life right now's a bloody pain,
When still young, I took the bitter pill,
Only he in comfort takes the strain.

No. 14 THE BALLAD OF THE EASY LIFE
(DIE BALLADE VOM ANGENEHMEN LEBEN)

Lucy and Polly meet in front of Mac's prison. Lucy is the daughter of police commissioner Brown; she, too, is secretly married to Mac the Knife.

No. 15 JEALOUSY DUET
(EIFERSUCHTSDUETT)

The quarrel quickly finds a conclusion. Mrs Peachum appears, clips Polly round the ear and drags her off. Lucy stands her ground.
    Mac succeeds [with Lucy's help] in escaping from prison. He makes a beeline for the whores. When Peachum wishes to pay him a visit he finds not Mackie but police commissioner Brown. In order to frighten him about the consequences of his carelessness, Peachum

tells the sheriff a story [about Queen Semiramis] with an obvious reference to the coronation celebrations taking place the next day.

Mac sings with [Mrs Peachum] the parable about what keeps man alive.

No. 16 SECOND THREEPENNY FINALE
(ZWEITES DREIGROSCHENFINALE)

[Act III]

That same night Peachum prepares to set off. His intention is to disturb the coronation procession with a demonstration of misery and squalor. He delivers a speech to his beggars.

Police commissioner Brown arrests the beggar king. The latter, however, warns him about being overhasty.

No. 17 THE SONG OF THE INSUFFICIENCY OF HUMAN ENDEAVOUR
(DAS LIED VON DER UNZULÄNGLICHKEIT MENSCHLICHEN STREBENS)

No. 18 SOLOMON SONG
(SALOMON-SONG)

Peachum has the police commissioner in the palm of his hand. He blackmails him, thus forcing his release. Moreover, he again puts Brown on the trail of Macheath, whom the whores have betrayed for a second time. Mac is once more put in jail in chains; once more he tries, by means of bribery, to escape.

No. 19 CALL FROM THE GRAVE
(RUF AUS DER GRUFT)

The bells of Westminster are ringing. It is just before six o'clock. All of Mac the Knife's acquaintances have appeared in the prison to bid him farewell as he is taken to the gallows. Beforehand Mackie begs everyone for forgiveness.

No. 20 EPITAPH
(GRABSCHRIFT)

Unlike the course of events in real life, however, the Threepenny Opera has a happy end. The King's mounted messenger saves Mackie from the gallows. The gratification of all concerned is expressed in the following verses.

No. 20a WALK TO THE GALLOWS
(GANG ZUM GALGEN)

Now, ladies and gentlemen, in our show
We should witness Mac's hanging,
For in the Christian world, as well you know,
Nothing comes from nothing.

But lest you might be tempted
To accuse us of some crass collusion
Mac will now be exempted
We offer instead an alternative conclusion.

Mercy, it's said, tempers justice
In opera, that's par for the course,
So let's have the theory in practice
And behold the King's envoy – on a horse.

No. 21 THIRD THREEPENNY FINALE
(DRITTES DREIGROSCHENFINALE)

CHORALE
(SCHLUSSGESANG)

Editorial note

The full synopsis normally expected in the Handbook series – an
account, that is, of the music's contribution to the unfolding of the
drama and the delineation of character – represents a mould of
conventional coherence which *The Threepenny Opera* emphatically
resists. The very impossibility of such a synopsis is, in fact, a key to
the work's significance. In accordance with Brecht's theory of Epic
Theatre, the musical and dramatic effects are not calculated to
constitute an overall unified structure. As one of several discrete
elements, the music neither serves nor makes the drama by carrying
the action forward (except in the parodic recitative in the third finale).
Rather, it stops the action in its tracks. To that extent it can be likened
to Handelian *opera seria*. Unlike in Handel, however, the music does
not contribute towards dramatic characterization in any general or
substantial way. If the music unfolds on a large scale, it does so as
an autonomous structure (as David Drew demonstrates in chapter 13).
When singing, the protagonists 'adopt attitudes' rather than tell us
anything about their true character or emotions, which strictly
speaking they do not possess, at least in any conventional sense. The
relationship between words and music is deliberately untautological
and ambiguous: the words can say one thing, the music something

else. Writing about the 'Zuhälterballade', Weill remarked: 'The charm of the piece rests precisely in the fact that a rather risqué text (not, by the way, as offensive as a lot of operetta texts) is set to music in a gentle, pleasant way' (cf. p. 188). The words put into the mouths of the singers are frequently in quotation marks, as it were. In the 'Barbarasong', for example, in which Polly 'gives her parents to understand that she has married the bandit Macheath', the scruff celebrated as the successful suitor can hardly pass for her nattily clad spouse (cf. p. 36). With its juxtaposition of narrative text, spoken dialogue and musical numbers, *The Threepenny Opera* is a montage, not an organic construction. For this reason it is uncommonly, if not intrinsically, susceptible to revision and rearrangement, as the account of the genesis in chapter 2 shows. It has even proved possible for characters to pilfer one another's material and create a new montage. At some point during the initial run of the Berlin première, for example, Lucy temporarily borrowed Polly's 'Barbarasong'; in his revised version of 1931 Brecht robbed Mrs Peachum of her lines in the second finale and gave them to Jenny instead; and Jenny's appropriation of 'Seeräuberjenny' (a practice started in G. W. Pabst's 1930 film) has become so habitual as to engender the widespread belief that she, rather than Polly, is the song's rightful owner.

Many of the narrator's passages in this hitherto unpublished concert version of *Die Dreigroschenoper* were lifted directly from the original stage work, where they also serve as an 'epic' summary of the action. In the 1928 libretto, which grew out of the original production, producers are instructed to project these connecting texts on to two large screens on either side of the stage, whereas in the 1931 'literary' edition, in which Brecht removed much of the stage business, no such instruction appears. Consequently, productions relying on this revised version of the work tend to assume that the connecting texts are to be spoken by a conférencier rather than appear as written captions in the manner of a silent film.

The present translation is abridged, containing as it does just the passages for narrator. The original document, which is held in the Bertolt Brecht Archive (BBA 1013), also reproduces the readily available texts of the musical numbers as well as slices of dialogue from the stage version. (The dialogue is interpolated at the following points: after no. 4, before nos. 6 and 7, before no. 9, in the middle of the narration before no. 11a, before nos. 13, 14 and 15, before the announcements of nos. 16 and 17, and before no. 20.) Although the typescript contains emendations in Brecht's hand, neither the extent

of his involvement in its creation nor the typescript's date has yet
been ascertained with any certainty. Nor is it clear what prompted
it in the first place. Brecht may well have had in mind less a live concert
performance than a gramophone recording, as with the short connecting texts he wrote in 1930 (published in Werner Hecht, ed.,
Brechts Dreigroschenoper, Frankfurt/Main, 1985, pp. 35f.). The
addition of new, post-1945 texts after nos. 5 and 14 points to a late
date, though certainly not later than 1956, the year of Brecht's death
(the texts in question are 'Der neue Kanonensong' and 'Die Ballade
vom angenehmen Leben der Hitlersatrapen', both of which are
printed in *Brechts Dreigroschenoper*, cited above, and also as part
of the appendix to Manheim and Willett's translation). Following the
change Brecht made in 1931, Jenny (rather than Mrs Peachum) shares
the second finale with Mac. At the same time there are signs that the
text was initially based on the 1928 libretto rather than any later
versions. Whereas the opening paragraph before no. 1 (retained for
the 1930 gramophone narration) was cut in 1931 for the *Versuche* and
in all subsequent editions, the following items, whose texts were not
published until 1931, are conspicuous by their absence: no. 12 in its
entirety, the second verse of no. 15, and a large part of Macheath's
valedictory speech before No. 20. The date of the action, '1730', is
a mystery (except for its proximity to Gay), since the première set the
work in the nineteenth century and the printed editions give no date
at all.

2 'Matters of intellectual property': the sources and genesis of 'Die Dreigroschenoper'

STEPHEN HINTON

Introduction

Of one thing we can be certain: when *Die Dreigroschenoper* opened in Berlin at the Theater am Schiffbauerdamm on 31 August 1928, the audience was left in no doubt as to the work's multiple authorship. The playbill indicated quite clearly the handful of sources and authors on which this, one of the great conflations of theatrical history, had liberally drawn: '*Die Dreigroschenoper* (The Beggar's Opera). A play with music in one prelude and 8 scenes after the English of John Gay. (Interpolated ballads by François Villon and Rudyard Kipling.) Translation: Elisabeth Hauptmann. Adaptation: Brecht. Music: Kurt Weill.' (See plate 1.)

A similar description was used in the 1929 edition of *Reclams Opernführer* (ed. G. R. Kruse), except that Weill was named as the principal author, with Brecht appearing last in the credits − after Gay, Villon and Kipling − as author rather than adaptor. Short biographical notes on all four men were also provided. For the first printed libretto, described below, the interpolated ballads and their creators were omitted; Weill was responsible for the music, Brecht for the 'German adaptation', and Elisabeth Hauptmann for the translation. All subsequent editions of the text designate Brecht alone as author, excluding on their title page any reference to the sources (except *GBF*, cited below), and merely allot Hauptmann and Weill fine-print credits as 'collaborators' (*Mitarbeiter*).

It might seem unusually self-effacing of Brecht initially to have cast himself in the role of mere adaptor, and hence inappropriate, even churlish, for anyone to accuse him of an 'offence' he had openly admitted, namely plagiarism. Many hands were at work − that much was clear from the outset. Even so, the list of co-authors did not end with those cited above, which is why the charge of plagiarism was in fact levelled. Brecht had omitted to acknowledge the translator of

9

Theater am Schiffbauerdamm

Direktion: Ernst Josef Aufricht

Die Dreigroschenoper

⟨The Beggars Opera⟩

Ein Stück mit Musik in einem Vorspiel und 8 Bildern nach dem
Englischen des John Gay.

⟨Eingelegte Balladen von François Villon und Rudyard Kipling⟩

Übersetzung: Elisabeth Hauptmann
Bearbeitung: Brecht
Musik: Kurt Weill
Regie: Erich Engel
Bühnenbild: Caspar Neher
Musikalische Leitung: Theo Makeben
Kapelle: Lewis Ruth Band.

P e r s o n e n :

Jonathan Peachum, Chef einer Bettlerplatte Erich Ponto
Frau Peachum . . . . Rosa Valetti
Polly, ihre Tochter . . . . Roma Bahn
Macheath, Chef einer Platte von Straßen-
banditen . . . . Harald Paulsen
Brown, Polizeichef von London . . . . Kurt Gerron
Lucy, seine Tochter . . . . Kate Kühl
Trauerweidenwalter . . . . Ernst Rotmund
Münzmatthias . . . . Karl Hannemann
Hakenfingerjakob . . . . Manfred Fürst
Sägerobert . . . . Josef Bunzel
Jimmie . . . . Werner Maschmeyer
Ede . . . . Albert Venohr

Filch, einer von Peachums Bettlern . . . Naphtali Lehrmann
Smith, Konstabler. . . . . Ernst Busch

Huren . . . . {Kuffner
Jeckels
Helmke
Kliesch u. a.

Bettler . . . . {Schiskaja
Ritter
Heimsoth u. a.

Banditen, Huren, Bettler, Konstabler, Volk.
⟨Ort der Handlung: London.⟩
Eine kleine Pause nach dem 3. Bild.
Große Pause nach dem 6. Bild.
Die Walzen des Leierkastens wurden hergestellt
in der Fabrik Bacigalupo.

1 Playbill of the Berlin première, Theater am Schiffbauerdamm,
31 August 1928

the interpolated Villon ballads, K. L. Ammer (pseudonym for Klaus Klammer), provoking as a result the intervention of one of the Weimar Republic's chief theatre critics, Alfred Kerr. Kerr's chiding article, entitled 'Brecht's Copyright' and published in the *Berliner Tageblatt* on 3 May 1929, elicited from Brecht the notorious reply in which, having conceded that he 'unfortunately forgot to mention Ammer's name', he excused the oversight with reference to his 'fundamental laxity in matters of intellectual property'.[1] The exchange enjoyed the status of a minor public scandal, becoming the first of the many *causes célèbres The Threepenny Opera* has produced. The Viennese moralizer and aphorist Karl Kraus, for example, a sworn enemy of Kerr's, jumped to Brecht's defence, pronouncing that he had 'more originality in the little finger of the hand with which he took the twenty-five verses of Ammer's Villon translation than that Kerr who has found him out'.[2] Money − a likely reason for the oversight in the first place − was at stake. Initially ignorant of the illicit use of his intellectual property, Klammer managed in the end to secure an arrangement whereby he received 2½ per cent of all royalties from performances of *Die Dreigroschenoper* in the original German. Thanks to the work's phenomenal success, he eventually earned enough to purchase a small vineyard in the Viennese suburb of Grinzing, Austria's best-known wine-growing district, where he produced a wine which he christened 'Threepenny Tipple' (*Dreigroschentropfen*).[3]

That was not the only windfall Klammer enjoyed from the plagiarism scandal. Such was the demand for his volume of Villon translations that a reprint edition appeared in 1930. Brecht was invited to supply the foreword, which he did in the form of a sonnet, closing with a characteristically forthright tercet:

> Wo habt ihr Saures für drei Mark bekommen?
> Nehm jeder sich heraus, was er grad braucht!
> Ich selber hab mir was herausgenommen ...
>
> (It's sour be cheap; you pay three marks for it
> And what a lucky dip the buyer gets!
> In my own case it yielded quite a bit ...)[4]

More precisely: Brecht took over wholesale large chunks of Ammer's Villon translations in 'Ruf aus der Gruft' and 'Grabschrift'; more or less freely adapted them in the 'Zuhälterballade', 'Die Ballade vom angenehmen Leben' and the 'Salomon-Song'; and conceivably left traces of Villon's influence in 'Die Moritat von Mackie Messer'.[5]

He also borrowed from himself: the texts of the 'Kanonen-Song', the 'Barbara-Song' and 'Seeräuberjenny' were written by Brecht and the latter two also set to music (by Brecht–Bruinier) many months before the idea of adapting Gay's *Beggar's Opera* had even arisen.[6]

Unsubstantiated legend has it that Karl Kraus made a creative contribution to the work in the form of an extra verse to the 'Eifersuchtsduett'.[7] If he did, which seems unlikely, the new material was almost certainly not performed at the première, since there is no evidence of the duet's acquiring its second verse until 1931; nor does Kraus seem to have claimed any remuneration for his rumoured (and unacknowledged) efforts. This particular portion of the work may indeed be bona fide Brecht. Yet there are others who plainly deserve their place on the roll call: the director, Erich Engel, and his assistants; the musical director, Theo Mackeben, and his musicians; and, last but not least, Caspar Neher, the set designer for the first production as well as several subsequent ones. All were instrumental in moulding a work that was not ready until literally a few hours before the curtain went up on that legendary opening night.

Nor, moreover, has the work been handed down to us in the original 1928 form. Weill and Brecht continued to make alterations even after the première. Most substantial were those made by Brecht (including the addition of that extra verse to the 'Eifersuchtsduett') for the first collected edition of his works, the *Versuche* (a term meaning 'Essay' in the dual sense of experiment and speculative attempt), published in 1931. Save for some minor modifications, it is this second, considerably revised version of *Die Dreigroschenoper* that is in circulation today, both in the original German and in countless translations.[8] The question of sources and genesis is, in short, an involved and intricate one, and the Ammer and Kraus anecdotes are just two of the many legends – some based on fact, some not – that continue to surround the work.

In the following discussion the documents cited, and identified by a grammalogue, are:

L   *The Beggar's Opera / Die Luden-Oper / Übersetzt von Elisabeth Hauptmann / Deutsche Bearbeitung: Bert Brecht. Musik: Kurt Weill.* Typescript prepared by Felix Bloch Erben in June 1928. Copy in Bertolt Brecht Archive (BBA 1782/1–66).

LE   Copy of *L* used by director Erich Engel, held in Bertolt Brecht Archive (BBA 2104/1–83).

LH   Copy of *L* used by Dr Halewicz, director's assistant. Also in Bertolt Brecht Archive (BBA 2106/1–146).

AS   *Die Dreigroschenoper.* Weill's autograph full score, completed in September 1928. Held in Stadtbibliothek Vienna.

T   *DIE DREIGROSCHENOPER / (Nach 'The Beggar's Opera' von John Gay) / von / Brecht / Musik von Weill.* Typescript used as the basis of *FE*. Held in the archives of Universal Edition Vienna (L1 UE 548).

FEP   *DIE DREIGROSCHENOPER / (Nach 'The Beggar's Opera' von John Gay) / von / BRECHT / MUSIK VON WEILL.* Galley proofs of *FE* with emendations by Weill and Brecht. Held in the archives of Universal Edition Vienna. Another copy in Bertolt Brecht Archive (BBA 1783/1−80).

FE   *Die Dreigroschenoper (The Beggar's Opera) / Ein Stück mit Musik in einem Vorspiel / nach dem Englischen des John Gay. / Übersetzt von Elisabeth Hauptmann. / Deutsche Bearbeitung von / BERT BRECHT / Musik von / KURT WEILL.* First edition of the libretto, published in an edition of 300 copies in October 1928 by Felix Bloch Erben and Universal Edition (UE 8850). Reprinted twice: 500 copies in November 1928 and another 500 in December 1929.

S   *Brecht / DIE SONGS DER / DREIGROSCHENOPER.* First edition of song texts, published in an edition of 10,000 copies in October 1928 by Gustav Kiepenheuer Verlag, Potsdam. Two reprints brought the total number of copies to 25,000.

PS   *KURT WEILL / Die Dreigroschenoper / (The Beggar's Opera) / Ein Stück mit Musik in einem Vorspiel und acht Bildern nach dem / Englischen des John Gay, übersetzt von Elisabeth Hauptmann / Deutsche Bearbeitung / von / BERT BRECHT / KLAVIERAUS-ZUG / (Norbert Gingold).* Piano vocal score, published in November 1928 by Universal Edition (UE 8851).

PCS   *Kurt Weill / DIE DREIGROSCHENOPER / (The Beggar's Opera) / Ein Stück mit Musik in einem Vorspiel und acht Bildern / nach dem Englischen des John Gay / übersetzt von Elisabeth Hauptmann / Deutsche Bearbeitung von Bert Brecht / Klavierdirektion.* Piano-conductor score, published in November 1928 as hire material by Universal Edition.

M   Copy of *PCS* together with the handwritten bandparts used by Theo Mackeben and the Lewis Ruth Band. Now in the possession of Mackeben's widow, Frau Loni Mackeben (West Berlin).

MFA   *DIE DREIGROSCHENOPER / VON / KURT WEILL.* Piano-vocal selection of 11 numbers published in 1929 by Ullstein-Verlag, Berlin, as No. 274 in the popular series *Musik für alle.*

VA   Copy of *FE* with Brecht's handwritten revisions for *V.* Held in the Bertolt Brecht Archive (BBA 1783/01−80).

V   *Die Dreigroschenoper.* In Bertolt Brecht, *Versuche*, iii (Berlin: Gustav Kiepenheuer Verlag, 1931), pp. 145−219. Also includes *ANMER-KUNGEN ZUR DREIGROSCHENOPER*; *DIE BEULE / EIN DREIGROSCHENFILM*; and *DER DREIGROSCHEN-PROZESS / (Ein soziologisches Experiment).*

C   'Pauv' Madam' Peachum!'. Autograph of one of the two additional chansons composed by Weill for the 1937 French production of *L'opéra de quat'sous*. Copy in the Weill–Lenya Research Center, New York.

BK   'Barbara Song' and 'Kanonensong'. Autograph of new piano-vocal arrangements made by Weill in 1942. Copy in Weill-Lenya Research Center, New York.

S2   *Bertolt Brecht / SONGS / AUS DER DREIGROSCHENOPER* (Berlin-Schöneberg: Gebrüder Weiss Verlag, 1949). New edition of song texts (incomplete), including post-1945 verses.

DO   *Die Dreigroschen-Oper*. Revised stage script prepared by Brecht and printed for distribution to theatres by Suhrkamp Verlag (Frankfurt/ Main, n.d. [1950]).

GW   *Die Dreigroschenoper*. In Bertolt Brecht, *Gesammelte Werke*, ii (Frankfurt/Main: Suhrkamp Verlag, 1967), pp. 394–486. Version by Brecht first published in *Stücke* (Frankfurt/Main, 1955).

PS2   New edition of *PS*, including 'Ballade von der sexuellen Hörigkeit', published in 1956 by Universal Edition (UE 8851).

FS   *KURT WEILL / DIE DREIGROSCHENOPER / Ein Stück mit Musik nach John Gays 'The Beggar's Opera' / von Elisabeth Hauptmann / Deutsche Bearbeitung von / BERT BRECHT*. Full score, edited by Karl Heinz Füssl. Published in 1972 by Universal Edition (Philharmonia No. 400).

MW   *The Threepenny Opera / after John Gay: The Beggar's Opera*. Trans. and ed. Ralph Manheim and John Willett, Bertolt Brecht, *Collected Plays*, vol. 2, ii (London, 1979).

GBF   *Die Dreigroschenoper / (Nach John Gays 'The Beggar's Opera')*. In Bertolt Brecht, *Grosse kommentierte Berliner und Frankfurter Ausgabe, Stücke 2*, ed. Jürgen Schebera (Frankfurt/Main and Berlin, GDR, 1988), pp. 229–322. Ostensibly the same as *V*.

Adapting *The Beggar's Opera*

The notion of adaptation admits of a wide variation of meaning. In the case of *The Threepenny Opera*, several major changes were made to the original, both additions and omissions, which have given the piece a complexion, purpose and message quite different from what started out as a literal translation of John Gay's *Beggar's Opera*, prepared in the winter months of 1927/28 by Brecht's diffident and devoted collaborator, Elisabeth Hauptmann. So much so that one commentator has observed that 'Brecht surreptitiously wrote a new piece'[9] – a remark which most certainly applies to Weill, who retained just one of the 69 popular melodies arranged by Johann Christoph Pepusch for *The Beggar's Opera*, the rest of the music being of his own invention.

The verbal matter of the piece – for which the American term 'book' is more appropriate than 'libretto' – underwent numerous reworkings before emerging as the version known today. But why the adaptation in the first place? In 1931, at a time of concentrated theoretical reflection, Brecht defined the piece retrospectively, in the *Versuche* edition (*V*), as 'an experiment in epic theatre'. And four years later, in 1935, he could look back on the 1928 production as 'the most successful demonstration of epic theatre'.[10] Yet the initial impulse for the adaptation appears to have been of a rather less experimental or theoretical nature. Brecht and Hauptmann were doubtless attracted, at least to begin with, by the prospect of repeating the extraordinary success that a revival of *The Beggar's Opera* had enjoyed in London a few years earlier. Frederic Austin's arrangement of the John Gay original, produced by Sir Nigel Playfair at the Lyric Theatre, Hammersmith, had opened on 5 June 1920 and run for a record-breaking 1,463 performances over a three-year period, eclipsing many times the previous record for a long-running show held by the first production of that work.[11] At the same time, Brecht had already shown an interest in adapting other people's work at a time when radical reinterpretations of classic plays were becoming fashionable. 'The art of vandalism', as W. E. Yuill has described it, was an integral part of Brecht's creative bent.[12] In 1923/24, assisted by Lion Feuchtwanger, he had already drawn heavily on another English play, Marlowe's *Edward II*, as the basis of his *Leben Eduards des Zweiten von England*, the première of which he directed himself in Munich in March 1924. Later, in the early 1950s, his interest in Elizabethan drama was to lead to his translating and adapting Shakespeare's *Coriolanus*, a project first mooted in the 1920s. And there are numerous other works by Brecht that also owe their existence to this principle of 'creative vandalism' − such as *Die Mutter* (after Gorky) and *Der Jasager* (after Arthur Waley's English translation of the Japanese Noh play *Taniko*).

The success of Playfair's revival had not escaped the music publishers Schott either. On 28 January 1925 they had written to the young composer Paul Hindemith (born in 1895, five years before Weill), proposing the idea of a new stage work based on *The Beggar's Opera*. Well acquainted with their rising star's previous flirtations with the idioms of modern dance music (or 'jazz', as it was then known), and in uncanny anticipation of some of Weill's music for *The Threepenny Opera*, they suggested to him that 'the way you drew the foxtrot of your Kammermusik No. 1 [1922] into the sphere of serious music would be the right thing in this case: refined popular music or a caricature thereof, at the same time a satire of the sort of

modern opera music composed by d'Albert'.[13] Hindemith appears
not to have responded to the suggestion, thereby leaving the field open
for Weill–Brecht *et al.* Rumour has it that the film director F. W.
Murnau had contemplated a film version of *The Beggar's Opera*.[14]
At any event 'Threepenny Fever' (*Dreigroschenfieber*) – an expression coined to describe the clamour and mania attending the early
performances of *Die Dreigroschenoper* in Berlin – was already in
the air.

Several of the people involved in the first production have
recounted in print the work's genesis and initial reception, each
contributing in his or her way to the many legends which continue
to circulate. The most substantial account is contained in the
autobiography of Ernst Josef Aufricht, the impresario of the first
production. Aufricht, however, relied heavily on Lotte Lenya, Weill's
widow, who in turn gleaned much information, including the wrong
date of the première, from an unpublished interview which her second
husband, George Davis, had conducted with Elisabeth Hauptmann
on 25 May 1955.[15] Heinrich Fischer, Aufricht's deputy, also published his own account, in 1957.[16]

Around the time that Hauptmann finished her working translation
of *The Beggar's Opera*, Aufricht, who had recently come into
possession of a good fortune, was in want of a play with which to
launch his new venture as impresario. He had rented the Theater am
Schiffbauerdamm, an early nineteenth-century theatre, a medium-
sized house with a gaudily mock-rococo interior in what was then an
unfashionable area near the centre of Berlin. (It now finds itself in
the Eastern Sector, next to the border, where since 1954, following
the city's division after the Second World War, it has served as the
home of Brecht's Berliner Ensemble.) The proposed date for the
opening was 31 August 1928, Aufricht's thirtieth birthday.

According to Hauptmann and Fischer, it was the latter who first
approached Brecht. Aufricht, who finds corroboration in Lenya's
version of events, claims also to have been there:

I now had a theatre in Berlin which I had to open in nine months' time. I
offered Erich Engel, whom I consider the most important director of the
1920s, the first production ... We [Aufricht, Fischer, and assistant Robert
Vambery] paid calls on authors living in Berlin. We went to Toller, Feuchtwanger and others, but none had a finished piece. 'If I don't find anything, I'll die. All we can try now is the artists' bars, the Schwannecke or
Schlichter's.'
We went to Schlichter's in the Lutherstrasse. On the walls hung pictures
for sale by the owner, the painter Rudolf Schlichter. There was someone

sitting in a second room. It was Brecht. I didn't know him personally, though I did know his literary experiments for the stage, and thought highly of his poetry. His long face often had the ascetic expression of a monk, occasionally the slyness of a gallows bird. He had dark, piercing eyes which greedily and hungrily absorbed everything presented to them. He was scrawny, with drooping shoulders. I have always considered his unkempt, proletarian turn-out, with cap, jacket and open neck, to be a Brechtian 'alienation'. Although his exterior tended to be repellent, he himself was pleasant.

We sat down at his table and posed the vital question. He began to relate to us a plot he was working on at the time. He noticed, however, that we were not interested, since we asked for the bill.

'There is always a minor work of mine. You can have six of the seven scenes tomorrow. It's an adaptation of John Gay's "Beggar's Opera". I've given it the title "Gesindel" ["Scum"]. The Beggar's Opera was given its première in 1728, not in London but in a barn in the suburbs; it deals with a corruption scandal: the notorious gangster is a friend of the chief of police and is in business with him. The gangster robs a very powerful man of his only daughter and marries her. The man is the boss of the beggars, he fits them out, trains them, and stations them according to their qualities. The end is in the seventh scene, which as yet I've only sketched.'

The story smelled of theatre. We arranged to collect the manuscript the next day in the Spichernstrasse, where Brecht had a furnished room.

Fischer went to the Spichernstrasse and, since it is not far from the Meinekestrasse, I waited for him there at my parents-in-law's. He came in the rain with the manuscript, wet through and beginning to disintegrate. We read it; I was immediately taken by the impudence and dry humour – today both have become blunted – as well as by the whiff of a new style, and was determined to open my theatre with 'Gesindel'. Fischer was of the same opinion. We telephoned Brecht, who informed us that a musician was also involved, Kurt Weill, whose two one-act operas 'Der Zar lässt sich photographieren' and 'Der Protagonist', with texts by Georg Kaiser, could be heard at the Charlottenburg Opera. Shortly afterwards I went along and found Weill's music too atonal for a theatre piece and asked Theo Mackeben, whom I had engaged as musical director, to get hold of the original music of 'The Beggar's Opera' by Pepusch so as to have a replacement ready.

Together with Engel, who also liked the Brecht text and who, as arranged, had taken on the direction of the opening production, we considered the question of casting. We saw the piece, as written, in terms of a comical literary operetta with a few flashes of social criticism. We took the only aggressive song, 'Erst kommt das Fressen' [2nd Finale], quite seriously. Political reality hadn't yet demonstrated in any drastic way that when morality disappears, food is also lost. Brecht and Weill were no classics. The profound explications of *The Threepenny Opera*'s socio-philosophical message, in which Brecht also later participated, have in retrospect given the piece a false significance.[17]

If Aufricht's memory had served him correctly on matters of chronology, then the above episode would have taken place in December 1927, nine months before the première. In the event, the information is perhaps only as authentic as the dialogue which Aufricht presents as direct speech. For all the atmosphere that such a stylistic device vividly evokes, Aufricht's words are, so to speak, too original to be true. According to John Willett and Ralph Manheim (*MW*), the encounter (if, indeed, it took place at all as described) must have been as late as March or April. They suggest, too, that the process of adaptation had probably not yet started. If so, then Aufricht's account of what Brecht offered him is guilty of yet further anachronisms, since his version of Brecht's synopsis already includes two of the major alterations made to the original: Gay's prison keeper (Lockit) has been replaced by the chief of police (Brown); and the eponymous beggars are no longer merely a part of the dramatic framework but feature prominently in Peachum's manipulations. Moreover, Aufricht remembers Brecht peddling the work at this stage under his own new title *Gesindel* ('Scum'), though this, as suggested, may also be a slip of his memory. Elisabeth Hauptmann's working translation has unfortunately not survived; nor does there appear to be a surviving manuscript of the work that bears this title.

In a letter dated 10 March 1928, Weill's publishers, Universal Edition in Vienna, 'learn from a newspaper notice that you are preparing with Brecht an adaptation of "The Beggar's Opera"'. The rival firm Schott must have read the same notice, since they too wrote to Weill with knowledge of his intentions. While Universal were merely keeping tabs on their young composer, Schott had more immediate business interests at heart. Their letter to Weill, dated 9 March, draws attention to the fact that they already have a version of *The Beggar's Opera* in their catalogue and that, understandably enough, they wish to 'eliminate mutual competition'. As Weill's reply of 14 March shows, the composer had already established some firm ideas about the nature and aim of his 'adaptation'.

During work on *The Beggar's Opera* I have rapidly developed the impression that it is out of the question to think of the piece as 'opera', and that one can best choose the form of a farce with music, which cannot be considered for opera houses because of the preponderance of dialogue. Our adaptation will probably be intended for a very famous Berlin actor; and Herr Brecht, who is heavily involved in the project, would therefore prefer it if the work were not given to a straight music publisher but rather to a theatre agency that liaises with the theatres and operetta houses for whom our work is intended.

The collaboration with Brecht was clearly underway, and Weill's description of the adaptation appears to be consistent with Aufricht's assessment of the piece as a 'comical literary operetta'. Furthermore, the mention of a 'very famous Berlin actor' suggests that the meeting with Aufricht may indeed already have taken place and the question of casting been discussed. Aufricht speaks of six completed scenes, with a seventh merely sketched. There were subsequently eight for the 1928 production and nine for the *Versuche* edition (*V*), following the interpolation of the discarded eighth scene, revised and reinstated under the title *Kampf um das Eigentum* ('Property in dispute').

The inception of *The Threepenny Opera*, which may or may not have initially been called *Gesindel*, can be located, then, in the first three months of 1928. And although it is still impossible to ascertain how much the adaptation of *The Beggar's Opera* had progressed by the time Aufricht or Fischer approached Brecht, and whether this meeting was before or after discussions with Weill had taken place, work on the piece did not begin in earnest until a few months later, as Lotte Lenya, the composer's wife, recalled in 1955:

it was decided that the only way Brecht and Kurt could whip the work still ahead of them was to escape from Berlin. But to where? Somebody suggested a certain quiet little French Riviera resort. Wires went off for reservations, and on the first of June, Kurt and I left by train, while Brecht drove down with Helene Weigel and their son Stefan ... The two men wrote and rewrote furiously, night and day, with only hurried swims in between. I recall Brecht wading out, pants rolled up, cap on head, stogy in mouth. I had been given the part of Spelunken-Jenny (Aufricht now says it was after my audition in the tango-ballad that he decided to forget about Pepusch).

Again, the vagaries of memory raise as many questions as they answer. Had Lenya really been given the part of Jenny before the trip to France? And if so, was the tango-ballad (*Zuhälterballade*) already composed before the auditions took place? (The picture of Brecht 'wading out, pants rolled up, cap on head, stogy in mouth' acquires a particularly piquant significance if one bears in mind the nature of the resort to which the young German artists had repaired. 'Le Lavandou was then a very small town but already ... the place for going out to Ile du Levant, which offered the leading nude beach in pre-war Europe.'[18]) The date of departure for the South of France cited by Lenya is certainly wrong, as Weill's correspondence with his publisher reveals. While a letter from Universal Edition dated 10 May was dispatched to Berlin, the next letter, dated 18 May, was sent to: Hostellerie de la Plage, Plage des Lecques, St.-Cyr-sur-Mer (Var). Weill replied from this address on 26 May, stating that he intended to stay there until 4 June and return via Frankfurt by the 8th. It is likely, then, that his next letter from Berlin, although dated 4 June, was really written on 14 June, especially in view of the 'received' stamp of 16 June (two days for delivery to Vienna being quite normal at the time). At any event he writes in that letter: 'Meanwhile I'm working at full steam on the composition of the Beggar's Opera, which I'm enjoying', adding that 'it is being written in a very easily singable style since it is supposed to be performed by actors.' He hopes 'to be finished by the end of June'.

Weill underestimated the time needed for the work ahead of him. His next letter is dated 22 July. 'You have not heard anything from me for rather a long time', he writes, 'as I'm working a great deal.' But he goes on to reassure his publisher: 'You'll be receiving by post in the next few days, via the publisher Felix Bloch Erben [the above-mentioned theatre agency], the piano vocal score of my Beggar's Opera (German title: "Des Bettlers Oper"). I would like to ask you, for the time being, not to reproduce this vocal score as a whole since the sequence of numbers is not yet fixed and two numbers are also still missing.' He adds that the study material for the Berlin production must be 'produced with the greatest possible speed since rehearsals begin on 10 August'.

On 26 April, with substantial portions of the work still to be written, Brecht and Weill had signed a contract with the theatre agents Felix Bloch Erben, whose responsibility it was, among other things, to produce duplicate copies of the stage script. Forthcoming royalties were to be divided among the authors as follows: Brecht 62½ per cent, Weill 25 per cent, and Elisabeth Hauptmann 12½ per cent. (The 2½ per cent later allotted to Klammer was docked from Brecht's share, albeit only for performances in German.) Bloch Erben wrote to Universal Edition on 5 June confirming the contract and including details of the royalty percentages due to Universal Edition.[19] At this stage, the piece was still referred to, in English, as *The Beggar's Opera*, with the subtitle, in German, 'A Traditional English Ballad Piece by John Gay'. On 1 May Bloch Erben's house journal, *Charivari*, had already announced the forthcoming production, using the same wording but beginning with the additional German title *Die Ludenoper* ('The Pimps' Opera'). This title also appeared, as a subtitle, on the stage script (*L*) subsequently prepared for the rehearsals in August (though without the additional 'ein altenglisches Balladenstück'). In a later issue of *Charivari*, dated 23 May, there is a brief column on 'the German version of Brecht's adaptation of the English play "The Beggar's Opera", written in 1728'; readers are informed that it is 'not an opera, but a prose work with music by Kurt Weill, using old English ballads'. By 18 July *Charivari* gives the main title in German as *Des Bettlers Oper*, as Weill did in his letter of 22 July; the original English title is now supplied in brackets, as it was for the première.

Lenya, following Hauptmann's recollections, stated that it was the writer Lion Feuchtwanger – one of 'the distinguished kibitzers who wandered in and out of the stalls' – who invented the final title: *Die Dreigroschenoper*.[20] Feuchtwanger has consequently been cited on numerous occasions for his creative contribution to the work. There is, however, reason to doubt this unequivocal attribution, as the recollections of Elias Canetti, another member of the literati present at rehearsals, make clear.

Karl Kraus was in Berlin at the time and he was friends with Brecht, whom he saw frequently, and it was through Brecht, a few weeks before the première of the *Dreigroschenoper*, that I got to know him. I never saw him alone but always in the company of Brecht and other people who were interested in this production ... The conversation concerned the *Dreigroschenoper*, which didn't yet bear this title; the name was being considered in this circle. Many suggestions were made and Brecht calmly listened to them, not at all as though it was his own piece; indeed, it was scarcely possible to see from the way he conducted himself during the conversation that it was he who had the final say. So many suggestions were made that I no longer remember who made which. Without appearing domineering, Karl Kraus made a suggestion which he threw into the debate, questioningly, as if he had doubts about it. It was immediately suppressed by another, a better one, which didn't win the day either. I don't know from whom the title did finally come; it was Brecht himself who proposed it, but perhaps he had got it from someone else who wasn't present and wanted to see what the assembled company thought of it. The freedom in his work with respect to demarcations and property labels was astonishing.[21]

Before *Die Luden-Oper* became *Die Dreigroschenoper*, there ensued the frantic weeks of rehearsal, during which countless alterations were made to the text. Nonetheless the pre-rehearsal text cyclostyled by Bloch–Erben already represents a considerable transformation of the English original. In an appendix to their translation (*MW*) of the standard (1931) text, Manheim and Willett have outlined the principal departures from Gay as follows:

Several subsequently discarded characters from Gay's original still remain (notably Mrs Coaxer and her girls), but Lockit has already been purged, together with all that part of the plot involving him, and replaced by the rather more up-to-date figure of Brown. Peachum's manipulation of the beggars is also new, as are the first stable and second gaol scenes. The main items retained from Gay in this script are, in our present numbering, scenes 1, 3, 4, 5 (which is not yet a brothel but a room in the hotel), 6, 8 and the principle of the artificial happy ending. There are no scene titles. However, Macheath's final speech before his execution is already there, much as in our version, as are several of the songs: Peachum's Morning Hymn (whose melody is in fact a survivor from the original, being that of Gay's opening song), Pirate Jenny, the Cannon Song, the Barbara Song, the Tango-Ballade, the Jealousy Duet, Lucy's subsequently cut aria (in scene viii), the Call from the Grave and the Ballad in which Macheath Begs All Men for Forgiveness; also the final chorus. Most of these are not given in full, but only by their titles, and some may not yet have been completed. There are also two of Gay's original songs, as well as two translations from Kipling: 'The Ladies' and 'Mary, Pity Women'.[22]

The Brecht Archive in East Berlin holds two especially valuable copies of the *Luden-Oper* prompt book: one (*LE*) used by the director, Erich Engel, the other (*LH*) by his assistant Dr Julius Halewicz. Both record in detail the cuts, amendments and interpolations to which the piece was subjected right up to and including the night of the première, thus offering a striking document of the extent to which *The Threepenny Opera*'s evolution was determined by the practical operation of putting the piece on the boards. The role of Mrs Coaxer, for example, which was to be played by Helene Weigel, Brecht's wife, had to be removed altogether owing to the actress's indisposition; she had gone down with appendicitis. The 'Moritat', on the other hand, one of this century's greatest evergreens, was a last-minute addition. Lenya relates the story of its genesis thus:

[Harald] Paulsen, vain even for an actor, insisted that his entrance as Mackie Messer needed building up: why not a song right there, all about Mackie, getting in a mention if possible of the sky-blue bow tie that he wanted to wear? Brecht made no comment but next morning came in with the verses for the 'Moritat' of Mack the Knife and gave them to Kurt to set to music. This currently popular number, often called the most famous tune written in Europe during the past half century, was modeled after the *Moritaten* ('mord' meaning murder, 'tat' meaning deed) sung by singers at street fairs, detailing the hideous crimes of notorious arch-fiends. Kurt not only produced the tune overnight, he knew the name of the hand-organ manufacturer – Zucco Maggio – who could supply the organ on which to grind out the tune for the prologue. And the 'Moritat' went not to Paulsen but to Kurt Gerron, who doubled as Street Singer and Tiger Brown.[23]

Aufricht's account of the Moritat's genesis is slightly different.

Harald Paulsen, who had mostly appeared in operetta, turned up in a black suit made by Hermann Hoffmann, a bespoke gentlemen's outfitters. He bounced across the stage in a double-breasted jacket which hugged his waist in turn-of-the-century style, tight-fitting trousers with straps, patent-leather shoes with white spats, in his hand a slender sword stick and a bowler hat on his head. The buttons on his jacket came up high and a wing-collar lent him an air of respectability. He completed the outfit, according to his own taste, with a large fluttering bow made of light-blue silk. The blue bow to match the colour of his eyes was indispensable – it meant tried-and-tested security with which he opposed the incomprehensible madness around him. He clung to it with both hands, preferring to part with his role rather than with his blue bow. A frightful uproar began which soon assumed catastrophic proportions, since Paulsen was already becoming hoarse and thus putting the show at risk. Brecht had an idea. 'Let's leave him as he is, oversweet and charming', he said in the office. 'Weill and I will introduce him with a "Moritat" that tells of his gruesome and disgraceful deeds. The effect made by his light-blue bow will be all the more curious.' That's how the most popular song of *The Threepenny Opera* was born.[24]

The 'Moritat' is inserted into Dr Halewicz's copy (*LH*), but not into Engel's (*LE*). In both copies a version of the wedding scene is deleted, and a new one interpolated. Scene 3, a straight translation of the encounter between Mrs Peachum and Filch from Gay's original (act 1:vi), appears in three versions, but is also cut three times. A translation of Kipling's poem 'The Ladies' ('Die Ballade von den Ladies') is still in. 'Die Zuhälterballade' is merely referred to as the 'Bordell-Ballade [Brothel Ballad] von François Villon'. The prison is still Gay's Newgate, not the Old Bailey as it later became. The other Kipling poem, a translation of 'Mary, Pity Women!' ('Maria Fürsprecherin der Frauen'), intended for Lucy, is already crossed out. The first refrain of the poem was subsequently used as the text of 'Pollys Lied' ('Nice while it lasted, an' now it is over'); it was cut for the première but later added to the version of the text (*V*) printed in 1931.[25] (The verses of the same poem were not permanently discarded, however: Brecht ingeniously recycled them a year later in the next collaboration with Weill, the 'play with music' *Happy End*, where they form the basis of the song 'Surabaya-Johnny'.) The 'Streben' (endeavour) in the title of Peachum's 'Lied von der Un-zulänglichkeit menschlichen Strebens' was originally 'Planen' (planning), as photographs of the captions used in the first production corroborate. Lucy's 'Aria' is still in; here it is indicated at the beginning of act 3 (later becoming, in revised form, the reinstated scene viii for the *Versuche* edition). It was deleted from the first production because it was technically beyond the actress (Kate Kühl) who eventually played the part. Moreover, as Weill later maintained, 'it had become apparent during the course of rehearsals that the whole scene was superfluous'.[26]

One of the most substantial cuts occurs towards the end of the final scene, just before Macheath's impending execution. The original intention was that the players should briefly step out of their respective roles and enter into a discussion with 'the voice of the author' — an obvious, if rather basic, alienation effect if ever there was one. The topic of discussion is the opera's ending.

The actor playing Macheath hesitates, turns round suddenly and discontentedly addresses the wings, right.

ACTOR PLAYING MACHEATH: Well, what happens now? Do I go off or not? That's something I'll need to know on the night.

ACTOR PLAYING PEACHUM: I was telling the author only yesterday that it's a lot of nonsense, it's a heavy tragedy, not a decent musical [*Melodrama*].

ACTRESS PLAYING MRS PEACHUM: I can't stand this hanging at the end.

WINGS RIGHT, THE AUTHOR'S VOICE: That's how the play was written, and that's how it stays.

ACTOR PLAYING MACHEATH: It stays that way, does it? Then act the lead yourself. Impertinence!

AUTHOR: It's the plain truth: the man's hanged, of course he has to be hanged. I'm not making any compromises. If that's how it is in real life, then that's how it is on the stage. Right?

ACTOR PLAYING MRS PEACHUM: Right.

ACTOR PLAYING PEACHUM: Doesn't understand the first thing about the theatre. Plain truth, indeed.

ACTOR PLAYING MACHEATH: Plain truth. That's a load of rubbish in the theatre. Plain truth is what happens when people run out of ideas. Do you suppose the audience here have paid eight marks to see plain truth? They paid their money *not* to see plain truth.

ACTOR PLAYING PEACHUM: Well, then, the ending had better be changed. You can't have the play end like that. I'm speaking in the name of the whole company when I say the play can't be performed as it is.

AUTHOR: All right ladies and gentlemen, you can clean up your own mess.

ACTOR PLAYING MACHEATH: So we shall.

ACTOR PLAYING PEACHUM: It'd be absurd if we couldn't find a first-rate dramatic ending to please all tastes.

ACTRESS PLAYING MRS PEACHUM: Right, then let's go back
    ten speeches ...
MACHEATH: ... has brought about my fall. So be it – I fall ...[27]

Engel's copy of the stage script (*LE*), which is less tampered with
than Dr Halewicz's (*LH*), still contains – uncut – translations of
two of Gay's airs (nos. VI and XI): 'Virgins are like fair Flower'
('Sehet die Jungfraun und sehet die Blüte!') and, in a rather freer
rendering, 'A Fox may steal your hens, Sir' (Wenn's einer Hur gefällt,
Herr). Engel's script may not have acquired the text of the last-minute
'Moritat'; it does however indicate that Macheath's initial entrance
is accompanied by 'soft music'. Brecht himself added a direction to
this effect in a typed manuscript of the work (*T*) that has hitherto
received no attention from commentators, apart from a cursory
mention in David Drew's *Kurt Weill: A Handbook* (London, 1987).
Now in the possession of the Universal Edition in Vienna, it was used
as the basis for the first printed edition of the work (*FE*), which was
published jointly by Universal Edition and Bloch Erben, ostensibly
as loan material to theatres, in October 1928.[28] The typescript
version probably reproduces more accurately than any other the actual
material used during those early performances of the work. Moreover,
additional handwritten instructions, most of which found their way
into the first printed edition of the work, disclose aspects of performance practice not contained in the 1931 version.

The instruction in Brecht's hand pertaining to Macheath's initial
entrance reads: 'Music of Moritat No. 2 very soft, as though as a
motif.' It is not the only instruction of its kind. There are others, all
in Weill's hand, which similarly prescribe such purely instrumental
passages but which completely disappear in Brecht's 1931 version.
In the 1928 version all of these instructions are retained, bar one.
In the sixth scene Weill requests: 'Here the orchestra can play the
Moritat No. 2 softly as a waltz' but for some reason this was over-
looked by the printers and not reinstated by Weill in the galley proofs
(*FEP*).

At the beginning of the final scene the orchestra is required to play
the 'Moritat softly, like a funeral march'. Several other numbers are
likewise recapitulated in instrumental versions. After the 'Liebeslied'
in scene 2, Weill indicates 'Entr'acte music. Repetition of No. 7 [i.e.
'Kanonensong'] for Orchestra'. At the end of scene iv there is a
similar instruction: 'Entr'acte music. No. 8 [i.e. 'Liebeslied'] for
orchestra.' The following Interlude between Mrs Peachum and Jenny,

including Mrs Peachum's 'Ballade von der sexuellen Hörigkeit', is missing: according to Lenya, Rosa Valetti refused to sing the song because of the text's 'filthy words'. It is also omitted from the first edition of the piano vocal score, published two months after the première, as it is from the 1929 edition of the song texts. It was first published, arranged for voice and piano, in Kurt Weill, *Song-Album* (Vienna, 1929, UE 9787). Weill also insists, incidentally, that the coronation bells at the beginning of the fifth scene should be tuned to F # and G. At the end of this scene he calls for 'Rem[iniscence]. No. 11 (Zuhälter b[allade].)' ('Rem.' is changed in the printed text to 'Entr'acte'; the song − 'Die Zuhälterballade' − becomes no. 12). There are two other small but interesting differences between the typescript (*T*) and the printed version (*FE*). In the former Brecht requires that the 'Salomonsong' be sung by Polly, whereas for the printed version Weill assigns it to Jenny: 'Jenny appears before the curtain with a barrel organ: No. 17. Salomonsong.' At any rate, according to Lotte Lenya, the 'Salomonsong' was cut from the first production. (It was subsequently published in *Die Musik*, 21 (1929), p. 432.) The 'Barbarasong' is first given in the typescript to 'Lucie'; a later handwritten amendment assigns it to Polly. This is additional support for the hypothesis advanced by Kim Kowalke (see chapter 4) that the 'Barbarasong' was sung in the early performances not by Roma Bahn but by Kate Kühl (possibly by way of compensating her for the suppression of Lucy's Aria). Although it is in its customary place in the manuscript (that is, effectively as no. 9), it is listed out of sequence as no. 12, thus indicating that it was previously placed after the 'Zuhälterballade'. This is where it occurs in Theo Mackeben's copy of the piano-conductor score (*M*), complete with the anonymous cue: 'Ich liebe ihn', followed by Brown's reply: 'Du auch − ja da kann man', an anticipation of the song's refrain ('Ja, da kann man sich doch nicht nur hinlegen').[29] In a letter to UE dated 10 September 1928, Weill himself still refers to the 'Barbarasong' as no. 12, and it is only after several further enquiries from UE that the matter is settled once and for all and the song's position verified, both in the stage script and piano vocal score, as no. 9.[30]

The musical directions included in the first published version of *Die Dreigroschenoper* document important aspects of the work's early performance history. In playing the Moritat 'as a motif' in various guises the musicians did not always stick to the letter of the score, as Mackeben's later recordings testify.[31] In the original band parts (*M*), however, many of these interpolations are written out and were doubtless supervised by Weill himself, who completed the full score only after the première. The most obvious significance of the motif would appear to be a rather crude parody of Wagnerian practices – something which certainly fits in with Weill's own proclamations on the work: 'This type of music', he declared in an interview in 1929, 'is the most consistent reaction to Wagner. It signifies the complete destruction of the concept of music drama.'[32] The reminiscences played during scene changes are also revealing about the role of music in the first production: first, that it was an even more substantial component than the score alone would indicate; and second, that it fulfilled an ironic, commenting function, such as in the repetition of the 'Kanonensong' after the 'Liebeslied'. Reporting on the first production for the journal *Melos*, Heinrich Strobel remarked: 'Entr'actes take up the song melodies, put them in a new light, give them a shifting backdrop by means of inspired counterpointing.'[33]

Part of the reason for many of the cuts and changes was purely practical: the piece would otherwise have overrun. And the fact that the première still ran about an hour longer than indicated on later copies of the programme, suggests (even allowing for encores) that some of the cuts were not made until afterwards. To cite an obvious example: Dr Halewicz's prompt book (*LH*) contains nine verses of the Moritat, as does the *Versuche* edition (*V*). Yet the post-première manuscript (*T*) and first edition (*FE*) print just six verses; verses 2, 3 and 7 are omitted.

Brecht's post-première revisions

On the whole, however, the changes made during the process of putting *Die Dreigroschenoper* on the stage and preparing for publication the version that ultimately emerged are of an entirely different nature from those Brecht subsequently made for his 1931 literary text. The business of making the piece stage-worthy was as much a matter of trial and error as of expediency. The preparation of the first printed text (*FE*) involved, above all, the clarification of matters other than the spoken and sung words. The principal concerns were the stage directions and specific details of musical performance, which in many cases were only transmitted orally. In the *Versuche* edition (*V*) many of Brecht's revisions reverse this process. The projected captions, stage directions and musical cues are substantially reduced. Instead, Brecht inserts new chunks of text which actually serve to alter the original complexion of the piece and ultimately to impose on it a new ideological slant. The change is also reflected in the theoretical commentary on the work, the *Anmerkungen* or 'Notes', that Brecht produced around the same time, which has not only informed subsequent readings of the work itself but also misinformed assumptions about its reception.

The Threepenny Opera is by no means an isolated example of Brecht's radically altering his works for later editions. He was a habitual reviser, a master of the work-in-progress. With works written before 1930 the purpose of revisions was at once aesthetic and political: to correct earlier 'aberrations' in the light of his current thinking, as regards both the theory of Epic Theatre and Marxist-orientated cultural strategies. *Lehrstück* (or *Das Badener Lehrstück vom Einverständnis*, as it later became) and *Der Lindberghflug* (later renamed *Der Ozeanflug*) are two cases in point. Both written in 1929, they were later reworked in accordance with Brecht's new ideas on didactic theatre in general and the *Lehrstück* as its principal genre in particular. The earlier versions, and hence traces of Brecht's evolution, were effectively suppressed. (With his revised versions the author could also meet contractual obligations for 'new' works.) When in 1930 Brecht's musical collaborator on both projects, Hindemith, supervised publication of the score of *Lehrstück* in which he included a preface outlining the creators' original intentions, Brecht took exception, vindictively censuring Hindemith's views in what was in fact a spirited but veiled display of self-criticism.

The connection between theory and practice in *The Threepenny Opera* is similar. As the Brecht scholar Ronald Speirs observed in his pioneering study comparing the first published version of the work and the 1931 'standard' edition, 'Brecht's "Notes on *The Threepenny Opera*" ... present a Marxist interpretation of the opera, based largely on [the] newly intercalated passages.'[34] The most far-reaching of these passages, and the one most frequently cited in commentaries, is Macheath's valedictory speech delivered before his reprieve. In order to distinguish the revised version (*V*) from the *Urtext* (*FE*), the newly intercalated material is printed here in italics:

MAC: We mustn't keep anybody waiting. Ladies and gentlemen. *You see before you a declining representative of a declining social group. We lower middle-class artisans who toil with our humble jemmies on small shopkeepers' cash registers are being swallowed up by big corporations backed by the banks. What's a jemmy compared with a share certificate? What's breaking into a bank compared with founding a bank? What's murdering a man compared with employing a man? Fellow citizens,* I hereby take my leave of you I thank you for coming. Some of you were very close to me. That Jenny should have turned me in amazes me greatly. It is proof positive that the world never changes. A concatenation of several unfortunate circumstances has brought about my fall. So be it − I fall.

The text of the interpolation first appeared in *Happy End*, written in 1929. It may not have been written by Brecht, though, whose chief contribution to that work was the initial outline of the plot and the lyrics of the songs. A likely candidate for authorship is the writer to whom Brecht entrusted his outline, Elisabeth Hauptmann. Be that as it may, the association of the practices of small-time criminals with those of big business becomes an important theme in Brecht's interpretation of *The Threepenny Opera*. It not only provided an afterthought to Macheath's farewell speech, but also informed Brecht's screenplay for the film version of the work (discussed below) and became a central idea in his *Dreigroschenroman* ('Threepenny Novel'). The way in which Brecht shifts the target of his critique of social relations is thoroughly characteristic of his development in the early 1930s. In his various reinterpretations of earlier works two overall tendencies can be detected. On a political level, the critique of capitalism becomes sharper, while, on an aesthetic level, the immediate functionality of his art receives greater emphasis, as in the *Lehrstücke*. The various adaptations of the *Dreigroschen* material bear witness to the first tendency: *The Threepenny Opera*'s message becomes progressively more radical. If the new dimension of big business, something quite foreign to the work's original spirit, could so alter Brecht's reading of the *Dreigroschenoper*, then there is a good chance that it will alter how others interpret the work as well (see chapter 15). In refashioning the book of *The Threepenny Opera* Brecht laid traps for philologists and exegetes alike. Anyone who has been involved in performing the work will probably have been struck by the discrepancies between the words in the printed versions of the music and those in the later versions of the book. By the same token, interpretations that discuss the work's original impact while basing their reading on Brecht's revised versions of the text lay themselves open to the pitfalls of exegetical anachronism.[35]

As Ronald Speirs has noted, many of the changes Brecht made in 1931 concern the role of Macheath. As Macheath's status as robber/bourgeois is altered so are his relationships with both his men and his women. The changes are at once small and substantial: the 1931 text cuts, for instance, the earlier description of Macheath as 'Leader of a band of highwaymen', while drawing attention elsewhere to his new career as a banker. 'Between ourselves', he confides to Polly in the 1931 version of scene iv, 'it's only a matter of weeks before I go over to banking altogether. It's safer and it's more profitable.' At the same time he is set further apart from his fellow robbers, who are made to seem more servile and submissive. In the new version he orders them to avoid bloodshed: 'It makes me sick to think of it. You'll never make business men! Cannibals, perhaps, but not business men!' (1:ii). In 1928 (*FE*) Peachum talked of Macheath's 'cheek' (*Frechheit*); in 1931 (*V*) it has become 'boldness' (*Kühnheit*). Revisions to the 'Salomon-Song' and the 'Zuhälterballade' also cast a different light on Macheath's character. In 1928 the final verse of the 'Salomon-Song' focussed on the dangers of passion. In 1931 the reason for Macheath's downfall is given an economic slant: 'passion' (*Leidenschaft*) is replaced by 'wastefulness' (*Verschwendung*). The first verse of the 'Zuhälterballade', which is sung by Mac, is similarly modified. In 1928 the third and fourth lines are nostalgic, with Mac invoking his former 'love' for Jenny.

> In einer Zeit, die längst vergangen ist
> Lebten wir schon zusammen, sie und ich
> Die Zeit liegt fern wie hinter einem Rauch
> Ich liebte sie und sie ernährte mich.

> (At a time, long since passed
> We lived together, she and I
> That time is now distant, as if behind smoke
> I loved her and she fed me.)

In 1931 Mac's sentiments in the third and fourth lines are different from before: they have become more prosaic and matter-of-fact, as has his manner of specifying them (with an '*Und zwar*').

> [In einer Zeit, die längst vergangen ist
> Lebten wir schon zusammen, sie und ich]
> Und zwar von meinem Kopf und ihrem Bauch.
> Ich schützte sie, und sie ernährte mich.

> (That is to say, from my head to her tummy.
> I protected her, and she nourished me.)

Macheath is not the only character to be affected by the revisions. Mrs Peachum's loss of the second finale is Jenny's gain, with a corresponding shift in their respective importance. Reviewing the première, the critic for the newspaper *Der Tag* described Jenny as a 'supporting role'. Since then, she has moved ever more into the limelight, especially on those occasions where, following the precedent of the 1930 film, she usurps Polly's 'Seeräuberjenny'. Polly and her father, Mr Peachum, also undergo a transformation. In 1931 Polly appears more independent, less wimpish: partly because of cuts in Macheath's part, partly because of the elimination of stage directions indicating her emotional response in the wedding scene (such as 'laughs along reluctantly'), and partly because she has now started to subscribe to the economic rationality propagated by husband and father alike. Having been instructed in matters of daily routine during Mac's impending absence, Polly acquires a new sequence of lines whose brazen materialism clearly unsettles her husband.

POLLY: You're quite right. I must grit my teeth and look after the business. What's yours is now mine, isn't it, Mackie? What about your rooms? Shouldn't I give them up? It's such a shame about the rent!

MAC: No, I still need them.

POLLY: But what for? It only costs us money!

MAC: You seem to think I won't be coming back at all.

POLLY: What do mean? When you do, you can rent them again! Mac ...

In the same spirit, Polly is given an extra speech in scene iii, in which she discloses to her alarmed parents the fact of her marriage to Macheath.

POLLY: Look at him. Is he, say, attractive? No. But he has his livelihood. He offers me an existence! He's an excellent burglar and a far-sighted and experienced highwayman to boot. That I know. I could let you have the current figure of his savings. A few successful enterprises and we could retire to a little country house, just like Mr Shakespeare whom father so admires.

Macheath no longer cuts the debonair and dapper figure he did in 1928. To cite Brecht's own 'Notes':

He impresses women less as a handsome man than as a well-heeled one. There are English drawings of *The Beggar's Opera* which show a short, stocky man of about forty with a head like a radish, a bit bald but not lacking dignity.[36]

This description stands in flat contradiction to Harald Paulsen's original incarnation of Macheath. 'The erotic attraction of dashing Mackie Messer', wrote Theodor W. Adorno in 1929, '[should not] be underrated.'[37] Similarly, Polly no longer shares so readily her mother's 'cheerful disposition', described by Walter Benjamin, which 'shields [the women] from the ethical problems with which their men have to concern themselves'.[38] In the 1931 version, Polly is more aware, and hence less shielded, than she was three years earlier.

Thanks to Brecht's revisions Mr Peachum similarly becomes more aware, more articulate − and more cynical. He is also allowed to appear a little more dignified: in scene iii Polly no longer repeats, to ironic effect, her father's words as he contemplates the prospect of life − or rather, business − without his daughter. When Peachum elaborates the basic types of misery in scene i, he does so at greater length. He and Mrs Peachum acquire a new last line to the 'Anstatt dass-Song'. Instead of repeating exactly Mrs Peachum's previous words: 'Wenn die Liebe anhebt und der Mond noch wächst' (When love springs forth and the moon still grows), they conclude on a decidedly gloomier note: 'Wenn die Liebe aus ist und im Dreck du verreckst' (When love is over and you're perishing in the dirt). Likewise the effect of a subtle change of diction in the seventh line of Peachum's opening verse in the first 'Dreigroschenfinale': the idea that someone actually gets what is theirs by right is now immediately countered by the resigned remark '*ach wo!*' − you must be joking. This cynical political awareness acquires an almost tub-thumping directness in scene vii with Peachum's newly inserted analysis of the legal system. Brecht has sharpened his sociopolitical critique; Wall Street has crashed; and Weimar Germany is in the grips of a reactionary backlash:

After all, we all abide by the law! The law was made solely for the exploitation of those who can't understand it, or who are prevented by sheer necessity from obeying it. And whoever wants a chunk of this exploitation must strictly abide by the law.

Peachum's summary dismissal of a beggar in scene iii now incorporates an excursus on aesthetic response.

My dear man, there's obviously a difference between 'tugging at people's heart strings' and merely 'getting on their nerves'. Yes, I need artists. Only artists can still tug at people's heartstrings. If you were to do your job properly, your audience would have to applaud! You're completely without ideas! Obviously I can't renew your engagement.

This last example is much more complex than the preceding one, and could be taken to illustrate both tendencies, the political and the aesthetic, in Brecht's development. While Peachum seems to be providing ironic justification for the artist's vocation, he may also be smuggling in a cryptic allusion to the idea of dramatic alienation (*Verfremdung*). 'Tugging at people's heartstrings' is precisely what Brecht's theory of Epic Theatre is at pains to proscribe.

The genesis of the music

Although the music of *The Threepenny Opera* has invariably been much more tampered with in performance than the verbal text, Weill himself did not change the work after 1928. His revisions were restricted to the period immediately following the première when he completed his autograph score. By 7 July, as mentioned above, he had finished all but two numbers of the vocal score (three, if one includes the last-minute 'Moritat'). The orchestration came last of all. On 21 August Weill wrote to his publisher giving the impression, at least to begin with, that he had finished this too. 'The orchestral rehearsals start on the 25th, the première is on the 31st.' Yet he admits with his closing words that he is not finished after all: 'I will tell you more when the score of the Beggar's Opera is completely finished.'

Since the last page of Weill's autograph full score (*AS*) bears the date '23 August 1928', one might readily infer that this was the day on which he completed the final draft of the entire work, in time for the first orchestral rehearsal two days later. The correspondence with his publisher informs us otherwise. On 6 September Universal Edition cabled Weill with a question: 'Where's the score of *Groschenoper*?' Weill replied the next day: 'I'm still busy at the moment completing the score following the experiences of the current production and also matching the vocal score exactly with the stage script.' A further two days had elapsed when Weill wrote:

I am sending under separate cover a large batch of music. You now have the complete vocal score. No. 6 (Seeräuberjenny), No. 2 (Moritat) and No. 13 (Ballade v. angen. Leben) will follow soon in full score. I enclose an exact list of numbers [unfortunately now missing]. The 'Ballade von der sexuellen Hörigkeit' has been cut completely. I am sending you No. 12 (Barbarasong) [soon to become No. 9], which is mainly set for piano in the full-score version, so that you can literally transfer the piano part to the vocal score. No. 17 (Salomonsong) [later 18] is set for harmonium in the full score version I'm sending you. Please transfer this version (not the one in the vocal score) to the printed vocal score. In the case of No. 5 ['Hochzeitslied'] please add to the vocal score the direction contained in the full score ['first of all sung a capella, embarrassed and bored. Later possibly in this version' – i.e. with instrumental accompaniment]. With No. 2 [Moritat] please add to the vocal score and full score the following: 'At Macheath's various entrances the orchestra can start playing this piece softly. At the beginning of the eighth scene it is played in a slow tempo as a funeral march.'

This last instruction was never carried out, and the absence of additional documentation leaves one wondering whether it was an oversight on the part of the publishers, which is quite likely, or whether the composer changed his mind. Nos. 6 and 13 followed the next day; no. 2 the day after that, on 12 September. As the covering letter explains: 'The delay has to do with my having to write out whole sections afresh, as they are still required in the theatre. Moreover, there are certain things I had to write down for the published edition which I only needed to pass on to the musicians here by word of mouth.'

Exactly to what extent Weill adjusted the full score 'following the experiences of the current production' we may never know, since not all of the materials have survived. Even where they have, it is difficult to tell the precise point at which the changes were made, or by whom. A good example is the opening of the 'Ballade vom angenehmen Leben'. By virtue of its being photographically reproduced as part of the preface to a popular vocal selection,[39] a full-score version of the opening has survived which consists merely of a dotted rhythm on the side drum (see example 1).

This must be the version from which the Mackeben parts (*M*) were copied, since they also contain the one-bar side drum introduction, with the dotted semiquaver melody being given to the tenor saxophone and piccolo. At some stage the familiar introduction was added. Whether the addition was made during rehearsals or once the show was already underway, and whether it was made at Weill's suggestion or not, remains unclear. Macheath's text 'Ihr Herren, urteilt jetzt selbst' is shown in the 1928 book (*FE*) as belonging to the song, though this in itself is no proof of the existence of the expanded instrumental introduction. In any event, this may well be a case where the musicians were initially instructed, 'by word of mouth', to improvise the introduction before it was committed to paper, particularly since it does little more than quote, as accompanists traditionally do *ad libitum*, the last four bars of the verse.[40] (See Geoffrey Abbott's discussion of the '*Dreigroschen* Sound' in chapter 14 for further comments on the genesis of individual numbers as reflected in the Mackeben band parts and other sources.)

Ex. 1

Faksimile aus der handschriftlichen Partitur (benutzt in Nr. 8 unseres Heftes).
Die hieraus ersichtliche Besetzung ist: Piccolo-Flöten, Alt-, Tenor- und Sopran-
Saxophon, Trompete, Posaune, Banjo, Hölzer, Becken und Klavier

It was stated earlier that although the book of *Die Dreigroschenoper* is a conflation of several sources, Weill's score is largely a new
composition. Writing to UE on 21 August 1928, ten days before the
première, Weill conveyed his own impression of the score's quality
and substance as follows:

I would like to ask you a favour. Now that work on the Beggar's Opera is
concluded, I think that I've succeeded in producing a good piece and also
that several numbers from it have the best prospects, at least musically, of
becoming popular in a very short time. To this end, it is absolutely necessary
that in all the publicity for the première the music is accorded its rightful place.
In the theatre (as ever in literature) people seem to be a little afraid of the
music's effectiveness, and I fear that the music will tend to be passed off in
announcements, press notices, etc. as incidental music [*Theatermusik*],
although with its 20 numbers it far exceeds such limits.

Weill therefore suggested that he be named as co-author so as to give
the music the best chance of success. 'You know that I personally
don't set great store by such things', he continued, 'but we must
seriously fear that the commercial possibilities of this music will be
wasted if it is not given adequate promotion at the première.'

The only music retained from *The Beggar's Opera* is Peachum's opening air, which Weill used for the 'Morgenchoral'. Otherwise there are no obvious borrowings, at least none for which the composer could be charged, like Brecht was, with plagiarism. Although Weill's conscious use of pre-existing material cannot be ruled out, the identification of any further sources necessarily entails an element of speculation. For if parody is a seminal device in *The Threepenny Opera*, then it is above all particular types of musical expression rather than actual compositions that are parodied. The Overture, for example, is 'Baroque-like', without actually quoting from a particular Baroque composer. The rising minor sixth employed – or rather quoted – throughout the work as the musical signification of yearning is not specifically Wagner's, let alone Tristan's: it is common, clichéd musical property. Nonetheless there are a number of occasions where Weill may well be making more specific allusions. A likely candidate here is the 'Barbara-Song', whose opening bars possibly put the première audience in mind of a popular melody from one of the 1920s' most successful operettas. The melody is 'Ich bin nur ein armer Wandergesell'; the operetta Eduard Künneke's *Der Vetter aus Dingsda* (1921)[41] (see example 2).

Not only are the rhythm and the melodic contour of the respective vocal lines similar but also the texture of their accompanying chords. Moreover, there is a textual connection which could scarcely have escaped Weill's notice. As regular correspondent for the weekly journal *Der deutsche Rundfunk*, he had himself written about *Der Vetter aus Dingsda* prior to the operetta's radio transmission in July 1926. The poor wayfarer (*ein armer Wandergesell*) deceitfully wins the unsuspecting heart of the heroine Julia. He is not who she thinks and expects him to be, namely the eponymous cousin from Dingsda (literally: 'whatsitsname'), but an impostor, in Weill's own words: 'a rather degenerate descendant of the family Kuhbrot'.[42] Rather than merely invite a direct analogy to Künneke's original, the text of the 'Barbara-Song' presents its own piquant variation. Polly's submission to a degenerate suitor is quite conscious and deliberate – a provocative snub to her parents' hypocritical sense of decorum.

But Polly, like the false cousin, is fibbing. The degenerate, impecunious suitor with the unclean collar in the third verse is no more the well-to-do Mac, famed for his sartorial elegance, than the Jenny of 'Seeräuberjenny' is his former concubine. As mentioned above, the texts of both these songs are Brechtian self-borrowings, which may partly explain the anomaly of the collar. A different, more

constructive explanation is that the 'Barbara-Song' affords Polly a
further opportunity to indulge her talent for play-acting (*Verstellerei*)
for which the irritated Mac has already reprehended her in the wedding
scene after her performance of 'Seeräuberjenny'. Having unsettled her
husband with her 'art', she now provokes her parents by the same
means. Within the theory of Epic Theatre such wilful disruptions of
the Aristotelian unities, in this case that of character, are less an
anomaly than an obligatory ingredient. Polly steps out of character to
'adopt an attitude', to use Brecht's later theoretical formulation,
intoning in both 'Seeräuberjenny' and the 'Barbara-Song' a kind of
anarchic *cri de coeur* on behalf of womankind — with a view to
political emancipation in the former and for the cause of amatory
autonomy in the latter.

While Brecht's setting of the 'Barbara-Song' seemingly left no mark
on Weill's music for *Die Dreigroschenoper*, his 'Seeräuberjenny'

Ex. 2

Weill. *Die Dreigroschenoper.* Copyright 1928 by Universal Edition A.G., Wien. Copyright renewed. Copyright assigned to European American Music Corporation. All rights reserved. Used by permission of European American Music Corporation.

possibly did. Both of these original settings were transcribed and arranged by Brecht's collaborator Franz S. Bruinier.[43] The parts of the arrangements bear the date '8 March 1927', although the 'Jenny-Lied' in the Brecht–Bruinier version must have been finished some months before, since Carola Neher (the future Polly of stage and film) performed it on Berlin radio on 31 December 1926 as part of the New Year festivities. Weill reviewed the event for *Der deutsche Rundfunk*, describing the song as 'splendid' (*vorzüglich*).[44] When he eventually composed his own immortal version of 'Seeräuberjenny' well over a year later, it is quite possible that Brecht's own refrain was still lurking in his mind (see example 3).

The similarity of the refrain, together with Brecht's later assertion that he 'dictated to Weill, bar by bar, by whistling and above all performing', has prompted the Brecht scholar Albrecht Dümling to accuse Weill of being 'inexact' in acknowledging co-authorship.[45] However, the Weill scholar David Drew has eloquently countered the

Ex. 3

und ein Schiff _____ mit acht Se - geln ____

____ und mit fünf - - zig Ka - no - nen ____

____ wird lie - gen am Kai.

[POLLY]

Und ein Schiff mit acht Se - geln und mit
Und das Schiff mit acht Se - geln und mit

fünf - zig Ka - no - nen wird lie - gen am Kai.
fünf - zig Ka - no - nen wird beschie - ßen die Stadt.

charge, identifying similar harmonic and melodic progressions to the
'Seeräuberjenny' refrain in several of Weill's early songs. And even if
Weill was responding in this particular case to Brecht's 'dictation', the
latter's idea – indeed, entire setting – is unremarkable. As Drew
writes: 'Bruinier may have been the first musician to board Brecht's
"Schiff mit acht Segeln" but it was Weill who took it to sea and
steered it to its destination with all its cannon blazing.'[46]

By way of underlining the speculative nature of identifying such
apparent borrowings, Wolfgang Ruf claims to hear at Seeräuberjenny's refrain, not Brecht's original Jenny, but a variation of
Madame Butterfly's 'Eccolo: ABRAMO LINCOLN!'; he also suspects a
textual parallel in that both women are singing about ships.[47] And
so one might go on. Which opera is the most likely source for the
King's Messenger's recitative in the third finale? And did Weill con-
sciously invoke the witches' curse 'Hokus pokus' (from his former
teacher Humperdinck's *Hänsel und Gretel*) when he set to music 'the
rabble, whores, pimps, thieves, outlaws, murderers, and female toilet
attendants' in Macheath's 'Epitaph'? (see example 4).
Ex. 4

Spin-offs

If *The Threepenny Opera* had gone the way of most modern operas, one could conclude here the discussion of the work's genesis and proceed to its stage history, which in most cases would comprise at most a dozen or so productions. But popularity dictated otherwise, engendering not just myths, but also spin-offs.

1 The first spin-off was an instrumental suite of numbers from the opera, much in the tradition of *Harmoniemusik*, arranged by the composer and entitled *Kleine Dreigroschenmusik*. The 'wind ensemble' consists of 16 instruments, including banjo, guitar, bandoneon and piano, the only instrument not used in the opera being the tuba. The suite's eight movements present seven of the

Dreigroschenoper's popular numbers that most readily shed their words (nos. 4, 2, 17, 14, 11b, 13, and 7), beginning with the Overture and concluding with a finale that artfully combines 'Ruf aus der Gruft', 'Grabschrift' and 'Chorale'. The solo instruments do not simply duplicate the missing vocal parts; they do their own kind of singing. The 'Kanonen-Song', in particular, is thoroughly reworked 'in the manner of an old operatic phantasy with much improvisation'.[48] By framing the 'Moritat' with the 'Lied von der Unzulänglichkeit menschlichen Strebens', the second movement reveals a motivic connection between these two numbers, which Peter Epstein first drew attention to in a review written to coincide with the suite's publication in March 1929: 'the beginning of the one is marked by the motion e−g−a, whereas the other (leaving out the upbeat) commences with the notes a−g−e'. Epstein began his perceptive piece by remarking that Weill was not merely exploiting the work's popularity, but also reacting against it.

The rapid dissemination of the modern 'Beggar's Opera' has given rise, here and there, to an unauthorized popularization, whereby numbers have been extracted from the stage music and played in the concert hall. The composer has rightly put an end to this: for it scarcely seems in keeping with the nature of these 'songs' when they are removed from their context and, robbed of their texts, presented as mere pieces of music.[49]

The official première of the *Kleine Dreigroschenmusik* took place at the Berlin Staatsoper on 7 February 1929, though it appears to have been preceded by an 'unofficial' première a few weeks earlier at the Berlin Opera Ball in the same building.[50] The conductor on both occasions was Otto Klemperer.

2 This is not the place to investigate in any detail the most celebrated spin-off of *Die Dreigroschenoper*, the film version made in 1930. Its genesis does, however, have particular relevance to the present discussion since both Weill and Brecht became embroiled in legal wranglings precisely over 'matters of intellectual property'. In fact, two versions of the film were made simultaneously, one in German and one in French. The cast for the German version starred Rudolf Forster (Mackie Messer), Carola Neher (Polly), Reinhold Schünzel (Tiger-Brown), Fritz Rasp and Valeska Gert (Mr and Mrs Peachum) and Lotte Lenja (Jenny). Their counterparts in the French cast were Albert Préjean, Odette Florelle, Jacques Henley, Gaston Mordot and Lucy de Matha, and Margo Lion. Otherwise director G. W. Pabst utilized for both versions the same sets and production team, and also engaged the same musicians, the Lewis Ruth Band

2 The two Pollys, Odette Florelle (*l*) and Carola Neher (*r*), from
the French and German versions of the 1930 film of *Die
Dreigroschenoper*

under Theo Mackeben. The filming took place in Berlin from 19
September until 15 November 1930.

On 21 May 1930, Nero-Film, under the auspices of Tobis and
Warner Brothers, had acquired from the agents Felix Bloch Erben the
exclusive film rights for *Die Dreigroschenoper*. The contract was to
last for ten years, and included a clause (§ 3) whereby:

The production company accords the authors the right of participation in adapting the material for the screen. Neither the publisher nor the copyright holders nor subsequent copyright holders may raise any legal objection to the form and content of the film as produced by the production company on the basis of the screenplay adapted in consultation with the authors. The composition of additional music and the arrangement of existing music may only be carried out by the composer Kurt Weill, who is to receive separate remuneration for this from the production company. By the same token, new lyrics to existing music or to any new compositions may only be written by the librettist Bert Brecht, who is to be engaged by the production company to collaborate on the screenplay. The production company is to remunerate the author Bert Brecht separately for this activity.[51]

In other words, the contract stipulated explicitly that both authors had a say in the film's production: Weill in the creation of the score, Brecht in the screenplay. Once they had given their blessing to these aspects of the film, however, their influence on the project ceased. As it turned out, §3 proved to be a stumbling block. Co-operation between Nero-Film and the authors went far from smoothly. Brecht and Nero-Film crossed swords over the production of the screenplay; and although Brecht had committed himself, in a supplementary clause which he himself had insisted on, to provide an outline for the screenplay, he failed to deliver on time. Nero, who also disapproved of the political turn that Brecht's initial sketch of the screenplay had taken, requested that he resign from any further collaboration on payment of the arranged fee. Brecht refused, whereupon Nero withdrew from its contractual obligations on the grounds that Brecht had failed to meet his. Filming commenced without Brecht having given approval of the screenplay. Weill, in turn, was unhappy about the production of the soundtrack, certain aspects of which he was not consulted about. Both authors therefore decided to take steps to sue Nero for breach of contract and, if possible, to place an injunction on the film's production and distribution. It was decided by Berlin's no. 1 district court to treat each author's case separately. The ruling, announced on 4 November, was also split: Weill won, Brecht lost. However, Brecht eventually came to an arrangement with Nero-Film whereby his legal costs as well as a fee for the initial collaboration were paid; and he was also to have his film rights returned earlier than previously agreed (at the latest within three years, or five years for a version in English).

In an article, which he later reprinted as part of his theoretical tract *Der Dreigroschenprozess: ein soziologisches Experiment*, Brecht stated that 'the aim of the trial was publicly to demonstrate the impossibility of a collaboration with the film industry, even given contractual protection. This aim was achieved – it was achieved when I lost the trial.'[52] Brecht's biographer Werner Mittenzwei has taken this to mean that 'the aim was to show that the trial necessarily had to be lost', which is clearly an exaggeration.[53] Weill won, thereby obtaining the right to block the film's distribution. When he eventually let the injunction drop, it was only after he had reached a settlement with Nero-Film which secured him payment of 50,000 Marks and the option of musical collaboration on three films.

Like the plagiarism scandal, the 'Dreigroschenprozess' was widely reported and commented upon in the press. In order to prevent misunderstandings and also to correct some, Weill published the following declaration:

Permit me to make a few remarks about the various commentaries concerning my settlement with Tobis. I did not reach the settlement because of the amount of compensation paid. I went to court in order to exclude from the production of the film any methods detrimental to the work of art or to the names involved, and I reached a settlement because Tobis guaranteed for future films the 'exclusion of methods detrimental to the work of art or to the names involved'. I went to court over the author's right of participation in the production, and I reached a settlement because Tobis made a commitment to include me in future productions. Until now all film authors have fought in vain for these concessions, morally and legally. I am the first to have attained them, for this reason my court case became superfluous. It is true: after two favourable decisions I on my own could not find the means, namely huge court and solicitor costs etc., to have the action withdrawn. And I also could not simply give away contractual rights which Tobis has acquired from me: for I have to live from my work and from the material value of my name as a composer. Yet anyone who knows me will know that I did not agree to the settlement because of material reasons but because I achieved the principal aim of the court case.[54]

Despite Brecht's condemnation of the film as a 'shameless botch' (*schamlose Verschandelung*),[55] there is no denying that it sticks more closely to his own outline for the screenplay, which he entitled *Die Beule* ('The Bruise'), than it does to his original stage version of *Die Dreigroschenoper*. The critique of big business retrospectively imposed on the stage version in 1931 informed the conception of the film from the start. During Mac's absence Polly and the gang leave large-scale petty crime behind them and found a bank. Rather than receiving the royal pardon, Mac escapes from prison during the beggars' demonstration to be joined in his respectable family enterprise not only by Brown, whose enrolment is celebrated with a rendition of the repositioned 'Kanonensong', but also by Peachum. The beggars, for their part, are menacingly out of Peachum's control.

The changes to the score, which is reduced in the film to 28 ½ minutes of music, are also substantial. All three finales are cut, for instance. Several songs are performed as purely instrumental numbers: 'Die Ballade vom angenehmen Leben' as a dance number played on the piano in the tavern scene; 'Pollys Lied' before Mac's disappearance; and the 'Zuhälterballade', performed on the piano during Mac's habitual visit to the brothel. (In this last case, it is quite possible that Pabst was keen to elude censorship, which had been urged by the chairman of the German film distributors' association, Ludwig Scheer. Apparently Scheer was not acquainted with the work as a whole, but having chanced upon a copy of the 'Zuhälterballade' lying on his daughter's piano, he had been morally impelled to publish a defamatory article about it.[56]) All of Lucy's music is missing, as is Lucy herself. Instead, it is a repentant Jenny who aids and abets Mac's escape. And it is here that Jenny inaugurates the tradition of her, rather than Polly, laying claim to 'Seeräuberjenny', which is sung as a reflection on her initial betrayal of Mac. In the wedding scene Polly therefore has to make do with the 'Barbara-Song' as a party piece. The gala première of the German version of the film, described as 'freely adapted from Brecht' (*frei nach Brecht*), took place in Berlin on 19 February 1931. UE also produced a song album (UE 1151) containing just four numbers ('Moritat', 'Seeräuberjenny', 'Liebeslied' and 'Kanonensong'). The première of the French version followed, in the same city and same cinema, on 8 June (with the French themselves having to wait until October).

3   It was not long after its Berlin première that the film of *Dreigroschenoper* became the object of Nazi protests. It was a foretaste of events to come, which would force Weill and Brecht into exile and prevent Weill from realizing his plan to collaborate with Tobis on further films. The form of Brecht's next reworking of the *Dreigroschen* theme was also conditioned by exile. While in Denmark, he did the most unusual thing of turning what had started out as an opera into a novel (examples of the reverse process are, of course, legion). *Der Dreigroschenroman*, which afforded Brecht the opportunity to expand on his aborted film project, was published in Amsterdam towards the end of 1934.[57] The English translation by Desmond Vesey was published in 1937 as *A Penny for the Poor*, with the interpolated lyrics from the original *Dreigroschenoper* awkwardly and in places unmusically translated by Christopher Isherwood.

4   When Ernst Josef Aufricht masterminded the second French production of *L'opéra de quat'sous* in the summer of 1937, he

commissioned Weill to set to music two additional chansons for Mrs Peachum. The texts of the chansons ('Tu me démolis' and 'Pauv' Madam' Peachum!', the first of which is now lost) were written by Yvette Guilbert, the diseuse who played the part. However, 'there is no evidence (and little likelihood)', as David Drew has noted, 'that she sang Weill's settings'; she may well have used her own.[58] Weill authorized Aufricht 'to use both chansons only for the Parisian production of the *Dreigroschenoper* and only for use by Madame Yvette Guilbert', thus appearing to entertain no further interest in their becoming permanent additions to the piece. Describing the second chanson to Aufricht (*C*), Weill remarked that 'It is very much in the style of the *Dreigroschenoper* to sing this rather obscene text to music that is very graceful and charming.'[59] This may be so. Weill's general approach to text-setting may not have altered too much in the intervening decade, but his musical idiom had – another reason, along with the foreign verbal language, to keep the French chansons as separate items.

5 By the time he made arrangements of the 'Barbara Song' and the 'Kanonensong' (*BK*) in 1942 Weill's idiom had changed even more, as a comparison of the new versions with the originals vividly illustrates (see fig. 3). What prompted Weill to revamp the songs remains unclear. The most likely explanation is that he prepared them for Lenya as one-off concert items. Yet this does not explain why he felt the idiomatic adjustments were necessary. Perhaps the *Verfremdung* of the cultural mix appealed to him. Conversely, it could have been that he was merely erasing the bolder, more surrealistic of his earlier European harmonies which he no longer endorsed. If that were the case, one might also be tempted to cast doubt over Weill's conviction that, unlike any of his other European works, the score of *Die Dreigroschenoper* could readily be transplanted to a new culture. Be that as it may, even though Weill and Brecht made repeated attempts in the 1940s to adapt the entire work for the American stage, the plans never materialized (see Kim Kowalke's detailed account in chapter 4).

6 The chief reason for the authors' failure to mount an American production of *The Threepenny Opera* was, put simply and euphemistically, the lack of mutual understanding that increasingly characterized their relationship. When, in 1948, Weill learned of a production of *Die Dreigroschenoper* for which Brecht had written additional material, he conveyed to his publisher serious reservations.

3 Kurt Weill, 'Barbara Song', first page of new arrangement made
   in 1942

A few weeks ago I received a report from Munich that in the new production
of [*Die Dreigroschenoper*] there the music had been considerably altered and
that new music had even been added. I would be most grateful if you could
find out whether this is true, since I would naturally forbid even the slightest
alteration to this score and, if repeated, would take legal action against it.

I have heard from another source that Brecht has revised the text of the
Dreigroschenoper. If the revised song texts have been made to fit to the music,
then we probably can't do anything about it. If, however, the music has been

altered, then you as publisher should lodge a severe protest and forbid any further performances of this version.[60]

Weill's fears were borne out. Brecht had revised small portions of the dialogue and also completely rewritten some of the songs (*DO* and *S2*). In scene i, for example, he reduced Peachum's exposition of the basic types of human misery in the knowledge that many physically disabled, namely 'victims of the art of war', would be sitting in the audience. Among the 'updated' songs are 'Der neue Kanonensong' and 'Die Ballade vom angenehmen Leben der Hitlers-atrapen', both written in the USA in 1946, which likewise take account of the immediate past with their references to National Socialist rule and the atrocities of the Second World War (*S2*).[61] Weill complained to Brecht that adding extra verses to songs would make for monotony, for example in 'Die Ballade vom angenehmen Leben', in which the composer had taken trouble to vary the accompaniment from verse to verse. The songs are not infinitely expandable, in other words, but self-contained musical entities. Brecht agreed.[62] The music in the production by the Munich Kammerspiele had also been altered, whereupon the composer took legal action. For the collected edition of his plays in 1955, however, Brecht reverted to the 1931 version, save for some minor alterations (*GW*). The prolonged and eventful genesis of *Die Dreigroschenoper* thereby ended, after 30 years of intermittent dissension over 'matters of intellectual property'. To judge from the current legal battles waged by the collaborators' heirs, the dissension has far from abated.

3 *The première and after*

STEPHEN HINTON

Introduction

According to the ledger kept by Weill's publisher Universal Edition in Vienna, the number of new productions of *Die Dreigroschenoper* in its first season exceeded 50. By 1933, and despite several glaring omissions, the ledger had recorded a total of 130, many of them abroad. The cities infected by *Threepenny*-fever, with varying degrees of susceptibility, included Brussels, Brno, Budapest, Copenhagen, Göteborg, Ljubljana, Milan, Moscow, New York, Paris, Prague, Oslo, Stockholm, Tel Aviv, Turku, Warsaw and Zurich. In due course the work was to be translated into most of the world's major languages, in many cases at least twice, into English no fewer than eight times. In his short article on the work, written around the time of the second French production in 1937 (and reprinted here as chapter 11), Walter Benjamin noted that as early as 1930 the work had played in Tokyo in three separate productions simultaneously. He quoted the current estimate of total performances in the world as 40,000. When *Threepenny*-fever hit America in the mid-1950s, the acclaimed production at the Theatre de Lys in New York alone clocked up 2,611 consecutive performances, becoming for a while the longest running musical show in history (see chapter 4 on '*The Threepenny Opera* in America').

The fever still rages. The 1986/87 statistics for new theatrical productions in West Germany may have placed *Die Dreigroschenoper* alongside *Hamlet* in only seventh position, with both plays receiving 10 new stagings in one season. In terms of audience figures, however, it was top of the list, attracting approximately 174,000 people − that is, twice as many as the Shakespeare play.[1]

Such record-breaking statistics indicate an area of unceasing and diverse activity so vast as to render the work's stage history effectively unchartable. The following chapter can do little more, then, than pick

50

out some of the pioneering ventures which secured *The Threepenny Opera* a prominent place on the cultural map. It begins with the première, continues with a whistle-stop tour of Europe, and ends on this chronicler's former home territory, Great Britain. Appended to this highly selective survey is a brief discussion of adaptations.

The première

One of the more recent accounts of the *Dreigroschenoper*'s opening night is that by Peter Härtling published in 1985.

> Thanks to her connections with the *Weltbühne*, Katja had got hold of tickets for the première of the *Dreigroschenoper* … After the 'Kanonen-Song' they sprang out of their seats, clapped their hands until they were raw, shouted 'encore', and succeeded, in unison with the frenzied audience, in getting the song repeated. They slipped into roles, and when on stage Jenny invoked the ship that was to liberate her, a ship with eight sails, Laura decided to be Jenny for that evening. And indeed she was, when at the Mampestube she recalled scenes and characters, hummed the songs, and when later, in the middle of the Kurfürstendamm, she stood with arms akimbo, the night wind tugging at her skirt, and she bellowed: *'Und ich mache das Bett für jeden.'*

Härtling has introduced an obvious but common infelicity in that it was Polly rather than Laura's new idol Jenny who originally performed the song. Yet in this case authenticity hardly matters. The above account comes from a piece of fiction, Härtling's pseudo-biographical novel *Felix Guttmann*.[2] The mythologizing process has come full circle: in using the première as an invocation of 1920s *Zeitgeist*, Härtling obviously relied for his information on one or more of the various published recollections of the event.[3] All report how the audience remained unmoved until the 'Kanonen-Song', which suddenly brought the house down. Some of the reminiscences contained in Härtling's sources may, however, be no more authentic than his own version's frankly fictional aspects. Lotte Lenya has suggested that they often are not.

> Perhaps the strangest note of all is that people who scornfully had passed up that opening night began to lie about it, to claim to have been there, primed for a sure-fire sensation! … And although I remember that the Schiffbauerdamm had less than eight hundred seats, I nod … Sometimes, remembering all that madness, even to that blank space in the programme, I'm not even sure that I was there myself.[4]

Unlike those who may only pretend to have attended opening night, Lenya most certainly was there, playing Jenny. But her name had inadvertently been left off the programme, which apparently so incensed her husband, Kurt Weill, that he threatened to stop the show. 'For the first and last time in his whole theatre career Kurt completely lost control ... Perhaps it was a blessing that I was the one who had to quiet him and assure him that, billing or no billing, nothing could keep me from going on.'[5]

By all accounts the final days of rehearsal were chaotic. Carola Neher, who was to play Polly, dropped out and had to be replaced by Roma Bahn. There were last-minute alterations, including the insertion of the 'Moritat'. Helene Weigel, who was to play Gay's Mrs Coaxer in a wheelchair, went down with appendicitis, so her part was removed altogether. Even at the dress rehearsal, which lasted well into the small hours, further cuts had to be made to trim the work down to a performable length. (For details see chapter 2.) When Lenya and the rest of the cast eventually did go on, it was to a house that was anything but packed. A copy of the programme booklet has survived on which the former owner has added Lenya's name, rated the individual cast members' performances with exclamation marks (on a scale from one to three) and appended the remark that 'on première evening the house was empty; whoever expected the huge success?'[6] The question is of course rhetorical. The general feeling in the theatre, according to impresario Aufricht, was that the show would close after the first night, if not actually during it. The actress playing Mrs Peachum, Rosa Valetti, was already making alternative arrangements.[7] Those who did attend were prepared less for a 'sure-fire sensation' than for a sure-fire flop. Small wonder, then, given the audience's size and apprehension, that it took a while to warm to the piece. Had Härtling's Laura really existed, and had she really wanted to go to the première, she would probably have had little trouble in acquiring tickets, even without her connections at the *Weltbühne*.

Although the production was put together in a hurry, its discrete elements – music, words and stage design – emerged from a collective effort. Just as Weill and Brecht wrote their portions of the work in close consultation, making alterations as rehearsals progressed, so director Erich Engel drew his production ideas from Caspar Neher's drawings, and vice versa. The set for the première, and also the philosophy behind it, were succinctly described in Brecht's note on 'Stage design for *The Threepenny Opera*' written in the late 1930s:

When it comes to designing a set for *The Threepenny Opera*, the greater the difference between its appearance for the dialogue and its appearance for the songs, the better the set. For the Berlin production (1928) a large fairground organ was placed at the back of the stage, with built-in steps on which the jazz band was positioned and with coloured lamps which lit up whenever the orchestra played. Right and left of the organ were two huge screens, framed in red satin, on to which Neher's drawings were projected. During the songs the appropriate song titles appeared on the screens in large letters and lights were lowered from the flies. So as to blend patina and novelty, opulence and shabbiness, the curtain was a small, none-too-clean piece of calico pulled open and shut on brass wires.[8]

As can be seen from surviving photographs, other early productions of *Die Dreigroschenoper* similarly employed the property described above (notably the organ pipes and the white half-curtain) as though it were as intrinsic to the work as the other elements.[9]

A close friend of Brecht's since their school days, Neher was a seminal influence on the evolution of Epic Theatre, whose anti-dramatic tenets can be most readily defined in terms of a style of production.[10] Just as Epic Theatre, at least in theory, deliberately subverts the so-called Aristotelian unities of character, place and time – hence Brecht's concept 'non-Aristotelian theatre' – so Neher's stage designs are, in terms of theatrical tradition, starkly unrealistic. In *Die Dreigroschenoper*, to quote the critic Paul Wiegler, the sets 'remove any memory of operatic scenery by means of a fantastic naturalism. The innards of the stage are laid bare.'[11] In this way the central fairground organ housing the musicians was both essential and incidental to the action. While all music-making was clearly distinguished from the dialogue with the help of special lighting, the members of the band were permanently visible as a constitutive part of the stage machinery. Any pretence to theatrical illusion was deliberately undermined, most blatantly by the captions projected onto the silk screens (see fig. 4). Appraising Engel und Neher's achievement in his article on 'The Psychology of the Stage Design', Ernst Heilborn stated that 'the backdrop ... replaced the image by its symbol, thereby demanding from the audience that they use their imagination to form the image from the symbol, in such a way that either the image emerged from the symbol or, rather, the image and symbol together led to inner perception'[12] (see fig. 6).

Whatever inner perceptions the stark images and symbols produced, they were soon in great demand. In his diary entry for 27 September 1928, Count Harry Kessler recorded what by then had

4 Theater am Schiffbauerdamm, 1928; calico half-curtain and captions on screens

5 Final scene from the Teatr Polski production (Warsaw), 1929

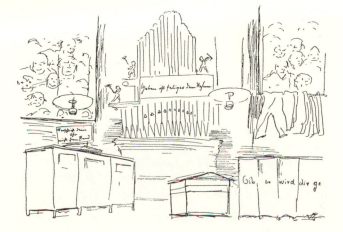

6 Décor at Schiffbauerdamm, drawn by B.F. Dolbin

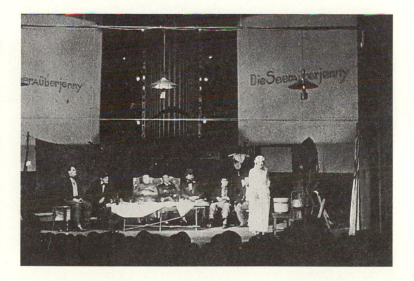

7 Polly (Roma Bahn) sings 'Seeräuberjenny' during the wedding
scene

become for the members of Berlin's smart society an obligatory visit to the Theater am Schiffbauerdamm.

> Very gripping performance, done in a primitive and proletarian way (*apache* style) à la Piscator. Weill's music enticing and expressive, the actors (Harald Paulsen and Rosa Valetti etc.) excellent. It's all the rage, permanently sold out. We bumped into the Prittwitzens (the ambassador and wife), the Herbert Guttmanns [member of the board of the Dresdner Bank and his wife], etc. 'One simply has to have been there.'[13]

Notwithstanding the unequivocal social success, the initial press notices which appeared on 1 September 1928 were predictably mixed, covering the whole critical gamut from unreserved adulation to outright dismissal.[14] One of the Republic's most noted theatre critics and a confessed Brechtian, Herbert Jhering, felt that 'the success of the *Dreigroschenoper* cannot be rated too highly'.

> It represents the breakthrough into the public sphere of a type of theatre that is not oriented towards chic society. Not because beggars and burglars appear in it, without a thriller emerging, nor because a threatening underworld is in evidence which disregards all social ties. It is because the tone has been found that neither opposes nor negates morality, which does not attack norms but transcends them and which, apart from the travesty of the operatic model at the end, is neither parodic nor serious. Rather, it proclaims a different world in which the barriers between tragedy and humour have been erased. It is the triumph of open form. (*Berliner Börsen-Courier*)

Jhering's rival, Alfred Kerr, was similarly complimentary.

> Under the pretext of an imitation of the forgotten *Beggar's Opera*, this is a very entertaining evening and an unquestionable success. Brecht is in his element when he includes ballad-like material. The composer Weill has written delightful music to all this, which provides a splendid parody. Excellent performance. (*Berliner Tageblatt*)

Like Jhering, the critic of *Der Tag* was attracted by the work's calculated ambiguity.

> Most important is what the thing as a whole attempts: to create from the dissolution of traditional theatrical categories something new that is all things at once: irony and symbol, grotesque and protest, opera and popular melody; an attempt which gives subversion the last word and which, leaving its theatrical claims aside, could represent an important phase in the otherwise directionless discussion about the form of the revue.

Reviewing the work for the *Berliner Börsen-Courier*, the opera critic Oskar Bie called the music 'completely new ... a model of modern operetta as it should be'. The communist *Rote Fahne*, on the other hand, was far from impressed.

If one is weak, then one leans on someone stronger; if one's attitude to the present is more or less one of incomprehension, then one seeks refuge in the past; if one does not know how to organize the revolutionary movement of the working class, then one experiments with the aimless and dull rebellious moods of the *lumpenproletariat*. (*Die Rote Fahne*, 4 September 1928)

The same critic went on to describe Brecht as a 'bohemian'. The work itself, he thought, compared unfavourably with Gay's *Beggar's Opera*: 'Not a trace of modern social or political satire. All in all, a varied, entertaining mishmash.' At the other end of the political spectrum, the right-wing *Neue Preussische Kreuz-Zeitung* merely indulged in a cheap critical joke:

Since I quietly fell asleep after the first five minutes I am unfortunately unable to say anything more about the content of the piece [except for quoting what was in the programme]. To anyone who suffers from chronic sleeplessness I can urgently recommend a visit to the Theater am Schiffbauerdamm. And if they are not overcome by fits of yawning during the course of the evening, they can rest assured that they are beyond help!

Within a few years the reactionary dismissals of *Die Dreigroschenoper* were to become no laughing matter. But in the meantime Berlin was under the *Dreigroschen* spell, and other German towns were quick to succumb. The first run at the Theater am Schiffbauerdamm finished on 11 April 1929 after 250 consecutive performances, whereupon the production transferred to the Komödienhaus, although Sunday matinées at Schiffbauerdamm continued for the entire run of more than two years. By the time it was in its second *en suite* run at Schiffbauerdamm in October 1929, the scene between Lucy and Polly (scene viii), which was cut for the première, had been reinstated, as had Carola Neher, who was originally meant to play Polly. Ever since the première, in fact, there had been regular cast changes. Charlotte Ander was soon sharing Polly with Roma Bahn. Carola Neher, in turn, was later replaced by Hilde Körber. Hans Hermann-Schaufuss and Frigga Braut regularly played Mr and Mrs Peachum. Theo Lingen, who took over as Macheath when Harald Paulsen was required for the Viennese première in March 1929, ended up relinquishing his part to Albert Hoerrmann.[15] Not that he left the cast altogether: he appeared as Tiger Brown instead. Lotte Lenya also changed roles. Having been replaced as Jenny by Cäcilie Lvovsky, she rejoined the cast for a third run at the Schiffbauerdamm as Lucy. According to the various newspapers that reported this brief recast revival in November 1930, the production by then had reached a total of 350 performances.[16]

Nor had the commotion been confined to the theatre. 'Berlin was shaken by *Dreigroschen*-fever', writes the composer Werner Egk in his memoirs.

Even my digs echoed with Brecht–Weill songs. These were reproduced most perfectly of all by my friend Peter Pfitzner, a son of the monomaniacal genius Hans Pfitzner. It gave me great satisfaction that Peter now breathed Brecht–Weill like others do oxygen.[17]

Several dance-band arrangements of the music were made, so-called 'Tanzpotpourris', some of them with Weill's explicit encouragement and approval. They were played by bands such as Marek Weber and his Orchestra, who in the late 1920s performed every afternoon in the 'Tanztee' room of Berlin's Hotel Adlon. In addition to the vocal excerpts featuring members of the Schiffbauerdamm cast, many of these popular arrangements were also committed to shellac and sold in considerable numbers. Apart from various jazz orchestra arrangements, Universal Edition published all the hit numbers individually as song sheets. They also carried in their catalogue 'Seven Pieces after the *Dreigroschenoper* for violin and piano' arranged by Stefan Frenkel (UE 9969), including a simplified version (UE 9969b).

Dreigroschen wallpaper was manufactured depicting and naming the work's principal characters. And a 'Dreigroschen-Keller' opened in Berlin's Kant Strasse. 'For a while', wrote one of its founders, the author Franz Jung,

this pub was all the rage in Berlin. It was the done thing, after the theatre, to end up in a group in the 'Dreigroschen-Keller'; not just the theatre crowd, who frequented the place in the first few weeks, soon the society snobs also turned up – whoever considered themselves part of culture, the diplomats and crooks of the strong-man and pimp type, journalists and police informers.[18]

The German town of Hildesheim is down on record as having given a première of *Die Dreigroschenoper* on 9 February 1933, just over a week after the seizure of power by the National Socialists. This, however, must have been the last production of the work in Germany until that by Karlheinz Martin at Berlin's Hebbel Theater on 15 August 1945.[19] During the Nazi period *Die Dreigroschenoper* was decried as the epitome of 'degenerate art'. This meant an effective ban, except when the work and its composer received official exposure at the exhibition of 'Degenerate Music' (*Entartete Musik*), which opened in Düsseldorf on 25 May 1938. Shellac recordings of the songs were played and a poster of Weill put on display. The latter contained the caption 'The creator of the *Dreigroschenoper*, in person', followed by the closing lines (in Weill's own manuscript vocal score) from the refrain of 'Die Ballade vom angenehmen Leben' — as if that, devoid of all irony, were the composer's own doctrine. Apparently the room devoted exclusively to *Die Dreigroschenoper* had to close because it attracted such large and appreciative crowds.[20] Unofficially, the work's popularity remained undiminished. Gramophone recordings of the songs were treasured possessions, played clandestinely as expressions of subversion as well as nostalgia. To quote a letter from Universal Edition to Weill of 5 July 1948: 'In certain private circles during the Nazi period, the songs of *Die Dreigroschenoper* were a kind of anthem and served as spiritual rejuvenation for many an oppressed soul.'

While West Germany (more precisely, Berlin's American Sector) was quick to reintroduce *Die Dreigroschenoper* to the repertoire after its twelve-year suppression, East Germany waited until 1958, when Fritz Bennewitz directed the GDR's first *Dreigroschenoper* in Meiningen. Rostock followed in 1959, where, according to the critic of *Theater der Zeit*, 'the director [Benno Besson] and the actors rigorously followed Brecht's *Anmerkungen*'.[21] Brecht's Berliner Ensemble finally added the piece to its repertoire on 23 April 1960, four years after the playwright's death. In order to justify his new production, Erich Engel, who had been responsible for the world première in the same theatre 32 years earlier, provided a note for the programme booklet. 'Today, as before [1928],' he averred, 'it is useful, by way of consciousness raising, to utilize such a satire in order to submit to the viewer's critique the adulteration of life under capitalism.'[22] In 1928 Macheath's receiving a knighthood was, Engel thought, operatic parody. In 1960, the idea of criminals (i.e. ex-Nazis) becoming part of the establishment had acquired a profound social relevance.

The solemnity of Engel's official enterprise stood in sharp contrast to a West German production in Cologne the following year, which André Müller of the East German *Theater der Zeit* declared 'a scandal'.

The show was a mixture of Anouilh, Ionesco, 'West Side Story' and Cologne carnival. Mac the Knife in a red dinner jacket and with an existentialist's beard. Polly, who was played by Belina, the star of EMI records brought in specially from Paris, appeared on stage in a long evening dress or in ultra-elegant trousers shot with gold. The beggar king Peachum in his black dinner suit looked like the director of a West German conglomerate ... The songs are scanned with *zicke, zacke, zicke, zacke, hei, hei, hei*. Tap dancing during the scene shifts; stagehands vacuum up non-existent dust with a vacuum cleaner à la Ionesco. The whores were charming call girls who advertised Dralon underwear. The text was mutilated and supplemented quite arbitrarily.[23]

Although Müller's condemnation derives from his cold-war campaign against the Federal Republic's decadent theatre, the West Germans were equally scandalized, particularly by the apparently anti-Semitic portrayal of Peachum, which provoked widespread protests.

Engel's new version openly acknowledged the influence of Giorgio Strehler's 1956 production in Milan (discussed below). Strehler, however, only saw in the imitation of his Italian success a sign of the East Berlin theatre's tendency towards 'museological ossification'.[24] The critique, which may or may not have applied at the time, has proved far-sighted, particularly in view of the *Dreigroschenoper*'s function at the Berliner Ensemble. The most recent production was the work of a collective which strove to return to the original text (but in fact the 1931 version was used) and based the sets on Caspar Neher's originals. Apart from a cosmetic overhaul in 1985, this production has featured regularly in the Ensemble's repertoire ever since it received its première on 2 October 1981. In the winter of 1988 it was showing definite signs of fatigue, appearing less like an exercise in 'consciousness raising' than a jaded exhibit wheeled out for bevies of western tourists.

Austria

Quick to follow on the heels of Hamburg, Frankfurt, Leipzig, Oldenburg, Prague, Augsburg and 24 other venues was Vienna. The première at the Raimund-Theater on 9 March 1929 was a gala cultural event. Universal Edition arranged for the composer to attend the dress rehearsal and to give both a press interview and a pre-concert talk on Radio Vienna.[25] Harald Paulsen was imported from Berlin to play Macheath. Karlheinz Martin (who later supervised the first postwar production in Berlin in 1945) directed, and Norbert Gingold, the arranger of the piano vocal score, conducted the 'Wiener Jazz-Symphonieorchester'. The press was unanimously effusive – in particular the critic of the *Neue Freie Presse* (and author of *Bambi*), Felix Salten, who had the benefit of having seen the original Schiffbauerdamm production.

Far be it from me to encroach upon the responsibilities of our music critic or to contradict his expert judgment. But I cannot ignore the perfect unity of Brecht—Weill, and my own artistic intuition senses that the young Weill's music is as characteristic as Brecht's language, as electrifying in its rhythm as the lines of the poems, as deliberately and triumphantly trivial and full of allusions as the popularizing rhymes, as witty in the jazz treatment of the instruments, as contemporary, high-spirited and full of mood and aggression, as the text, which occasionally spills over into readily avoidable and even more readily dispensable brutality.

Some of these excesses were toned down in the Viennese performance. This is probably Karlheinz Martin's best work since his production here of Wedekind's *Franziska*. He has managed to shift the whole thing into the realm of unreality — something which is startlingly in evidence from the very beginning in the scene with the 'Moritat'. It is hard to imagine a group of beggars, invalids and destitutes who, bathed in music and song, create such a harmonious, almost pleasing impression, look so lively and remind one such of puppets. The platform which twice comes into view during Mackie's song, a revolving platform on which Mackie's fellow gangsters perform a waxwork-like roundelay of crimes, is a superb idea of the director's, touching as it does the very nerve of the audience. (10 March 1929)

The production, maintained Salten, 'tactfully subdues those elements that are harsh, and successfully intensifies those that are effective'; its overall character, he concluded, was 'refined' (*gepflegt*). Although (or perhaps because) the provocatively 'primitive and proletarian'

8 Final scene from Raimund-Theater production (Vienna), 1929

style which had so impressed Count Kessler in Berlin seems to have yielded in Vienna to polish and discipline, and although (or perhaps because) Martin's production was one of very few in Austria prior to the *Anschluss* in 1938, *Die Dreigroschenoper* at the Raimund-Theater found great favour with the public and critics alike, with performances soon reaching treble figures.[26]

Switzerland

Zurich had in fact beaten Vienna by two months. Switzerland's first *Dreigroschenoper*, directed by Max Semmler, opened at the Neues Theater Zurich on 29 January 1929, and closed 6 days later. Whether commenting favourably or unfavourably on the work, the Swiss critics were particularly bothered by the work's uncertain generic identity. The next production at the Stadttheater Basel (director: Oskar Wälterlin), which opened four months later on 31 May, ran for just three performances (receiving two repeats during the next season). 'It is in no way an opera, even less a traditional play. Still less, in our opinion, is it an operetta', wrote the critic of the newspaper *Vorwärts* (3 June 1929).

Zurich's Stadttheater was the next to try, with a production that opened on 22 September 1929. It closed five performances later, after director Paul Trede had received anonymous threatening letters. Trede was the most obvious exponent of the Swiss tendency to engage for all the major parts trained singers from opera and operetta. 'The opera', he wrote in his brief to the performers, 'is an experience for singers.'

Whoever has not been endowed by mother nature with a sonorous and indefatigable throat has no business being here. That is to say: what principally matters in Zurich is the beautiful voice, artistically treated and shaded by natural feeling.[27]

Nonetheless the press, and the author of the threatening letters, perceived a critical intention. 'The most convincing mockery of bankrupt operetta imaginable', wrote the critic of the *Tagesanzeiger Bern* (24 September 1929). Nor was Bern any more successful with its production, which opened on 30 March 1930. In its preview the *Neue Berner Zeitung* (27 March 1930) expressed optimism: 'At a time when good operettas are so scarce that almost all operetta theatres have closed down, such a work, placed as it is between opera and operetta, is bound to be greeted by Bern's theatre-goers.' In the event, the show disappeared after six performances.

France

France's first *Dreigroschenoper* had its première in Paris at the Théâtre Montparnasse on 13 October 1930. Translated by André Mauprey, the well-known adaptor of Lehár's operettas, *L'opéra de quat'sous* became one of the biggest failures of director Gaston Baty's career − partly because the piece itself was criticized as an unworthy adaptation of the John Gay original (which had been revived in Paris with considerable success in 1921) and partly because of poor musical performances. In the programme booklet Baty introduced his work under the heading 'Dreaming and Forgetting'. He had directed it 'in a peculiar way, in an unreal sphere, like a nocturnal charade which bordered on a dream'.[28] After trouble with the censors, the French version of the Pabst film was eventually shown to Parisian audiences in October 1931. The music in particular met with considerable critical acclaim. The same cannot be said, however, of the next stage production of *L'opéra de quat'sous*, which opened in Paris at the Théâtre de l'Etoile on 28 September 1937. Ernst Josef Aufricht, the original impresario at Schiffbauerdamm, engaged as director Francesco von Mendelssohn, who had been responsible for the flop of *The 3-Penny Opera* in New York four years earlier (see chapter 4). He also persuaded Weill to write two extra chansons for the diseuse Yvette Guilbert (see chapter 2) and even invited Brecht, who accepted, to come from Denmark to attend rehearsals. But the press and public largely rejected what was to be the last *Dreigroschenoper* in France until the 1950s.

Russia

News of the *Dreigroschenoper* first reached Russia via the Soviet Commissar for Enlightenment, Anatolij Lunačarskij. Passing through Berlin on his way to a disarmament conference in Geneva in 1928, he managed to include a visit to Schiffbauerdamm, where the performance sufficiently impressed him to warrant a laudatory report in a Russian newspaper. Rather than pay tribute to the work's provocative innovations, however, as most of the *Dreigroschenoper*'s apologists had done, Lunačarskij chose to invoke tradition, in this case the work of Moscow's own theatre company TRAM (Teatr rabočej maladeži − theatre of working-class youth).

Of course the similarities are purely coincidental; the performance of the opera is especially realistic and presents a lifelike, high-quality portrayal of the

64   *Stephen Hinton*

London underworld. However, just like with TRAM, which also champions realist theatre, music suddenly occurs on stage, people dance or sing songs or cabaret ditties, and in the same way a transition is made to 'defamiliarized theatre' (*uslovnij teatr*).[29]

But it was to Alexander Tairoff's Kamerny Theatre in Moscow, rather than TRAM, that the task fell of presenting the Russian première of *Opera niščich* (The Beggars' Opera, as it was first called) in 1930. Like the Enlightenment Minister, reviewers were able to draw on facets of their own contemporary culture to write notices with a critical assurance unparalleled in the work's early stage history. In mirroring current shifts in Soviet aesthetics, however, they adopted positions variously and precariously poised, as Brecht himself was at the time, between formalism and the nascent socialist realism. The following comment is an interesting case in point. Suggesting that the Kamerny production employed 'formalist' elements, the reviewer teasingly eschews any direct value judgment.

The innovations of the Kamerny Theatre, which contribute towards the development of complete theatrical mastery, are still cultivated on the basis of a playful aesthetic in pieces without any social content, whereby self-sufficient theatrical effects emerge.[30]

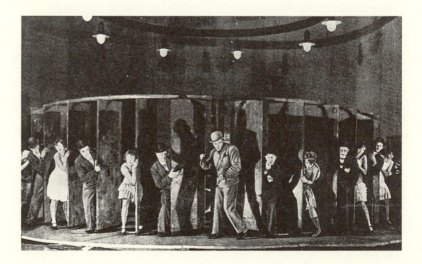

9 Scene from the Kamerny Theatre production (Moscow), 1930

The critic of *Izvestija* (16 February), on the other hand, unequivocally disapproved, suggesting that to show on stage policemen collaborating with gangsters was ideologically suspect. 'It is high time,' he wrote, 'that our theatres ceased playing homage to petit-bourgeois bad taste and instead turned to more relevant themes.'

On yet a different level, another commentator discovered in the piece a forceful critical realism.

Die Dreigroschenoper is a peculiar German paraphrase on the theme of Gorky's *The Lower Depths*. Like the Gorky piece, it is written in premonition of monumental social conflicts. As in Gorky, the rabble appear in an unmasking role. It is on them that we pin our faith – they are destined to proclaim the downfall of society, to fling in its face the bitter truth and issue a barrage of curses.[31]

Of Brecht's works, *Die Dreigroschenoper* is the only one to have been staged in the Soviet Union during the playwright's lifetime. By the time of its Moscow première in 1930, its first Russian champion, Lunačarskij, had already resigned in the midst of political shifts which were to reverse the eclectic cultural radicalism he had done so much to foster. *Trechgrošovaja opera* (to use the title of the new translation) was not performed in Moscow again until over thirty years later. S. Turmanoff directed it in 1963 at the unlikely venue of the Stanislavsky Theatre. 'Brecht's ideas about theatre were', Eva Kreilisheim has tersely noted, 'if anything, foreign to the traditions of that house.'[32]

Italy

The Threepenny Opera's stage history in Italy also began in 1930. In an interpretation by the noted avant-garde director Anton Giulio Bragaglia, *La veglia dei lestofanti* (trans. Corrado Alvaro and Alberto Spaini) opened in Milan's Filodrammatici on 8 March. Bragaglia, whose work enjoyed the Duce's approval before fascist censorship stiffened its guard, was a committed Futurist. His 'Teatro della Rivoluzione' primarily concerned itself with formal experiments which deployed revolutionary aesthetic means influenced by the cinema. In a celebratory article, Walter Benjamin quoted Bragaglia's comparison of himself with the German director Erwin Piscator. The latter, Bragaglia asserted, 'uses technology to political ends, whereas I put it at the service of art'.[33] Photographs of this 'commedia-jazz', as it was styled, show the antiquated world of operetta visited by incongruous stereotypes from such motley spheres as *commedia*

10 Page from the programme booklet of *La veglia dei lestofanti*
    at the Filodrammatici Milan, 1930

dell'arte, revue and Oskar Schlemmer's Bauhaus theatre, all viewed
through Futurist spectacles. Fidelity to the text was sacrificed under
the weight of the director's fertile and domineering imagination. The
dialogue was shamelessly bowdlerized and the score rearranged. When
Bragaglia took the show on tour, the 'moral and intellectual reserve'

of Verdi's native Parma lodged its protest against this 'festosa caricatura del melodramma all'italiana', as the programme booklet described the work.[31] In general, however, *La veglia dei lestofanti* (literally: 'The swindlers' vigil') was a considerable success with both press and public.

The next Italian production of *The Threepenny Opera* was in more ways than one a clandestine affair. It was given just once, to an invited audience of intellectuals, at the Teatro Argentina in Rome on 11 February 1943. In order to elude the attention of fascist censors, the director Vito Pandolfi outwardly presented the work as *L'Opera dello straccione*, 'The Beggar's Opera', even though it bore even less resemblance to Gay than the Brecht–Weill adaptation does. Nor did Pandolfi offer a faithful rendition of the latter work either. The musicologist Roman Vlad completely rewrote the score, and the songs included texts by Sherwood Anderson, Jack London, Apollinaire and Villon.

The director turned the figure of the hero Mac the Knife into a kind of embodiment of the regime; typical of the orientation of his interpretation was the mimed epilogue, something foreign to the original text, in which Mack is condemned to a picturesque demise ('Addio, Mac ...'). In a boat he slowly disappears from the scene.[35]

Pictures of the production show the influence of Brecht's 'literarization of the theatre' as introduced in the German premières of *Die Dreigroschenoper* and both the 'Songspiel' and opera versions of *Mahagonny*. Incorporated in the painter Scialoja's sets were laconically provocative statements displayed on placards. One of these, in English, declared: 'Liberty is delicious'. For the select audience attending this disguised adaptation in the politically oppressive climate of 1943, the target of Pandolfi's message would have been anything but secret.

Since its première on 2 February 1956 at the Piccolo Teatro Milan, Giorgio Strehler's highly successful production of *L'opera da tre soldi* (as it is titled in the translation by Ettore Gaipa, Gino Negri and Giorgio Strehler) has been revised and revived three times – in 1958, 1960 and 1973. The Piccolo Teatro had opened in 1947 as Italy's first municipally financed theatre, and aimed to realize the dictum, inspired by Gramsci, that theatre should begin before the performance and end only after it.[36] The choice of *The Threepenny Opera* was clearly influenced by Brecht's post-1929 concept of theatre as an institution with pedagogic and didactic obligations. While planning the forthcoming production, Strehler travelled to Berlin 'with 27 exactly

11 Scene from *L'Opera dello straccione* at the Teatro Argentina Rome, 1943

formulated questions' to discuss his concept with the playwright himself.[37] Brecht, in turn, travelled to Milan with his assistant Elisabeth Hauptmann to attend the final rehearsals and the première. In a letter of 11 February 1956 to his former mistress Ruth Berlau, he wrote that the performance was splendid in conception and detail and very aggressive — lasted from half-past nine until two in the morning; the opera is uncut . apparently it was a great success and the piece does indeed seem very fresh. Strehler, probably Europe's best director, has moved the piece to 1914, and Teo Otto has created wonderful sets (a garage instead of a stable, etc.). A very good idea; after the Third World War one would have to move it to the year 19..'.[38]

Like Brecht, Strehler was anxious that the catchy melodies might all too easily undermine, as he saw it, the playwright's enterprise. As a pre-emptive measure he had the music reorchestrated in a way that accentuated the jazz component and, he felt, intensified the work's aggressive character. 'If the predominant role that music plays in Brecht's work is accepted and confirmed', he later observed, 'it turns out to be one of the most difficult and fascinating barriers that has to be overcome. And it is not the only one.'[39]

Strehler's new production in 1973 introduced yet a further up-dating of the action, to the year 1928, with Macheath being turned from one of Al Capone's ancestors into a contemporary brother-in-crime. The language, which in 1956 had been translated with a view to avoiding censorship of the text's more indelicate passages, was given a harsher, cruder edge. The overall style of the show took a decided shift towards revue and musical. Stars from the entertainment industry such as Milva, who played Jenny, were cast in the principal roles. Once again the score was mutilated.

Strehler's productions of *L'opera da tre soldi* have served as controversial models for the postwar Italian reception of Brecht. As such, their idiosyncrasies need to be seen in the context of efforts associated with the Italian Communist Party to formulate a Marxist aesthetic. In Italy, as in Germany, the forum for such theorizing was the so-called 'Realism Debate', in which Brecht's writings were tapped as an authoritative, canonized source. Yet the fact that Strehler should have chosen *Die Dreigroschenoper* with which to introduce his audience to Brecht as a theatrical practitioner of exemplary political commitment smacks of compromise, an attempt to sugar the didactic pill. Perhaps this is why he found it necessary, in a prologue which he later discarded, to instruct the audience of the work's socially critical relevance. It is also a telling irony that at least one critic could mistake this for a dispassionate attempt at historicization.[40]

Britain

The first full-scale British staging of *The Threepenny Opera* took place in the same year as Strehler's Milan première, in 1956. Before then, apart from a few isolated screenings of the Pabst film, a handful of critical articles, and an anonymous reorchestration of the score in 1938 for Antony Tudor's ballet *The Judgement of Paris*,[41] there were just two performances of the work – one of them a complete concert version, the other semi-staged excerpts. The first of the articles was a review of the German première written by the Berlin correspondent of *The Times*, A. Ebbutt (reprinted here as chapter 7). Ebbutt's review is remarkable in that it evinces an unusual grasp of trends in contemporary German theatre, such as the work of Erwin Piscator, with which it legitimately compares the Schiffbauerdamm production, and also resists the temptation simply to dismiss the work by means of an unfavourable comparison with 'our' *Beggar's Opera*, as so often happens with subsequent writers. The most dismissive, in many ways the most 'British', and certainly the most entertaining of the early commentators is Eric Blom, whose essay entitled 'Three-groats opera' was published in *The Sackbut* in 1931 (reprinted here as chapter 10). Beside Blom's piece, with its complaints of 'distressing insipidity', 'vertical *Katzenjammer* atmosphere' and the 'unrelieved poverty of the libretto', Constant Lambert's reservations about the Weill–Brecht collaboration, as recorded in his popular survey *Music Ho! A Study of Music in Decline* (1934), acquire an air of positively urbane judiciousness. Before discussing directly *The Threepenny Opera*, Lambert advances the thesis, as remarkable as it is truly prophetic, that Weill was a quintessentially American composer even before he had set foot on that continent.

Weill is undoubtedly the most successful and important of the Central European composers who have experimented with the jazz idiom. It is curious that a German should be the first to sum up in musical synthesis certain phases of American life. American jazz is either too Hollywood or too Harlem – it rarely suggests the dusty panorama of American life which gives such strength to even second-rate films. Weill is almost the only composer who can evoke in music the odd, untidy, drably tragic background that is presented to us so forcibly by William Faulkner in *Sanctuary* and *Light in August*.

Unlike so many composers who have taken up jazz as a stunt and dropped it the moment they felt it was no longer the most daring fashion, Weill has gradually evolved from disparate German and American elements a style of highly individual expressiveness. Even in his early and crude *Drei Groschen Opera* [sic] there is a certain Hogarthian quality, a poetic sordidness, which gives a strength to what otherwise might have been a completely worthless

work. Just as the *Drei Groschen Opera* in spite of its crude American-
isms catches the ramshackle charm of the poorer quarters of London, so
Mahagonny in spite of its Teutonic traits sums up the inverted poetry of
American 'low life'. *1 he Seven Deadly Sins* marks as great an improvement
on *Mahagonny* as *Mahagonny* did on the *Drei Groschen Opera*.[42]

Although it was not until 1936 that the London Film Society gave
the first public screening of the Pabst film, it had twice been shown
privately in 1932 and 1933.[43] The original stage work had to wait
until 1935, when it was broadcast, on 8 February, as one of the BBC's
Contemporary Music Concerts.[44] The announcement in *The Listener*
(8 February) read as follows:

The contemporary music to be heard from the B.B.C.'s concert at Broad-
casting House to-night is the German version of the 'Beggar's Opera'. This
performance, which is the first one over the wireless in Britain, will be a
complete one, and Mr. Denis Freeman will be in charge as producer. The
text is a free adaptation of John Gay's, and the music, except for one melody
taken from the original, is entirely the work of that brilliant young German

12 Scene from G.W. Pabst's film of *Die Dreigroschenoper*;
Macheath (Rudolf Forster) makes the acquaintance of Polly
(Carola Neher)

musician Kurt Weill. He has used the title 'Die Dreigroschenoper', which the B.B.C. translate as 'The Tuppenny-Ha'penny Opera', claiming that this emphasises the satire implied. The cast includes Charles Victor, Marie Dainton, Tessa Deane [Polly], Robert Chisholme [presumably the same Macheath as in the 1933 New York production], Norman Shelley, Vivienne Chatterton, Dorothy Leigh, Edwin Ellis, Reginald Smith, Arthur Goullet, Ernest Sefton, Samuel Worthington, and Wilfred Grantham. Mr. Edward Clark will conduct.

Apart from a well-informed and sympathetic preview in the *Radio Times* (1 February) by the German émigré musicologist Alfred Einstein, the British press gave the work a rough ride, their critical stance fluctuating between blatant jingoism and inapt classicism. A short notice for *The Musical Times* remarked that

Goethe and Gay have a bond of sympathy. Each can look down on a foreign perversion of his best work and gain a modicum of consolation from the shudderings of his compatriots. There was plenty to shudder at in the concert version of 'Die Dreigroschenoper' ... Bert Brecht the librettist, and Kurt Weill the composer, have done a queer thing. The one has lifted and altered Gay's plot, the other has thrown away the well-loved tunes and substituted his own post-war jazzy inanities. It is all very crude and painful. But (to be fair) they know nothing of Gay and Playfair in Germany. They lack our touchstone and our sensitiveness. So we may concede that, coming from the blue, this cynical, out-of-the-way frivolity may have had some piquant attraction, and we need not grudge it a few years of popularity. After all, ours has gone on for two hundred.[45]

The great Wagnerian Ernest Newman, writing in *The Sunday Times* (10 February), was equally – perhaps predictably – appalled.

'The Beggar's Opera' we all know, to our delight. On Friday night the B.B.C., in one of its concerts of what it calls contemporary music, treated us to an opera that can only be described as beggarly. The 'Dreigroschen Oper' of Bert Brecht (text) and Kurt Weill (music), which was all the rage in Germany a little while ago, is described by its authors as 'after "The Beggar's Opera" of John Gay'. It may be after that masterpiece, but it will certainly never catch up with it: these two dull dogs achieve the almost incredible feat of making even crime boring. It is difficult to say which is feebler, the libretto or the music – perhaps the latter, which has the worst faults of more than one bad style and the qualities of not a single good one, even at second hand.

Part of the fault must have lain with the performance. In this respect, Weill himself was the most scathing critic of all. 'It was the worst performance imaginable', he protested in a letter (dated 14 February, presumably to UE) from the Park Lane Hotel. 'The whole thing was completely misunderstood, it was compared of course with the ''Beggar's Opera'', and hence torn to pieces by the press.'[46]

C. Denis Freeman's translation received its second and last public performance three-and-a-half years later on 28 July 1938, when The Opera Group in London presented semi-staged excerpts as part of the Festival of German Music. The concerts, four in all, were organized to accompany the Exhibition of Twentieth-Century German Art at the New Burlington Galleries, mounted as an explicit protest against the Nazis' exhibition of 'Degenerate Art', which had been touring Germany since 19 July 1937. The conductor of the *3 Groschen Opera* (as it was billed) was Ernst Schoen, former director of Frankfurt Radio. (The first half of the programme featured 'Songs and Satires by Wedekind, Kaestner, Brecht–Eisler'.) If the theatrical property used was necessarily makeshift, then the uncommissioned backdrops by Barlach, Beckmann, Dix, Ernst, Grosz, Kandinsky, Kokoschka, Schlemmer, *et al.* must have more than made amends.[47]

When *The Threepenny Opera* opened at London's Royal Court Theatre on 9 February 1956, the British had clearly become more receptive to the work than hitherto. The New York success of the Blitzstein version (also used in London) had doubtless prepared the way. But as with Strehler's Milan production in the same year, Sam Wanamaker's 'Soho musical' (as the piece was billed) must also be seen in the context of postwar Brecht reception: less within the cerebral confines of Marxist ratiocinations, however, than as part of the anarchic revolt of the Angry Young Men. To quote the music critic Peter Heyworth: 'Those were intoxicating days when, led by Ken Tynan, we drove through the Brandenburg Gate in search of a form of theatre that was revolutionary in style as well as content.'[48] London's middlebrow press felt obliged to warn its readers: 'a show with a violent, shocking difference … don't take your maiden aunt' (*Daily Herald*). 'I think you had better leave your aunt at home' (*Evening Standard*). *The Times* hated it: 'Most of [the music]', protested that newspaper's critic, 'could have been turned out by a hack in the Charing Cross Road.' Heyworth and his fellow critic on *The Observer* Kenneth Tynan loved it. Tynan began his review by remarking that 'this promises to be a good year for Brechtians'.

A Brechtian, let me explain, is one who believes that low drama with high principles is better than high principles with no audience, that the worst plays are those which depend wholly on suspense and the illusion of reality; and that the drama of the future will be a wedding in which neither partner marries beneath itself.

'Mr. Wanamaker's production', Tynan went on to observe, 'is loyally Brechtian.'

He retains Caspar Neher's brilliant, fragmentary scenery, and uses signboards and lantern slides to tell us what is going to happen next. Daphne Anderson is a sweetly cheating Polly, and Georgina Brown, pouting and slouching, gives Lucy the full sensual treatment. George Murcell and Warren Mitchell are the best of the cut-throats. One shrinks only from the embarrassing grimaces of George A. Cooper as the corrupt Commissioner, and from the abject mis-casting of Bill Owen as Macheath. Mr. Owen gives us a bantamweight swell, whereas what is wanted (and this is the whole satirical point) is a heavyweight grandee who might pass for a banker. [Ewan MacColl, from the world of traditional folkmusic, was the Street Singer. Berthold Goldschmidt, a Schreker pupil who emigrated to Britain in 1935, conducted.] But I would forgive much in return for a musical show in which no word or note is coy, dainty or sugary. These qualities are lies; beguiling lies, perhaps, but denials of life. Brecht's honesty, tart though it tastes, is an affirmation. It says that whoever we are, and however vile, we are worth singing about. (*The Observer*, 12 February 1956)

Peter Heyworth was convinced less by the book than by the score. 'Bert Brecht and Kurt Weill were angry men', he began, 'when in the troubled Berlin of the late twenties they wrote the *Dreigroschenoper*. But if Brecht's text has not come through the passage of time unscathed and if in Marc Blitzstein's adaptation most of the pungent bite and precision of the German original has been lost, Weill's score emerges as a masterpiece of its kind.' Like Heyworth, Hans Keller openly took exception to the glib dismissal of Weill's score by the critic of *The Times*, producing for *The Music Review* a vigorous defence (reprinted here as chapter 12), which characteristically combines Viennese music-analytical organicism and Freudian psychoanalysis.

It was another sixteen years before London saw another *Threepenny Opera*. Of Tony Richardson's realization of Hugh MacDiarmid's loose translation, which opened at The Prince of Wales on 10 February, Irving Wardle wrote in *The Times* that 'instant theatricality is its sole objective. Together it is a smart, slick, punchy production of the kind which invites applause as each star appears.' Vanessa Redgrave as Polly danced a spoof Trocadero. She appeared, accor-ding to the *Evening News*, 'to have strayed from a Wimbledon garden party. In a wide-brimmed black hat, Joe Melia was a Twenties gangster.' 'If I'm less sure about Barbara Windsor's Lucy, all bounce and curls', remarked *The Observer*'s Helen Dawson, 'it's because at the moment it seems to add a discordant "Carry-On" note at odds with the cynical humour of the rest of the production.' For the present writer, it was his first encounter with the work, and although Barbara Windsor's performance may have been at odds with the cynical humour of the piece as such, it seemed quite in keeping with the rest of the production. *The Threepenny Opera* had been transformed into a glossy West End show.

By way of illustrating not just the diversity of the British approach but also the extent of *The Threepenny Opera's* astonishing malleability, whether intrinsically or extrinsically determined, brief mention should be made of two more recent productions. First, the Glasgow Citizens' licentious romp of 1978, described here by *The Times'* theatre critic Ned Chaillet:

Philip Prowse's production of *The Threepenny Opera* is set 'deep in the *Herz* of old Soho', at least in part, which gives some idea of the direction the play has taken. Brecht turned the English of *The Beggar's Opera* into German, with new morals, plot twists and Kurt Weill's music. Mr Prowse has turned an uncredited English translation of Brecht halfway back into German and set the scenes of underworld struggle in a Louis-Quinze drawing-room. Brecht's dislocation of the English original, fragmented in so many new ways by Mr Prowse, takes on new power to disturb.

The pastel prettiness of the room, in blue, pink and white with a chandelier, a grand piano and paintings on the ceiling, is invaded by beggars in black-and-white rags. The room's sole occupant, an elegant woman played by David Gann in drag, is abused, beaten, forced to sit with the prostitutes and finally knifed by Macheath. None of that, not even the room, is anywhere in the script, but it focuses the ideas of class struggle with unsettling vigour.

With the alien sound of the German-English dialogue and the gradual destruction of the room as bits of it are used to tell the story − the top of the piano becomes Macheath's prison and when he is about to be hanged the rope dangles from the chandelier − there is a distance that keeps the increased aggression watchable. It is at moments like a Stanley Kubrick picture of society, a sort of 'Clockwork Threepenny', but because of the liberties in Mr Prowse's production, it is sometimes a closer approximation of Brecht's Germanic England than many a more dutiful performance. (*The Times*, 2 October 1978)

One such 'dutiful performance' was the one by the National Theatre, directed by Peter Wood and given its première on 13 March 1986. Robert David MacDonald provided a new − accurate as well as bland and unsingable − translation. Dominic Muldowney directed a first-class band of professional instrumentalists who played, both faithfully and spiritedly, every note of Weill's full score. (Glasgow had made do with a 'prepared' piano.) The star-studded cast, headed by Tim Curry as a foppish Macheath, may have been stronger on acting than singing, but talent and resources were in abundance − the latter regrettably too much so. *The Threepenny Opera* is a chamber piece. To transfer it to a stage as vast and grand as the National's Olivier Theatre, notwithstanding laudable fidelity to the text, is a production

decision in a sense more inauthentic in approach than some of the
more preposterous liberties taken by the Glaswegian company.

Adaptations

With a work such as *The Threepenny Opera*, itself an adaptation,
the dividing line between interpretation and adaptation is often
blurred. Günter Krämer's production at West Berlin's Theater des
Westens in 1987 is a case in point. (Krämer's, incidentally, was the
first production in West Berlin since 1945; in the interim all other
attempts to stage the work had been impeded by the Brecht estate.)
Krämer so supremely ignored the musical demands the work places
on performers that inspired interpretation, an epithet which by all
means applies in his highly watchable case, might just as well be
described as free adaptation. The same goes for the productions,
discussed above, by the Glasgow Citizens in 1978 and Bragaglia in
1930, both extreme examples of what can happen to *The Threepenny
Opera* in the inventive and frequently capricious arena of director's
theatre. In conventional opera or music-drama, the director may feel
at licence to divorce the score, sometimes quite brutally and unmusically, from the action on stage. The music nonetheless remains
intact. With *The Threepenny Opera*, however, the victim of novel
interpretation may well be the score itself. How many performances
of the work have there been for which (i) musically inept performers
were engaged, (ii) Weill's instrumentation was treated as optional,
or (iii) the music was simply suppressed? At the Theater des Westens
(i) certainly applied, as did − to a lesser extent − (iii), and (ii) would
have applied had Krämer's alterations to the score not been vetoed
by the copyright holders. The director's principal concern was with
theatre as opposed to music theatre, the music thus treated as
incidental rather than essential.

In Wolfgang Staudte's film version of *Die Dreigroschenoper*, shot
in 1962, it was not only the screenplay (by Staudte and Günter Weisenborn) that necessitated the description '*after* the theatre piece by
Bertolt Brecht and Kurt Weill' (italics added) but also Peter Sandloff's
re-scoring of the music. The actors included Curd Jürgens as
Macheath and Hildegard Knef as Jenny. Having taken over the
direction of the film from Helmut Käutner, Staudte was forced to
shoot against the clock before the licence on the film rights expired.
No sooner had he finished, though, than an adaptation of the
adaptation was made: after acquiring the American rights on the film,

Joseph E. Levine/Embassy Pictures shot new scenes with Sammy Davis Jr as the Street Singer which they interpolated without Staudte's consent.[49]

There have also been two even freer adaptations, one for the theatre and one for the screen. The Nobel prize-winning Nigerian writer Wole Soyinka wrote his *Opera Wonyosi* in 1976 as a satire on a handful of African tyrants and the numerous vices he saw present in Nigeria and the Central African Republic at the time. The Gay/Brecht plot becomes fused with the local colour of African politics, with Captain Macheath's marriage to Polly being set against the background of preparations for the coronation of Emperor Boky. Apart from the 'Moritat', which he retained, Soyinka rewrote all the other songs, thus requiring completely new musical settings.[50]

For a description of the film *Opera do Malandro*, the present writer must defer to the magazine *Time Out* (No. 884, 29 July 1987):

Take 'The Threepenny Opera', relocate in Rio, replace Kurt Weill's score with Brazilian sambas, and embellish with dancing and dreamy décor. What do you have? An almost totally successful studio-shot musical from Mozambique-born director Ruy Guerra. In an *extremely* loose adaptation of Brecht's classic, Guerra tells a tale of fairy-tale simplicity: the year is 1941, and the Brazilian government are backing the Nazis against the wishes of the US-obsessed population at large, one of whom − white-suited pimp Max − is developing his own capitalistic practices ... Hollywood ancestors − notably Hawks's *Scarface* and Gene Kelly's musicals − are refracted through a double prism of Brechtian modernism and traditional Brazilian culture.

At the time of writing (February 1989) yet a further adaptation is in the offing: a multi-million dollar film of *The Threepenny Opera* (to be called *Mack the Knife*) produced and directed by Menahem Golan. Shot in Hungary, it is set in Dickensian London with Roger Daltry as the street singer whose role has been expanded to that of epic conférencier and with décor that could have been inherited from the film version of *Oliver*. In view of the announcement that the orchestra has been augmented to thirty-five players, including strings, one might well speculate who, if they had lived to witness it, would be more put out − Weill or Brecht?

4 'The Threepenny Opera' in America

KIM H. KOWALKE

> What, in your opinion, accounted for the success of *Die Drei-groschenoper*?
>
> I'm afraid it was everything that didn't matter to me: the romantic plot, the love story, the music ...
>
> And what would have mattered to you?
>
> The critique of society.
>
> *An interview by Brecht with himself, c. 1933.*[1]

After Weill's death in 1950, the attorneys representing his estate sought advice from several colleagues who had prepared the federal tax returns for the Estates of Jerome Kern, George Gershwin, and George M. Cohan. Following the precedent established for estimating the monetary values of the artistic legacies of these American songwriters, the firm of Paul, Weiss, Rifkind, Wharton and Garrison hired Max Dreyfus to appraise the copyrights in Weill's compositions. Dreyfus, the doyen of publishers of American popular song and theatre music (and at the time, president of Chappell Music), assessed the 'fair market value' of Weill's *oeuvre* at $25,000, exclusive of anticipated ASCAP income, also estimated at $25,000. (In comparison, in 1945 Kern's had been appraised for $183,500.) Because Weill had received no money from either his publishers or Brecht for scattered performances in Europe after the war, Dreyfus claimed in his affidavit that the 'Moritat vom Mackie Messer' and *Die Dreigroschenoper* as a whole were, practically speaking, 'worthless':

It is my opinion that none [of Weill's compositions] can be considered 'popular' music in the sense that they have been or will be widely played; furthermore, I cannot foresee any widespread market for any such musical compositions. From my personal familiarity with the decedent's compositions published abroad and based on my knowledge of, and familiarity with, foreign music markets and the value of foreign copyrights, I would state that such foreign works have no present value at all as they carry a very limited appeal and, on a financial basis, would have no salable value.[2]

Ten years later Marc Blitzstein's American adaptation of *Die Dreigroschenoper* closed its run at the Theatre de Lys after 2,611 consecutive performances, eclipsing *Oklahoma!* as the longest-running musical in the history of the American theatre. The show had drawn more than 750,000 people into the 299-seat house and had grossed more than three million dollars on an initial production cost of $8,792. The cast album, the first of an off-Broadway musical, had sold over 500,000 copies, and more than forty 'pop' renditions of 'Mack the Knife' had spun off ten million pressings.[3] Blitzstein's version of *The Threepenny Opera** guaranteed for Weill what his Broadway works had not: a posthumous impact on the course of American musical theatre and the impetus to resurrect some other works composed before his arrival in the United States. *Die Dreigroschenoper* had preceded Weill across the Atlantic, but it took twenty years longer than its composer to adapt successfully to the new cultural setting. A chronicle of its struggle evinces both the challenges Weill faced as an émigré composer and the changes in social, political, theatrical and aesthetic values necessary for the posthumous acceptance of his European works in America.

Die Dreigroschenoper first crossed the Atlantic during May 1931 in G. W. Pabst's film version. Opening in New York three months after its première and lacking the pre-release notoriety a lawsuit had assured it there (see chapter 2), the film showed in the Warner Theater at Broadway and 52nd Street. Billed as an 'All-Talking GERMAN Musical Drama', *The Beggar's Opera* (subtitled 'Die Dreigroschenoper') was competing with John Barrymore as *Svengali* and James Cagney and Jean Harlow in *The Public Enemy*, playing in Warner theatres a few blocks down Broadway. An English synopsis printed in the programme characterized the film's hero, Mickie [sic] Messer, as 'the Al Capone of olde England' and described the 'Barbarasong' as 'a ditty about a girl who says "No!" until the right man comes along'.[4]

Reviewing the film for the *New York Times*, Mordaunt Hall deemed it 'a moderately entertaining offering', but only 'for those

---

* To differentiate the various English-language translations and productions of *Die Dreigroschenoper*, this essay preserves the orthography of their respective titles: *The 3-Penny Opera* (1933), *The Three Penny Opera* (1946), *The Threepenny Opera* (1952), and *Threepenny Opera* (1976). Titles of songs are cited in English only when they refer to a specific translation.

familiar with the Teutonic tongue'. His otherwise bemused critique concluded:

> The melodies are quite agreeable and one would not complain if there were more of the singing and less of some of the action. It is, however, a fantastic affair which has none of the charm, vitality, and bitter satire of Gay's *Beggar's Opera*. The vocal recording is for the most part exceedingly good, except when those players with penetrating voices were obviously too close to the microphone.[5]

The film found few enthusiasts among an audience hungry for escapist musical fare in the new medium. Needless to say, its box office showing did nothing to encourage a stage production of the alien play in America. The recordings of songs from *Die Dreigroschenoper* made by Lenya and other cast members in 1930 likewise appealed to only a limited circle of aficionados. George Gershwin, for one, told Weill and Lenya at a party shortly after their arrival in New York in 1935 how very fond he had become of the Telefunken recording, except that he had never liked the 'squitchadickeh' voice of the leading lady; Lenya never forgave the remark.[6]

When *Die Dreigroschenoper* was first mounted on stage in the United States in 1933, it had already been produced in virtually every major European city, except in England, which resisted until 1956 what was generally viewed as an unpardonable crime against *The Beggar's Opera*. The 1920 London revival of Gay's ballad opera, which had persuaded Elisabeth Hauptmann to translate it into German for Brecht's consideration, also spawned two New York productions of what had been George Washington's favourite play. The first, at the Greenwich Village Theater in 1920, included a few members of Nigel Playfair's original company in its cast; it fared better than its 1928 Broadway successor, a Playfair touring production which opened (and quickly closed) at the 48th Street Theater, just five months before *Die Dreigroschenoper* received its première in Berlin. But the fact that *The Beggar's Opera*, the most successful play-with-music in the English language, had not found an audience in New York during the previous decade did not discourage two enterprising producers from trying their luck with a retranslation into English of the Brecht/Hauptmann adaptation. Hoping to duplicate the theatrical sensation of Central Europe in depression-ridden America, the two novice producers, John Krimsky and Gifford Cochran, travelled to Berlin in January 1933 to obtain the stage rights from Felix Bloch Erben, to meet with Weill and Brecht, and to hire as director Francesco von Mendelssohn, who had assisted Erich Engel with the production at the Theater am Schiffbauerdamm. The programme credited Cochran and Krimsky's brother Jerrold with 'adaptation of the play into English'. The forty-two members of the cast were mostly unknowns or newcomers: Robert Chisholm, an Australian operetta baritone, as Macheath; Steffi Duna, a Hungarian 'concert ballet dancer' fresh from a stint of Noël Coward, as Polly; and as Peachum the jovial ventriloquist of 'Brother, Can You Spare a Dime' fame, Rex Weber. A young actor named Burgess Meredith abandoned his portrayal of the Dormouse, Duck and Tweedledee in Eva Le Gallienne's *Alice in Wonderland* to play the minor role of Crooked Finger Jack.

Little is known about the particulars of the English adaptation, since no copy of the script seems to have survived. In 1942 Weill suggested to Brecht that 'one of the principal reasons for the failure in 1933 was that [Krimsky and Cochran] had made a literal trans-lation' instead of an adaptation geared for the American theatre.[7] But if the programme booklets for the production accurately reflect its outlines, the adaptors and director by no means merely recreated what had been presented in Berlin. Their adaptation also apparently diverged considerably from both the libretto published by Universal Edition in October 1928 and Brecht's revised 'literary text' published by Kiepenheuer in the 1931 *Versuche*. The list of musical numbers in the booklet, for example, omitted Peachum's 'Morgenchoral' and the 'Anstatt-dass-Song', as well as the 'Salomonsong' and 'Ballade von der sexuellen Hörigkeit', both of which had been cut during rehearsals in Berlin too.[8] Krimsky and Cochran retitled the 'Barbara-song' the 'Lucy Song', as Lucy (rather than Polly) sang it in act 2, scene iii.[9] Additional changes were implemented between the week of 'tryout' performances in Philadelphia and the New York open-ing: the first scene in Peachum's Beggars' Establishment disappeared (the songs therein had evidently already been cut). The 'Second Finale', sung in Philadelphia by Mrs Peachum (Evelyn Beresford) and Macheath, as specified in both the libretto and score published in 1928, was reassigned in New York to Jenny (Marjorie Dille) and Macheath, as in Brecht's 1931 version.

In November 1932, Weill had already made plans to attend the final rehearsals and première in order to oversee the production. On 6 February 1933 he wrote to his publisher, Universal Edition: 'I firmly intend to go to New York for the *Dreigroschen*-première. If the music is done well and my name properly promoted there, after six months I could have the same position in New York that I have in Paris.

Brecht absolutely wants to go, which means, of course, that the music would be pushed completely into the background.' But after rehearsals had begun, Weill reported that Mr Wreede, the director of Felix Bloch Erben, 'had put forward certain arguments against my trip'. Wreede, relieved that Brecht had now decided not to go, feared that he would change his mind again if he heard of Weill's plans. Weill wrote to Universal Edition on 2 March:

> Obviously there is great fear in New York that B., the author of the text, will come and that the whole thing, not only the production but also the public image, would be pushed in that direction, which would very much prejudice the reception of the work. It appears that Wreede has similar fears. I have told him that I don't share them, as I won't beat the drums here for publicity about my trip. I want to go there only to ensure that my music will be performed well; and in case of a success I'll be in position to follow up on the consequences.

Weill's publisher urged him to go and pledged full support: 'positive results such as commissions, concerts, and additional productions are probable'.

On 14 March Weill advised Universal Edition that Wreede still opposed his trip: 'he says I should wait to see if the production is a success.' Ignoring the increasing threat to his person in Germany, Weill feared for the fate of his music in New York:

> I have written in detail again to Mendelssohn and implored him to provide for a respectable performance of the music. Perhaps it would be helpful if you would send him (Hotel Ambassador) my original full score of *Die Dreigroschenoper*. The printed score is really full of errors and gives rise to many false impressions on account of its being a reduced piano-conductor version. We must do everything to assure a first-class performance of the music. I also ask that you write Mr. Dreyfus, the head of Harms, who, Wreede tells me, is himself a very good musician, so that he attends the musical rehearsals of *The 3-Penny Opera* with the same care he devotes to the Gershwin works. Give him a description of the musical idiosyncrasies of the piece − that it is not jazz-music in the American sense but rather a quite special, new sound, which can be achieved only by a meticulous realization of the original full score.

A week later, on Potsdam Day, Weill fled Berlin to Paris. Brecht and his family had already left on 28 February, the day after the Reichstag fire. If Weill still entertained any thoughts of a trip to New York during these dark days, they were forgotten almost immediately upon his arrival in Paris, when he was commissioned to compose a ballet score for Balanchine's *Les Ballets 1933*. After Cocteau declined his invitation to collaborate, Weill summoned Brecht from Switzerland.

By opening night of *The 3-Penny Opera* in New York, they were already working on *Die sieben Todsünden*.

The first performance of *The 3-Penny Opera* at the Garrick Theater in Philadelphia, originally scheduled for 3 April, had been moved up inauspiciously to 1 April to avoid conflict with the first nights of Ethel Barrymore's *An Amazing Career* and George M. Cohan's *Pigeons and People*. In retrospect, the next day's notices were both surprisingly receptive and predictably uncomprehending. Writing in the *Philadelphia Public Ledger*, Arthur B. Waters found *The 3-Penny Opera* 'a rich and racy diversion, plentifully supplied with good music and people who could sing it, gay and colorful in its settings and costumes, and quaint and provocative in its story'. In contrast, the *Inquirer*'s Linton Martin thought it 'quite the "roughest" night on theatrical waters within the memories of the oldest and most sophisticated sailors of the playhouse seas':

This modern version of the most ancient English ballad opera ... with music by Kurt Weill, whose tone poem of 'Lindbergh's Flight' provided a storm center of discussion when presented by Leopold Stokowski at Philadelphia Orchestra concerts two years ago, might have brought blushes to the blasé cheeks of even the gayest blades of Restoration England, when language had no limit ... Self-conscious snickers and embarrassed giggles punctuated the performance last night as demure lassies ... uttered and sang, with the utmost insouciance, words relegated to the dictionary by polite society today ... Some mock-apprehensive souls declared they expected the patrol wagon to back up any minute and let ladies and children in first ... As the saying goes, 'Don't take the kiddies.'

The 3-Penny Opera had been scheduled to open in New York on 10 April at the elegant Empire Theatre, Broadway and 40th Street, an incongruously posh setting for an opera for beggars. Apparently all was not well, however, as the official première was postponed for three days, with the invitation-only preview rescheduled for 12 April. Several New York newspapers printed excerpts from the generally favourable Philadelphia reviews in an attempt to whet theatre-goers' appetites near the end of an otherwise dreary season, darkened at its beginning by the death of Florenz Ziegfeld. Only three 'book musicals' had survived more than a few weeks: Kern's and Hammerstein's *Music in the Air*, Porter's *Gay Divorce* (Fred Astaire's farewell to Broadway), and De Sylva's and Brown's *Take a Chance* (featuring Ethel Merman's show-stopping 'Eadie Was a Lady').

The first-night audience of *The 3-Penny Opera* included Fannie Brice, Billy Rose, Martin Beck, and Howard Dietz, but it was not the hit everyone had been waiting for. New York critics roasted it.

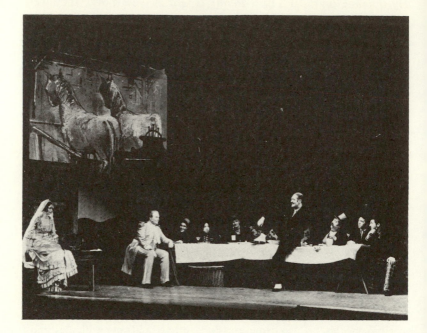

13 The Wedding Scene in the production at the Empire Theatre New York, 1933. Robert Chisholm (Macheath), Rex Evans (Tiger Brown), Steffi Duna (Polly), and the Gang, including Burgess Meredith as Crooked Finger Jake. Directed by Francesco von Mendelssohn and designed by Cleon Throckmorton

In the *New York Herald Tribune,* Percy Hammond called the play a 'torpid affectation, sluggish, ghastly, and not nearly so dirty as advertised'. Gilbert Gabriel labelled it a 'dreary enigma' that was 'not funny enough, flashing enough, sharp enough to cut through its own attendant atmosphere of squalor, muss, and gloom'. But he liked the score:

Its music is, by all odds and ears, the best thing about *The 3-Penny Opera.* In the modern idiom Mr. Weil [sic] has composed a collection of ballads, duets, and finales which are stormily insinuating, mocking, stinging, memorable for their curiously bold, macabre tunefulness, fretting the story with a most interesting and distinguished score. You have heard its equal for originality in precious few operettas of our day ... The cast has able artists in it, but the wrong ones ... up to their noddles in a calamitous piece of awfully arty misdirection.

Newsweek (15 April 1933) characterized the production no more favourably, but described elements of its 'epic' staging in some detail:

The part [of Brown] is played by Rex Evans in flamboyantly effeminate fashion and the idea of his being called 'Tiger' is supposed to raise a laugh ... *The 3-Penny Opera*'s most interesting feature is the stage setting, executed by Cleon Throckmorton after the German designs by Caspar Neher. Upstage center a representation of a pipe organ stands throughout, behind which the orchestra is concealed. When it is desired to change the scene, a curtain about eight feet high is drawn across the stage and the various flats and props needed are frankly dragged on, usually drowning out the orchestra ... Robert Chisholm is robust as Macheath and has the only good singing voice in the company ... The lyrics are clumsy and jarring on the ear.

The critic for the *New York Times* seemed genuinely baffled by the 'gently mad evening', while *Variety* suggested that only 'one melody may linger after the show has gone – it is called "Ballad of the Easy Life"'. By far the most sympathetic theatre critic, Robert Garland, reported in the *New York World Telegram* that the 'first-night audience seemed determined not to like it in a great big way':

A rebel of an operetta, it walks boldly and bitterly through the autumn in which we all reside, kicking up the leaves and applying lighted matches where lighted matches are sure to do the greatest harm. The trouble is that it does not laugh as it is doing so ... You'll know what I mean when I say that *The 3-Penny Opera* is as humorless as Hitler.

In an attempt to counteract the poisonous reviews and the failure of the show's advance publicity to attract a New York audience with rumours of its naughtiness (which Philadelphia had found so titillating), the press department placed an unsigned promotional piece in the 15 April edition of the *New York Evening Post*. Entitled 'Germany's Young Radicals', the article is filled with *de rigueur* hyperbole as well as staggering misinformation; while reliably recounting little about either Germany or its young radicals, it nevertheless unwittingly reveals much about the America which *The 3-Penny Opera* encountered in 1933:

On the opening night of *The 3-Penny Opera* in Berlin, when the Nazis staged a riot in the gallery and it seemed inevitable that the curtain would have to be rung down, Brecht leaped into action behind the scenes, urged the terror-stricken actors to go on with the show and forced it through to the final curtain. The Nazis retreated at the end, while the cast responded to thirty curtain calls from a slightly hysterical audience.

According to all reports, Brecht is now in prison by order of Chancellor Hitler. Brecht is described as a gaunt man of frightening mien, with his close-cropped head, piercing eyes, and violent manner. He is regarded as a mouthpiece for the modern German spirit.

Kurt Weill, who is conductor of a symphony orchestra in Berlin, has been guest conductor in many European cities ... Weill's wife is Lotte Lenya, the singer and actress who played nearly every feminine role in *Die Dreigroschenoper* during its Berlin run. Weill is described as a humorous young man, short and dark. He has never been able to turn out a conventional score.

The sensationalist strategy didn't bolster ticket sales; *The 3-Penny Opera* closed on 22 April after twelve performances. Stephen Rathbun eulogized its passing in the *New York Sun* on 24 April:

The lovely music and the bitter, grim satire of *The 3-Penny Opera* have died away ... The fact that Bert Brecht's modernization of *The Beggar's Opera* is somber and depressing is, no doubt, the reason why it was unsuccessful on Broadway. In these days, if people want to be depressed, they can be depressed at home! Why should they pay money to be depressed in the theatre? ... Let us be Gay, but let us not be Brecht at the expense of gayety. When gloom on the stage meets gloom in the audience, the result is failure for any play. At least that's what happens in America.

The work would not be staged again in America until 1946, when the aftermath of worldwide events far more depressing than any foreseeable in 1933 would add yet another subtext to *Die Dreigroschenoper*.[10] On 5 May Universal Edition informed Weill that '*The 3-Penny Opera* has closed after just 10 days. To be sure, this is especially unfortunate and catastrophic news.' Weill blamed Mendelssohn for the disaster; in 1937 he articulated to Lenya his appraisal of Mendelssohn's (and Brecht's) ability to stage *Die Dreigroschenoper* in a foreign cultural setting:

I find Francesco more repulsive than ever. I am simply flabbergasted by this dilettante's nerve to mount *Dreigroschenoper* again in Paris. It will be a tremendous flop, to be sure. He's totally untalented and only backbites. In casting the principal roles he's mainly concerned with who will be able to get along with him. Unfortunately I can't forbid it, since Aufricht is having him come and he pays Aufricht for that. But Brecht is also coming and he'll spoil [*versauen*] the whole thing anyway.[11]

Three days after *The 3-Penny Opera* had closed, Lehman Engel conducted a single performance of *Der Jasager* at the Grand Street Playhouse in New York. In December 1934 Bruno Walter programmed Weill's Symphony No.2, retitled 'Three Night Scenes: A Symphonic Fantasy' for two subscription concerts of the New York Philharmonic. Nearly unanimous in their scathing reactions to Weill's symphony, New York's music critics reinforced the theatrical and cultural bulwarks that would confront Weill when he docked in

New York the following September. Although he initially planned only a short stay to supervise rehearsals of his music for Max Reinhardt's production of *The Eternal Road* (the English version of the biblical pageant *Der Weg der Verheissung*), repeated postponements of opening night prevented an early return to France. In fact, Weill was to return to Europe only once, in 1947, on stopovers to and from Palestine, where he visited his parents, brother, and sister. He avoided Germany. During his fifteen years in the United States, he would not see a production of *Die Dreigroschenoper*, despite repeated efforts to adapt his most popular work to the requirements of American commercial theatre. Indeed, not one of his stage works completed in Europe would be produced professionally in America before his death.

Weill was formally presented to the American branch of 'New Music' at the Cosmopolitan Club on 17 December 1935 in a concert devoted entirely to his works. The unlikely sponsor of the programme was the League of Composers, whose periodical, *Modern Music*, had consistently published negative reviews of Weill's music — after Copland's initial report of the 'very dull' Violin Concerto in 1926 — until Virgil Thomson's appreciative 'Most Melodious Tears' appeared in the November–December 1933 issue, which designated Weill as 'a new model of German composer'. Earlier that year, echoing Schoenberg's diatribe about the music of *Die Dreigroschenoper* in his masterclass in Berlin, Marc Blitzstein had dismissed what he called Weill's 'super-bourgeois ditties' as 'real decadence: the dissolution of a one-time genuine article, regurgitated upon an innocent public, ready, perhaps even ripe to learn'. But in the March–April 1935 issue of *Modern Music*, Blitzstein reported that he had just visited Weill in Paris and heard a private piano-performance of the 'huge oratorio-spectacle': 'it is Weill's best score, and also his most uneven. Weill has one theatre-attack. It has long-range communicability, and sufficient variety inside its own curious limitations.' Weill, however, described this first meeting with Blitzstein rather differently:

An American musician visited me and asked me to play him some of [*Der Weg der Verheissung*] ... He asked me if he might be permitted to work on the musical adaptation required by the English translation ... I don't know if any such collaboration is necessary, and also I know Mr. Blitzstein too little to be able to judge whether he could do it. He seems to be more of a writer-about-music [*Musikschriftsteller*] than a musician.[12]

Blitzstein reviewed the 17 December concert, which Thomson had actually helped to arrange; entitled 'New York Medley, Winter,

1935', Blitzstein's essay in *Modern Music* opened with a prelude about Thomson, segued into a Weill-section, and concluded by adding Eisler in counterpoint:

Kurt Weill's music suits Thomson's public even better than Thomson's does; it is much more ordinary, and as cunning in detail ... Parts of *Mahagonny* are stunning music of the faux-populaire school; on the other hand, Lenja is too special a talent, I am afraid, for a wide American appeal; but she has magnetism and a raw lovely voice like a boy-soprano ...
    One can talk of Eisler and Weill together. They write the same kind of music, although their purposes are completely at variance. Both use severely simple melodies, regular two-four stepping tunes, to hum on your way out; perfect cadences, symmetrical phrase-lengths, unvaried *oom-pah* accompaniments. But Eisler's music for the Theatre Union's *Mother* revealed (even though a wretched performance) that both in temperament and knowledge he is the superior. Weill is flaccid (he wants to 'entertain'); Eisler has spine and nerves (he wants to 'educate').[13]

Five months later, Blitzstein suggested in *Modern Music* that 'Weill's natural sweetness and softness are probably the cause of the *Dreigroschenoper*'s enormous and mistaken success.'[14] Most of the members of the League, committed to new music of sorts very different from Weill's, probably shared Blitzstein's distrust of 'mistaken success'; only a handful stayed past intermission.

The following summer, Blitzstein attended the Group Theatre's seminars at Pine Wood Lake Lodge in Trumbull, Connecticut, where Weill lectured on 'Music in the Theatre'. In his lecture notes, Weill described *Die Dreigroschenoper* as 'a new type of musical theatre' with 'real appeal to all circles of the audience'. After addressing larger aesthetic and sociological issues, he suggested that 'technical questions' would be better studied in practical work: 'I have chosen a number of songs and scenes from *Die Dreigroschenoper* (in a bad translation) and will first teach you the music and then work on the style of singing and acting.' The first assignment required each member of the class to perform one of the three roles in the First Finale. In his next contribution to *Modern Music*, a review of *Johnny Johnson*, Blitzstein recanted, almost paraphrasing passages from Weill's lecture:

I have written some harsh things in the past about Kurt Weill and his music. I wish now to write a few good things. He hasn't changed, I have ... I think Weill feels that certain ways of being expressive never die; and I think he believes he can crack open, make plastic, even re-form a mold which has hardened in the memory for other composers. If in listening one can make the first hurdle (I used to say 'You *can't* write like that!'), then one finds the music fresher and more appealing than all the smart-striving social-climbing Broadway songs. Weill has practically added a new form to the musical theatre. It is not opera, although it partakes of the 'number' form of Mozart ... This almost elementary, uninhibited use of music, seemingly careless, really profoundly sensitive, predicts something new for the theatre.[15]

Although Weill himself made few efforts on behalf of his European works, his project lists from the period repeatedly include a new version of *Die Dreigroschenoper*, to be adapted specifically for the American theatre by a leading playwright.

During his first trip to Hollywood in 1937, Ernst Toch had introduced Weill to Ann Ronell, who had played rehearsal piano for Flo Ziegfeld's Broadway productions of the Gershwins' *Rosalie* (1928) and *Show Girl* (1929) and now hoped to become George's protégé. Ronell was supporting herself in Hollywood by writing English lyrics for productions of European operas and operettas and also had provided several lyrics for the film score which Weill was composing. He then invited her to furnish lyrics for an American version of *Die Dreigroschenoper*, using his own rough English translations as a basis. Ronell finished only three songs before Weill summoned her to New York early in 1938 for a backers' audition. At their apartment on East 62nd Street, Weill accompanied Lenya in the three numbers for Bennett Cerf and Jed Harris, who had just directed the Broadway première of *Our Town*. The audition failed to generate further interest, except from an enthusiastic guest – Marc Blitzstein.

Brecht and Weill had met again in New York in the autumn of 1935, when Brecht arrived to supervise the Theatre Union's production of *The Mother*. Banned from the theatre after just two weeks for his abusive behaviour and threats of legal action, Brecht characteristically refused any compromise, even with the theatre company in America ideologically most disposed toward his plays. Later, during his period of American exile from 1941 to 1947, Brecht again effectively barred his own works from the professional stage by insisting that the American theatre would have to adapt to Brecht and Brecht's works, rather than *vice versa*.[16] After Brecht returned to Denmark in 1936, Weill and he had no further contact until 1939, when Weill wrote to suggest that the contract with Felix Bloch Erben for the stage rights of *Die Dreigroschenoper* should be terminated, since he had not received any royalties from the productions in Paris or Stockholm, apparently because Nazis now controlled the firm. Brecht agreed, but neglected to mention in his reply that he had received from other sources, on behalf of both of them, some money for performances in Europe.[17] In June he inquired from Weill, 'what are the real chances for *Die Dreigroschenoper* in America?' Weill answered:

I believe that it wouldn't be impossible to mount *Die Dreigroschenoper* again in America at some point, assuming that we can free up the rights, because no one will make a contract with a German publisher. One could risk it, of course, only with a completely new adaptation (which must be made by someone first-class) and with one of the best Broadway producers. I will be busy with this project in the course of next season and will keep you informed of any progress. As soon as I get back to New York, I'll undertake the necessary steps to get back our rights.

No correspondence between Weill and Felix Bloch Erben dating from this period has been traced.

For the next two years Weill and Brecht did not communicate. In March 1941, Elisabeth Hauptmann, then living in Los Angeles, wrote to Weill asking him for a contribution, after his enormous success with *Lady in the Dark*, to support Brecht's travel to America with his family.[18] Weill sent one hundred dollars to Brecht's bank in Finland. Although Brecht arrived in Los Angeles during July 1941, he did not contact Weill until the following February, even though he had entered into negotiations, soon after his arrival, for an all-black production of *Die Dreigroschenoper*. The entry in his *Arbeitsjournal* for 22 November 1941 states: 'The Negro Clarence Muse has done an adaptation of *Die Dreigroschenoper* and wants to put on an all-Negro production.' When Brecht did resume correspondence with Weill early in 1942, he casually asked how things stood with the rights for *Die Dreigroschenoper*, particularly the American rights, and suggested that he 'would gladly try the piece at some point with Negroes, since there are splendid Negro actors here who are naturally better suited than Americans'. (Recent productions in the long tradition of all-black theatre and opera on Broadway included *Porgy and Bess*, which both Weill and Brecht had seen in 1935, and the 1939 adaptations of Gilbert and Sullivan, *The Swing Mikado* and *The Hot Mikado*.) On 5 March Weill received a cryptic telegram from Brecht's agent in Hollywood: 'Negotiating between Brecht and Clarence Muse for musical version "Dreigroschen Oper". Please wire immediately your share in stage royalties and motion picture rights.' An explanatory letter from Brecht arrived the next day:

Some Negroes are very interested in a production of *Die Dreigroschenoper*. Clarence Muse (who, I think, produced *Run, Little Children* here), together with Paul Robeson (who is helping to start a National Negro Theater and wants eventually to play Peachum), wants to produce it here with Katherine Dunham as Polly. Muse has made an adaptation, almost nothing changed, except the setting (now Washington) and the inauguration of the President instead of the coronation. They want to make their own instrumentation of your music for their band ... I will send the contract on to you as soon as I get it.[19]

On 7 March Weill wired George Marton, Brecht's agent, to express doubts about the feasibility of the project and to request additional information for his agent and publisher. Two days later Weill answered Brecht's letter:

I hope that you are not yet too deeply entangled in these matters ... It's a shame that you didn't give me the opportunity to advise you at an earlier stage of negotiations. I believe that I could have advised you better than most people in Hollywood; especially in the matter of an American revival of *Die Dreigroschenoper* I am sort of an 'expert', since I've been engaged with this problem continuously during the last seven years. Because of the overall structure of the American theatre, it is very tricky to revive a play that has failed once before, even if it has as good a reputation as *Die Dreigroschenoper*. But no doubt we will have a first-class revival of *Die Dreigroschenoper* if we wait for the best combination of translator (for the play and, what is especially difficult, for the lyrics), director, producer, and actors. In recent months I've had many negotiations with Charles MacArthur, one of the best young dramatists in America and a long-time collaborator of Ben Hecht. He was very interested, and my plan was to get a really first-class American adaptation either from him alone or together with Hecht, with whom I am very friendly.

Weill also reminded Brecht that he had already been working for years with an American writer on an all-black version of *Die Dreigroschenoper*, but there were real problems to be solved: 'It became apparent that the idea of having American Negroes performing a German adaptation of a seventeenth-century [*recte*, eighteenth-century] English ballad opera was so "sophisticated" that it would totally bewilder the audience. We then attempted to rework the piece so that the problems became genuine problems of the Negro − but that meant we'd have to write a whole new play.' Weill did, however, empathize with Brecht's position:

It goes without saying that I can very well understand that you're eager to get something going here and also that your financial situation makes a quick theatrical success desirable. But I had hoped that you would find a start in film through your friends in Hollywood so that we could wait with *Die*

Dreigroschenoper until we could really take advantage of the best prospects which this 'property' holds for us. But you will probably say that this is a typically capitalist viewpoint.

As for me personally, of course I must see the translation of the book and lyrics before I can make any decision. The songs from *Die Dreigroschenoper* are extremely well-known and loved in specialist circles here. Again and again I've tried to get translations of the lyrics that fit the musical style and preserve the qualities of your original verse. Up to now I've had no success, and I will not free the music until the question of translation is absolutely solved. Also please send me the book. I can well imagine how my music would turn out if I were to agree to the theatre's desire to make its own instrumentation. I have always, especially here in America, insisted that my music be played only in my own orchestrations in the theatre, and I must hold to this principle in this case as well.[20]

Weill's cool response precipitated a torrent of telegrams and letters from Brecht and his agent, reiterating their confidence in the project and emphasizing Brecht's dire financial straits. (Brecht claimed that he and his family were subsisting on a stipend of $120 a month from the 'European Film Fund'.)[21] In his second letter to Brecht, dated 13 March, Weill again asked to see a copy of the translation but assured him that meanwhile he would discuss the matter directly with Paul Robeson, for whom Weill intended his recently completed 'Walt Whitman Songs'. Ten days later Weill received a letter of recommendation for Clarence Muse from Mrs Robeson, who suggested that Weill might wish to contact Muse directly. Robeson apparently was not so involved in the project as Muse and Brecht had implied.

On 31 March Theodor W. Adorno sent Weill a letter in support of Brecht's project. After first proclaiming that he hoped 'to keep their valued relationship alive', Adorno told Weill that 'he was spending a lot of time with Brecht' and was writing now 'to express his own opinion' on the Negro production of *Die Dreigroschenoper*. He suggested that 'the ideological situation in America could not be compared to the German one of 1929'; America was 'not yet ready to accept the authentic *Dreigroschenoper*, which is so inseparably tied to a climate of crisis'. Consequently, a faithful rendition of the score must be abandoned in favour of a sociological 'refunctioning', which could be achieved by allowing 'a Negro jazz ensemble the greatest and most radical improvisatory freedom' with the score – an unlikely argument from Adorno, whose disdain for jazz was well known.

Although Weill's response has not been traced, on 8 April he gave Lenya a progress report on recent developments in the matter and summarized his outraged reply to Adorno's 'completely idiotic letter':

Clarence Muse, that poor old negro fellow who wants to do 3-Gr.-O., wrote a desperate letter. I am sick and tired of this whole affair and wrote him I would be willing to make a contract for a production *in California only*, but that I don't allow to show it outside of Cal. unless I have seen and passed it. That would be completely harmless for me because nobody cares anyhow what they are doing out there. If they don't accept this, to hell with them! But at least I have shown my good will. Muse writes me that Brecht had told him last summer he had written to me and I didn't answer! The good old swinish Brecht method. Well, I wrote Wiesengrund a letter which he won't forget for some time. I wrote him: It is a shame that a man of your intelligence could be so misinformed. Then I explained to him that the American Theatre isn't as bad as he thinks and in the end I said: 'maybe the main difference between the German and the American theatre is the fact that there exist certain rules of "fair play" in the American theatre. Three cheers for the American Theatre!'[22]

Meanwhile, Weill's letter to Brecht of 7 April had outlined the terms under which Muse's company could mount a production in California; it concluded: 'I want to assure you again that I will do everything in my power to make it possible for you to go through with this project, and you can believe me that I am doing this only because you seem to expect great things for yourself from this production and because I like Mr. Muse's enthusiasm which is something very rare and very precious.'[23] Brecht replied in mid-April with a lengthy, apologetic account of the history of his involvement with the project; he concluded:

I write at such length because I understand that you could easily misunderstand all of this, since I always write only out of extreme necessity and then too briefly. I'd like to suggest that we take up our collaboration again and simply erase all the misunderstandings and longstanding semi-quarrels, which so easily arise out of these troubled times, separation, etc. Till now I have lost none of my friends, and in our work we've always had so much fun and made such progress.

Weill sent Brecht's letter to Lenya:

Here is a letter from Brecht which came yesterday. It sounds very pitiful and I feel sorry for him. Maybe we are a little unjust with him. He probably went through so much that his nicer side is on the surface again. I just hate to triumph over someone who is down on the floor, and I don't want anyone to feel that I am cruel or egotistic. I would rather have the reputation of being a sucker than of being greedy or stingy or 'kleinlich' ... I'm inclined to offer him some financial help — something like $50 a month for a few months. What do you think?[24]

Lenya replied immediately by telegram: 'Don't send money to Brecht.' On 19 April she answered at length:

I know Darling how easely [sic] you forget things but I do remember everything he ever did to you. And that was plenty. Of course he wants to collaborate with you again. Nothing better could happen to him. But I am convinced after a few days, you would be so disgusted with him, I could just write it down for you what would happen. Think of people like Moss [Hart] and John Steinbeck and Max [Anderson] and all the rest we know and compare them, than [sic] you know it's impossible for you to take up that relationship again.

George Marton responded to Weill's proposal of 7 April with a copy of a letter agreement between Brecht and Muse dated 24 February 1942 (note that the date of the agreement antedates Brecht's first contact with Weill). Weill was to 'send it back with his signature'. His telegram to Marton on 20 April sizzled: 'This is the most shameful proposition that ever has been made to me. My agent and my publisher did not find one paragraph in this document that would serve as a basis for discussion.' Marton then suggested that Weill send a draft agreement of his own; Weill did not respond. Instead, he wrote to Brecht that he could not 'waste any more time on this ridiculous affair'. Weill also pointed out that the terms which Brecht had accepted in February ceded worldwide rights for *Die Dreigroschenoper* in all media in perpetuity to Muse, for which Brecht would have received 4 per cent of the adaptor's share of royalties, a sum Weill estimated at ten dollars per week, providing he donated his own share to Brecht as well. After a brief 'I told you so' lecture on the complexity of the American theatrical system, Weill closed by reciprocating Brecht's conciliatory gesture: 'I was very happy that you have explained to me the circumstances of this entire *Dreigroschen*-affair. I too would like to avoid, without fail, any misunderstandings coming between us, since I always recall our collaboration with great joy and I hope that soon we will find the opportunity to resume it.'[25] But he wrote to Lenya: 'I guess you are right about Brecht ... The whole thing is as crooked and "ausbeuterisch" [exploitative] as only contracts with communists can be.'

The clear-cut conflicts between Weill's and Brecht's attitudes toward the nature and appropriate future of *Die Dreigroschenoper*, apparent throughout the Muse affair and so reminiscent of the very issues which had made further collaboration in Berlin impossible, did not dissuade Weill, despite Lenya's misgivings, from proceeding once again as if their differences were indeed reconcilable. Both men continued to explore the possibilities for *Die Dreigroschenoper* in

America. Brecht's entry in his *Arbeitsjournal* for 1 June reported that 'MGM is seriously considering filming *Die Dreigroschenoper*.' In November Weill wrote the Justice Department's Office of Alien Property in an effort to free the rights to the work from its European publishers:

There are several groups both in New York and in Hollywood who would be interested in a revival of this successful play. The copyright for the play was owned by Felix Bloch Erben in Berlin, the musical rights by Universal-Edition in Vienna. These two publishing houses have been taken over long ago by the Nazis, and since *Die Dreigroschenoper* was one of the first plays which were banned by the Nazi Government, the original copyright owners have been unwilling and unable for years to fulfill their contractual obligations ... I would be very glad if the Alien Property Custodian would take over the copyrights for the play and the music so that all future sales or production contracts could be negotiated by this office.[26]

For the next year and a half, Weill and Brecht attempted without success to collaborate on an American musical adaptation of *Der gute Mensch von Sezuan*, which Weill was also to produce, and a musical treatment of *Schwejk*.[27] But by October 1944 all of their joint projects had collapsed. In his first letter to Caspar and Erika Neher after the war (2 July 1946), Weill reported: 'I almost never see Brecht. He is still the old egomaniac and obsessed with his idiotic old theories, without any sign of a more human development.'

Although their efforts to promote *Die Dreigroschenoper* had failed, the music had been enjoying a life of its own. Lenya, who made her American radio debut in 1937 in Blitzstein's *I've Got the Tune*, sang several songs from *Die Dreigroschenoper* (as well as one of Blitzstein's) in her nightclub show that year at Le Ruban Bleu. In January 1940 Antony Tudor staged *The Judgement of Paris*, with an instrumental score excerpted from *Die Dreigroschenoper*, for the Ballet Theatre in New York. First presented in London during 1938, the ballet updated Paris's meeting with Venus, Juno, and Minerva to a café where three gaudy hostesses each try to seduce a customer and then eventually join forces to rob him of his possessions. Tudor apparently chose the musical selections himself, for Weill had no role in the two-piano arrangement of his music that was used in London. When Tudor and Hugh Laing were preparing the New York production, however, they asked Weill to make an orchestral version of their score. Weill declined; the resulting anonymous orchestration is lushly (and incongruously) scored for full orchestra with a complete string section. Although Weill made new piano-vocal arrangements of the

'Kanonensong' and 'Barbarasong' for Lenya, they were not included on her recording of six Weill songs for the BOST label in 1942.[28] The following year she and Weill did, however, perform the 'Moritat vom Mackie Messer' for 'We Fight Back', a programme at Hunter College organized by Ernst Josef Aufricht and Manfred George to recruit the emigré community for the war bond drive.

    With the end of the war in sight, Weill again turned his attentions to a 'Brecht-less' American adaptation of *Die Dreigroschenoper*. Back in Hollywood, this time to work on the film score of *One Touch of Venus* (which was about to close on Broadway after 566 performances) and to discuss another film project with Maxwell Anderson and George Cukor, Weill wrote to Lenya on May Day 1945:

I just had my breakfast with the Andersons. We thought they would announce the end of the war in Europe today, but it seems now that all those peace rumors were a German trick again. So we'll have to wait a little longer, but it might happen any day now. Did you see that picture of Mussolini's death? Isn't that exactly like a Goya? What a perfect 'death of a dictator!' No Shakespeare could have invented it better. I wonder now what kind of death fate has in store for Hitler and his friends ... I tried to call Walter [Huston] to ask him over for dinner, but couldn't reach him. My dinner with René Clair has been postponed. Max got suddenly all excited about the idea of doing an American version of *Dreigroschenoper*, laid in the Bowery around 1900, as a satire on Tammany and the election machine. We would use only a few songs from *Dreigroschenoper* and write new ones — and I wouldn't give [it] to Cheryl [Crawford]. I would rather work with the Playwrights [Company]. — A possible show with René Clair also sounds quite exciting. I suggested to him that wonderful French comedy 'Le chapeau de paille' which I read last year at the Milhaud's. It is a French classic, and Clair's first picture was based on it. He was very enthusiastic about the idea. Yesterday I had a letter from Paul Robeson, with 2 different ideas for an opera for him, and that's another thing I'll follow up because I feel more and more like writing opera again — opera for Broadway, of course. So you see, I am in no way discouraged and full of ideas.

Weill scribbled a postscript at the bottom of the second page: 'If you could find in the library room (or in my room) a little book (unbound) of John Gay's "Beggars Opera", please send it.' Having just spent two years squabbling with Brecht on various projects, Weill now apparently intended to bypass him altogether by having Anderson adapt *The Beggar's Opera* anew. But on 11 May, Weill reported to Lenya that Anderson was having second thoughts:

Max read the 'Beggar's Opera' (thanks for sending it), but he just doesn't understand this kind of negative humor and is always afraid of anything that is not on the line of straight idealism. He sees everything in the light of today's events, and he forgets that it is the privilege of the theatre to see the world in a mirror. By showing with biting humour what the world would be like if it were inhabited by crooks and hypocrits [sic], the 'Beggar's Opera' does more good than all the dramas of 'noble souls'. But I guess one needs the background of an old civilisation to see that – and of all American playwrights Max seems to be the closest to it. I think I'll get him to write a book for an opera for me some day. But I have to get the idea as usual.

In July 1945 *Die Dreigroschenoper* opened to a packed house at the Hebbel Theater in Berlin – a symbolic gesture, made even more so with Kate Kühl, the original Lucy, now playing Mrs Peachum. Brecht unsuccessfully attempted to persuade American occupation officers to stop the production on the grounds that he wasn't there to supervise it. He noted in his *Arbeitsjournal* on 25 September 1945 that 'I never would have allowed a performance. Without a revolutionary movement, the "message" is pure anarchy.'[29]

A year later *The Three Penny Opera* was finally performed again in the United States – largely through the efforts of Eric Bentley, who was then acting as Brecht's agent and teaching at the University of Minnesota. A few progressive college theatres were beginning to assume roles that left-wing organizations such as the Group Theatre and the Theatre Union had played before the war. Bentley recalls that he had failed to interest Minnesota's music and theatre departments in producing the work: 'I played and sang all the songs for the chairmen of the two departments. When I'd finished, the music chairman said: "My, how Central European. It will never go in the U.S.!"'[30] Undaunted, Bentley sent a script to the University of Illinois in Urbana; the Illini Theatre Guild presented four performances in November 1946. The production utilized a translation by Desmond Vesey, which dated from 1937 but remained unpublished until 1949, when it appeared in a revised version with Bentley sharing translator's credit. Weill and Brecht each received a copy of a fascinating four-page report on the production from its director, Charles Shattuck:

The production was, on the whole, a very successful and a very popular one ... [but] the weak spot ... was the music. We couldn't, under the circumstances, arrange for an orchestra, and had the accompaniment performed on an electric organ. This should have been a good substitute; the results were not up to expectation, however, so that aspect of the production must be written off as an artistic loss ... The actors had a good deal of trouble in grasping the basic style, but I think in the long run they achieved it very well. The system of 'illustrating' rather than 'being' is not essentially different from the artifices of melodrama, and for the most part they learned to accept the script

14 Act II, scene ii in the first post-war production in America, presented by the Illini Theatre Guild in Champaign, Illinois, in November 1946. Charles Shattuck, director

as melodrama and play it high ... The play is too long as it stands, at least for amateur uses. The first night we played it all – it ran 3 hours and 15 minutes – which is too long for a funny play to last. By removing scene 3 and cutting several stanzas of songs, and also, by more efficient playing, we gained approximately half an hour in successive performances.

Shattuck also reported on his 'smallish unit sets', the tinted white lighting, the 1920s costuming, and the use of sign-boards for scene and song titles. In place of the Overture, the organist introduced Jenny's (!) 'Ballad of Mackie the Knife' with a *fortissimo* chorus of the song. The most curious musical adaptation, though, was the 'Ballad of Sexual Slavery': 'No music for this is published, and Mr. Weill could not supply any. By very minor revision it was made to fit the tune of the EASY LIFE and was so rendered.' Mr Shattuck's report concluded:

In the finale we seriously reduced the length of the musical score, much damaging the musical satire here, but doing so because we were not especially interested in the musical joke, and not skilled enough to execute it. We inserted part of Polly's 'Happy Ending' song, which appears on the old Radio-funken [Telefunken] records, though not in the script.

We are very grateful to Messrs. Brecht and Weill for their generosity in making available to us the opportunity to produce this extraordinary and very valuable piece of theatre ... We hope that the author and composer can find some way for a New York production soon. It should be very good box-office, and add its item of good to the social programme of the contemporary world.

Any reasonable hopes for a New York production disintegrated when *Beggar's Holiday*, John Latouche's and Duke Ellington's updating of *The Beggar's Opera*, opened on Broadway on 26 December 1946 (two weeks before *Street Scene*). Its distinguished cast and production staff were racially integrated: Alfred Drake played Macheath; the Lockits were black, the Peachums white. After a disastrous tryout in New Haven with neither score nor script completed, the producers had replaced director John Houseman (Weill's neighbour on South Mountain Road in Rockland County, New York) with George Abbott, who also failed to resolve the inherent conflict between Latouche's highly theatrical book and Ellington's highly untheatrical score. Although the production closed after only fourteen weeks in New York, any possibility of a commercial production of *The Three Penny Opera* had been pre-empted, at least for the time being.

Northwestern University, however, presented six performances of Vesey's translation in Evanston, Illinois, during February 1948. Director Claudia Webster had borrowed Charles Shattuck's German and French recordings of the score and profited from his experience with the earlier production at the University of Illinois. The student musical director, Thomas Willis, recalls that he ran into some of the same problems described by Shattuck: he borrowed a piano-vocal score from the New York Public Library; the orchestra comprised only a piano and Hammond Solovox, which Willis played, and a drummer; an instrumental arrangement of Peachum's 'Futility Song' replaced all but seventeen measures of the Overture; many of the numbers were transposed or rearranged; the third finale had to be simplified and shortened; the music for the 'Ballad of Sexual Slavery', omitted from the German piano-vocal score, was transcribed from a recording. But the cast of this college production was extraordinary: Paul Lynde played Tiger Brown; Joe Bova, Peachum; Robert Wright, Macheath; Mary Boatner, Polly. The Mrs Peachum was Charlotte Lubotsky; six years later, as Charlotte Rae, she would play the same role at the Theater de Lys. During lunch hours the cast recorded all the musical numbers on disc, and although only the Lucy and Mrs Peachum had studied voice, the performance is remarkable for its

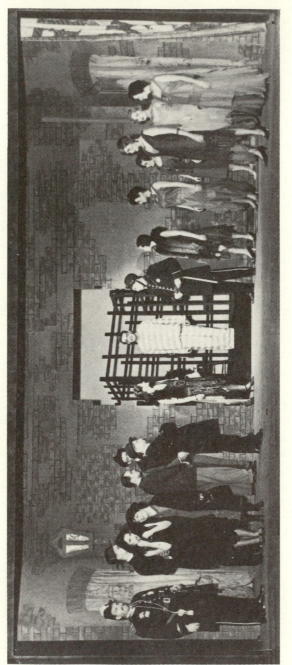

15 Macheath (Robert Wright) awaiting execution in Northwestern University's production (February 1948), directed by Claudia Webster.

musicality, stylistic conviction, and clarity of diction. A review in the *Chicago Journal of Commerce* confirms the professionalism of the rest of the production: 'N.U. has come through with a crisply-paced, ingeniously mounted, and competently acted production ... almost never amateur or "little" theatre in style.'[31]

Late in October 1949, during the rehearsals for *Lost in the Stars*, the Metropolitan Opera Guild sponsored a workshop production of *Der Zar lässt sich photographieren*, with a Shah standing in for the Cold War-sensitive Czar. Weill attended the dress rehearsal at Juilliard with his musical assistant, Lys Symonette. As the only production of a German opera by Weill since his arrival in the United states, the *Zar* was a tangible reminder of what he had left behind. Mrs Symonette recalls that during the cab ride back to the Music Box Theatre Weill was uncharacteristically silent, until they passed the marquee of the theatre where Marc Blitzstein's *Regina* was in final rehearsals – with Weill's own perennial conductor, Maurice Abravanel, as musical director. Weill then repeated his 1935 appraisal of Blitzstein, 'He's a better writer than a composer,' and continued matter-of-factly: 'I wish he'd stop trying to imitate me. Now he wants to translate *Dreigroschenoper*.' Both Abravanel and Cheryl Crawford recall being so impressed with Blitzstein's first efforts on the lyrics that they recommended to Weill that he look at them, but he refused. In a colourful account written four years later to publicize the New York première, Blitzstein recalled that he finally telephoned Weill at Brook House in January 1950:

'I've made a translation of the "Pirate Jenny" song from your *Dreigroschenoper*. When can I show it to you?'
Weill said: 'Right now, Sing it to me.'
'Over the phone?'
'Why not? Wait. I'll put Lenya on the extension' ...
   After the first line, Weill at the other end began drumming his fingers to accompany me with the beat. I finished. He said in the mild, quiet tone so characteristic of him: 'I think you've hit it. After all these years! ... Marc, do it all, why don't you? The whole opera.' ... I was happy at their enthusiasm but other work called.[32]

On 2 March Weill and Blitzstein celebrated their 50th and 45th birthdays respectively. A month later Blitzstein attended Weill's memorial service at Brook House and his burial in Mount Repose Cemetery in Haverstraw:

Coming home, I found myself haunted by another number from the *Dreigroschenoper* – this time the 'Solomon Song'. That one took me all night. Soon I was translating still other songs and snatches from Brecht's original text ... I had reached the point of no return and had to do it all.

In July, the League of Composers again sponsored a Kurt Weill Concert, this time 'as an expression of tribute to their late colleague, who made such a notable and lasting contribution to theatre music of our times'. Ten thousand people attended the event at Lewisohn Stadium – as opposed to the 150 at its 1935 predecessor. During the evening there was no performance or mention of any of Weill's European works – an imbalance redressed the following February, when Ernst Josef Aufricht, the original producer of *Die Dreigroschenoper* in Berlin, produced a 'Kurt Weill Concert' at Town Hall in New York. Originally scheduled for one performance, it was repeated two additional times by popular demand. The second half comprised a concert version of *Die Dreigroschenoper*, sung in German and accompanied by two pianos, with Lenya listed in the programme as Polly. Lucy and Jenny had been deleted from the cast. Virgil Thomson used his review of the Town Hall concert as an occasion to survey Weill's *oeuvre*, to differentiate his German works, which had 'made musical history', from his American ones, 'thoroughly competent but essentially conformist'. Lamenting that Weill had 'ceased to work as a modernist' and had 'renounced his intellectual position' in America but suggesting that his German works 'belong in the constantly available repertory', Thomson adumbrated the continuing debate over the relative worth of 'the two Weills'.[33] A year later, Aufricht revived the event in Town Hall, with a more *Mahagonny*-weighted first half and Kitty Carlisle Hart featured in a set of three French songs.

Meanwhile, Blitzstein had been working on his adaptation. Having dedicated to Brecht *The Cradle Will Rock* (1936–37), the best-known of his stage works in the agit-prop tradition of the American Left, Blitzstein was perhaps uniquely qualified as both dramatist and composer to realize an American performing version of *Die Dreigroschenoper*. Soon after Weill's death, he showed Lenya drafts of some of his English lyrics, which she found 'extraordinary' in their musicality and colloquial turns of phrase. By October 1950 Cheryl Crawford had taken concrete steps to realize her longstanding plans for an American production of *Die Dreigroschenoper*. She had obtained Brecht's permission, pending final approval of Blitzstein's, but then gradually lost interest in the project when other rights couldn't be cleared. In November 1951 Eric Bentley wrote to

Blitzstein, 'even though I collaborated on a literal version made for the British public by Desmond Vesey, in all probability your version is the one for the American public.' He offered to direct a New York production, if one materialized, or to arrange for one in Philadelphia, if it didn't.[34]

On 9 January 1952, *Variety* announced that 'a new version of Kurt Weill's "Three Penny Opera", with a fresh libretto, lyrics, and some new music, which Marc Blitzstein completed about six weeks ago, is being considered by several Broadway producers. It's also reported that the New York City Opera Co. is interested in the work for its coming season, at the City Center, N.Y., with Leonard Bernstein as conductor.' Indeed, the New York City Opera had announced that its spring season would include new productions of *Wozzeck* (the first performance in New York since 1931), *Amahl and the Night Visitors*, and *The Threepenny Opera*. Coinciding with the peak intensity of Joseph McCarthy's 'witch hunts' for Communists, the announcement provoked a storm of protests from the right. In the 4 February 1952 issue of *The New Leader*, Kurt List, an Austrian-born composer/critic who had studied with both Webern and Berg, marshalled an attack, reminiscent of Goebbels' but which now utilized both the ammunition and tactics characteristic of McCarthy's troops:

For its spring production, the New York City Opera Company has announced a new version of the Kurt Weill—Bert Brecht *Dreigroschenoper* — this time in an adaptation by Marc Blitzstein. As most readers will recall ... Brecht belonged to the fringe of Communist sympathizers. He has since become the literary pope of Eastern Germany, though not without having been rebuked several times for pacifist deviations, and the like. Mr. Weill, as far as I know, never had any Communist sympathies, though his feeling unquestionably tended toward the left. I do not know what Mr. Blitzstein is going to make of the original; but in view of past performances, such as *The Cradle Will Rock* and *No For An Answer*, there can be little doubt that the opera will have a leftist tinge.

I have no particular objection to this. However, I fail to see why a more or less publicly supported institution should lend itself to any kind of political propaganda if its specific purpose is the artistic enlightenment of the people of New York. The available choices included a number of other contemporary operas which were not only better but free of an odious political stigma ... The morality of the *Dreigroschenoper* is completely out of place in our America of today ... Mr. Blitzstein will have to do a lot of adapting in order to make this story morally acceptable. I do not know what he plans to do with the music, but I do not see how it could be materially changed from its meaningless and filthy innuendo to a more elevating experience.

I have no intention of advocating that this piece be banned from the City Center stage. But I think if those of us who are opposed to its basic premises are willing to have it displayed publicly, with public funds, in New York City, then the gentlemen responsible for the production should announce it as what it essentially is — a piece of anti-capitalist propaganda which exalts anarchical gangsterism and prostitution over democratic law and order.[35]

On 7 February, the chairman of the board of directors of the City Center announced tersely that the production 'had been postponed from this spring until next fall because of financial troubles'. In April Blitzstein informed the *New York Times* that 'a Broadway producer, who prefers to remain anonymous for the time being, will take over *The Threepenny Opera* after the City Center engagement.' But announcements for the fall schedule of the New York City Opera made no mention of the piece.

Instead, Blitzstein arranged for his longtime friend Leonard Bernstein to programme a concert version of *The Threepenny Opera* during Brandeis University's Festival of the Creative Arts. On 14 June 1952, just two days after the première of his own *Trouble in Tahiti*, (which he had dedicated to Blitzstein), Bernstein conducted *The Threepenny Opera* on a programme with Stravinsky's *Les Noces* and Pierre Schaeffer's *musique concrète*, 'Symphonie pour un homme seul', both choreographed by Merce Cunningham. Nearly five thousand people filled the new Adolph Ullman Amphitheatre in Waltham, Massachusetts, with Blitzstein himself narrating the amplified performance with witty summaries of scene and plot interspersed between numbers. A recently catalogued private recording of the concert is revelatory in many respects. The performance included the entire score, with the exception of Mrs Peachum's 'Ballade von der sexuellen Hörigkeit', which still would not have been printed in the UE-parts rented for the occasion from Associated Music Publishers. Bernstein conducted Weill's original orchestrations, except for an electric organ substituting for the harmonium and bandoneon throughout and in a few sections for some of the original 'doubles': bassoon, flute, cello, string bass. None of the numbers had been transposed, except for Lenya's: 'Pirate Jenny' and 'Tango Ballad' down a minor third, 'Solomon Song' down a major second. Lucy (Anita Ellis) sang the 'Barbarasong' (see note 9) at its original pitch, not as a 'torch' number. Although a baritone, the Macheath (David Brooks, who later directed *Trouble in Tahiti* on Broadway) sang his solo numbers in their original keys, with only the phrase in the third finale with the high A♭ and a line in 'Love Song' sung an octave lower than written. The Messenger rendered the recitative in the third finale as spoken dialogue. Although the internal dance breaks in 'Tango

Ballad' had been shortened and a stanza of 'Call from the Grave' omitted, Bernstein and Blitzstein otherwise remained remarkably faithful to Weill's autograph full score. 'Mack the Knife' received polite applause, but Lenya stopped the show with 'Pirate Jenny'. A thunderous ovation followed the third finale; the gratuitous reprise of 'Mack the Knife' had not been added yet.

Many Boston-area newspapers and several New York critics covered the event. In his review for the *Christian Science Monitor* on 16 June 1952, Harold Rogers quoted Hans Heinsheimer (the head of the opera division of Universal Edition in the late twenties), who had served as 'discussant' for the evening: 'Marc Blitzstein's English adaptation was so true to Bert Brecht's German original that we are hearing essentially the same piece that had taken Germany by storm 24 years ago.' Howard Taubman noted in the *New York Times* that *The Threepenny Opera* had been the most important event in the festival and suggested that surely some producer would mount a fully staged production in New York during the forthcoming season. As a follow-up to the Brandeis performance, Decca Records planned to record excerpts at the Pythian Temple in New York on 17 October 1952. With Bernstein conducting, Jo Sullivan (Polly) and Lenya were to recreate their Brandeis performances, while John Raitt had been signed to sing Macheath; Randolph Symonette, Mr Peachum; and Burgess Meredith, the Streetsinger. After the cast had already started coaching with Blitzstein, the project was abruptly cancelled because mechanical rights could not be cleared.

Four days after the performance in Waltham, Lenya wrote to her attorney: 'I just returned from Brandeis, where I sang (if you want to call it that) at the Festival. We did *Threepenny Opera* (this time in English). It was a big success and might very well lead to a Broadway production.' In fact, Blitzstein and Lenya rejected offers from Billy Rose, Roger Stevens, and other major producers who insisted that the show would have to be rewritten and rescored. Remembering the 1933 debacle, Rose encouraged Blitzstein to take more liberties with Brecht's text, urged him to go back to Gay's ending, and suggested that Oscar Hammerstein's rewrite of *Carmen* could serve as a useful model. When more than a year passed without an acceptable offer from a commercial producer, Lenya and Blitzstein agreed to give the option to the Phoenix Theatre, which then reneged. Finally Stanley Chase and Carmen Capalbo, two young employees in the Story Department of CBS Television in New York, came upon a review of the Brandeis performance and contacted Blitzstein.

In October 1953 the neophyte producers went to his small apartment in Greenwich Village, where he played and sang the entire score for them. A subsequent meeting included Lenya and her second husband, George Davis; as a test, they shrewdly sent a copy of Blitzstein's script home with Chase and Capalbo so that they could determine 'what would have to be changed'. Lenya was disarmed by the young men's understanding of the piece and their eagerness to do it 'just as it was'. Having initially hoped to produce Camus' *State of Siege* with Marlon Brando, Chase and Capalbo had already reserved the intimate but run-down 299-seat Theatre de Lys in Greenwich Village by advancing a week's rental of $600; with Lenya's and Blitzstein's blessings, plans now went forward for a limited run of *The Threepenny Opera* during the next season. The producers also tried to convince the 55-year-old Lenya to play the role of Jenny; she insisted that she was too old for the part. Finally she agreed, at George Davis's urging, but only with the proviso that the director should feel free to replace her during the rehearsal period.

Capitalizing the production at just under ten thousand dollars raised from twenty-three investors (considered an astronomical sum for off-Broadway) Chase and Capalbo recalled working eighteen hours a day and scouring thrift shops for costumes and properties:

We did everything ourselves, built props, sewed costumes, did publicity, fell into bed exhausted and got stuck with pins from the night's work on the costumes. We had no office, couldn't afford one, no regular phone. Most of the money was raised from a phone booth in Cromwell's Drugstore.[36]

Meanwhile, Blitzstein was making substantial changes to his adaptation: he sharpened and polished a number of lyrics, with extensive revisions to the 'Ballad of the Easy Life', 'Solomon Song', and 'Call from the Grave'; he abandoned his original notion of setting the play in Boss Tweed's New York during the 1870s and restored the action to Victorian England – but not until Philadelphia, New Orleans and San Francisco had been tried and rejected. To compensate for Lenya's claim to 'Pirate Jenny', he wrote new lyrics for 'Bilbao Song' and patched the resulting 'Bide-A-Wee in Soho' into the wedding scene to fill the gap in Polly's role. (The London production also included the song; its omission from the cast album and materials rented for stock and amateur performances avoided copyright problems with *Happy End* and allowed 'Pirate Jenny' to be restored to Polly when Lenya was no longer involved.)

Capalbo himself directed and assembled a cast of 25, most of whom were young and willing to work, as Lenya did, for off-Broadway minimum salaries that had been specially negotiated with Actors' Equity: five dollars per week for rehearsals and a sliding scale, with a guarantee of twenty-five dollars per week, for performances. The principals included Scott Merrill, hitherto known primarily as a dancer, as Macheath; Jo Sullivan again as Polly; Leon Lishner, an opera singer who had appeared in *Regina*, and Charlotte Rae as the elder Peachums; Beatrice Arthur as Lucy; Gerald Price as the Streetsinger; George Tyne, blacklisted and only recently back from Europe, as Tiger Brown. Once the cast had been selected and rehearsals were underway, Blitzstein had to make additional musical changes as well as concessions necessitated by financial exigencies. Since Bea Arthur was almost a female baritone, she simply sang the 'Barbara Song' an octave lower than Weill had intended. But the 'Jealousy Duet', originally conceived for two caterwauling sopranos, also had to accommodate Arthur's lower range, so Blitzstein made a new arrangement. He also restored the 'Ballad of Sexual Dependency' to the score,

16 Lotte Lenya (Jenny) and Scott Merrill (Mack the Knife) in Capalbo and Chase's production of Marc Blitzstein's adaptation at the Theatre de Lys in New York, March 1954

added a (lower) harmony part for Macheath in 'Love Song', transposed 'Solomon Song' even lower for Lenya (a perfect fourth), and
rewrote some of Macheath's solo lines for the baritone range. At some
point, he appended to the concluding chorale two of the three 'Happy
Ending' stanzas of 'Mack the Knife' that Brecht had written for the
film version to replace, not supplement, the third finale. Ironically,
this reprise of the show's hit song now closed the evening in conventional Broadway fashion. Finally, Blitzstein reduced the doublings
in the original orchestrations to the standard ones covered by
American Federation of Musicians guidelines and reassigned the parts
of the missing instruments, while increasing the number of players
from seven to eight. (Blitzstein apparently had borrowed Weill's
autograph full score from Universal Edition in Vienna, as it now bears
his annotations as well as some made by Bernstein.) These musical
changes joined forces with the 'typically Broadway' vocal skills of
most of the company to minimize the impact of both the overt operatic
(and operetta-like) moments and the subliminal operatic referential-
models of the original score. All in all, the final version of Blitzstein's
adaptation followed Brecht's script more literally than it did Weill's
score. Although he had softened the tone of the original language in
a number of places, made a few judicious cuts in the dialogue (the
first preview still lasted nearly four hours), reordered some passages,
and reinstated Gay's opening to the brothel scene, Blitzstein's script
undermines the sense and shape of the 1928 libretto less obviously
than does Brecht's own literary version published in 1931 – the
'authorized' text, now often mistaken as the historically 'authentic'
one.

Reflecting Weill's posthumous clout as a successful Broadway
composer, Brecht's absence from the scene, and Lenya's authoritative
presence, the production was billed as 'Kurt Weill's *The Threepenny
Opera*', with his name above the title and Marc Blitzstein's in the same
size, typeface, and boldness just below it. Brecht shared third billing
for 'original text' with a redundant 'Music by Kurt Weill'. Blitzstein
deferred to Lenya on virtually all points of interpretation, and
ultimately the director asked him to stay away from rehearsals
altogether. Some of the cast worried that the FBI might close the
production or that, at the very least, McCarthyites might picket the
theatre. Although the première had been set initially for 2 March,
Weill's and Blitzstein's birthday, the show opened on 10 March 1954
without incident, but to mixed reviews from theatre and music critics
alike. One groused about the tiny orchestra, another about the seedy

sets and costumes, still another about the uneven performances. Harold Clurman found the direction 'labored and awkward instead of sprightly and bright', and Olin Downes criticized the 'crowded, smelly little theatre' itself.[37] But on 21 March, Brooks Atkinson, drama critic of the *Times*, and Virgil Thomson, music critic for the *Herald Tribune*, devoted their Sunday columns to *The Threepenny Opera* and the Phoenix Theatre's *The Golden Apple*. Atkinson asserted that 'the brains, taste, and inventiveness of the musical theatre have moved off-Broadway this season', while Thomson praised Blitzstein's translation of 'one of our century's most powerful creations' as 'the finest thing of its kind in existence':

He has got the spirit of the play and rendered it powerfully, colloquially, compactly. And his English versions of the songs are so apt prosodically, fit their music so perfectly that one can scarcely believe them to be translations at all.

In the *Saturday Review* (27 March), Henry Hewes told New York theatre-goers that they would 'find a trip to Christopher Street the most rewarding of the season'. Indeed, the company reportedly played to standees at every performance for twelve weeks; it closed after 96 performances.

The production was forced to vacate, because the Theatre de Lys had previously been booked by other producers throughout the summer and the entire next season; the first successor lasted one night. Although Capalbo and Chase received offers to move their unexpected hit musical uptown to a Broadway theatre, it would have meant restaging and redesigning the production at the expense of an intimacy that was one of its chief assets. None of the seven other off-Broadway houses was available, so the producers put the entire production into storage and simply waited for the Theatre de Lys to open up again. During the 1954–55 season, Brooks Atkinson ended each of his reviews of subsequent flops at the theatre with the same plea: 'Bring back *The Threepenny Opera*!' Meanwhile, Blitzstein and Lenya were besieged by requests from theatres around the country for performance rights; they declined most but allowed Harvard's Lowell House Musical Society to present four performances in April 1955.

With Lucille Lortel, the new owner of the Theatre de Lys, joining the team of producers, *The Threepenny Opera* finally reopened after a hiatus of 15 months on 20 September 1955. During its absence, *The Pajama Game*, *The Boy Friend*, *Fanny*, *Plain and Fancy*, *Silk*

Stockings, and *Damn Yankees* had installed themselves uptown. Nevertheless, *The Threepenny Opera* ran consecutively for 2,611 performances, outlasting all of them to become (temporarily) the longest running musical in history. Although the production itself was unchanged and the original cast largely intact, now the critics were nearly unanimous in their acclaim. In the first issue of a new weekly, *The Village Voice* (26 October 1955), Jerry Talmer described two shows at the Theatre de Lys:

One has a cast of twenty ebullient and engaging actors and actresses ... The other show has a cast of one, and her name is Lotte Lenya ... When Miss Lenya shambles front and center to exhale the first weary, husky, terrible notes of her husband's famous song about the Black Freighter ... we are stark up face to face against a kind of world and a kind of half-century that no one born this side of the water can ever quite fully make, or want to make, his own. Hogarth and Gay, Goya and Lautrec, Koestler, Malraux, Traven, and even such as Remarque and George Grosz – all of it, all of them, and a hundred others, are packed into this one hot hellish instant, with the smoke still rising from the crematories and Bert Brecht's old friend Uncle Joe Stalin just sitting there, waiting, far to the north.

In April Lenya won that season's 'Tony' award for 'best featured actress in a musical', while the production garnered a special 'Tony'. During its run, Louis Armstrong, Dick Hyman, Bobby Darin, Frank Sinatra and Ella Fitzgerald successively climbed the pop charts with renditions of what became one of the biggest 'hit tunes' of the century. In January 1956, Lenya wrote to a friend: 'The "Moritat" has been recorded by 17 different companies. You hear it coming out of bars, juke boxes, taxis, wherever you go. Kurt would have loved that. A taxidriver whistling his tunes would have pleased him more than winning the Pulitzer Prize.'

Success brought its own problems. Despite generally packed houses, with just 299 seats to sell, the producers could offer only modest increases in salaries, even to principals. (Lenya's salary escalated to sixty-five dollars per week.) The production contract with Actors' Equity stipulated a five-day notice by an actor leaving the show to accept a better job. As a result, *The Threepenny Opera* served as an amazing springboard for talent; during its run, 709 different actors played the twenty-two roles, with many cast members moving up to larger roles within the company before leaving to do Broadway shows or national tours. The company's roster of alumni included, besides the original cast, Jerry Orbach, Ed Asner, Jane Connell, Nancy Andrews, Estelle Parsons, Grete Mosheim, Martin

Wolfson, Georgia Brown, Frederic Downs, Leon Janney and Jo Wilder, to name only a few. Since each replacement required at least one rehearsal, the production seldom went more than two weeks without a 'brush-up'. Programme copy seldom kept up with the casualties of the latest raids on the cast. Only two actors stayed with the company from opening to closing night.

Once it had become clear that *The Threepenny Opera* could become a veritable gold mine for its producers, the relatively informal agreements that had previously sufficed could not withstand the onslaught of new claims. Although Lenya and Blitzstein had signed a contract with the producers specifying equal shares for Weill, Brecht and Blitzstein, Brecht never returned his copy. He did send formal approval of Blitzstein's adaptation (he called it 'magnificent') via Elisabeth Hauptmann on Berliner Ensemble stationery. But after the opening in 1954, Brecht's European agent informed the producers that he would approve 30 per cent for Blitzstein, but Weill's share could not exceed the 25 per cent specified in the original contract with Felix Bloch Erben. After unsuccessfully attempting to persuade Brecht of a more equitable division of royalties, Lenya and Blitzstein signed their own bilateral agreement stipulating that, other contracts notwithstanding, they would divide equally all proceeds remaining after Brecht's and Elisabeth Hauptmann's shares had been deducted. Lenya refused, however, to grant Blitzstein's adaptation exclusivity: 'Marc, like Mr. Bentley, wished to have his version made the one authorized English-language version, but I would not agree to this, despite the admiration I have for his work and my feeling that no other existing version gives a hint of Brecht's poetry and power.'[38]

Shortly after the production reopened in 1955, John Krimsky and Edmond Pauker claimed exclusive ownership of English-language production rights on the basis of their 1933 contracts and sought a court injunction against further performances at the Theatre de Lys. They eventually settled out-of-court with Chase and Capalbo for a lump-sum payment and a small percentage of box office receipts. Scattered unauthorized productions of the Vesey–Bentley translation infringed upon the exclusivity promised to Capalbo and Chase and irritated Lenya:

Mr. Bentley had hopes that Kurt would give his blessing to the Bentley–Vesey version. Needless to say, that Kurt refused. Their version seemed to Kurt stilted, flavorless, the lyrics unsingable, the score quite distorted. Last winter, several unauthorized performances of this work were given in Chicago, to very bad press. Nevertheless, Mr. Bentley is bitter about the Blitzstein version; attacking it cautiously in print, and viciously in private.[39]

Universal Edition demanded five per cent of Weill's share, but the Office of Alien Property impounded those royalties, as well as those due to Brecht, who was then 'a German national residing in the East Zone'. (Eventually the money was remitted to Brecht's son, Stefan, who was an American citizen.) When negotiations commenced for the London production, which opened at the Royal Court Theatre on 9 February 1956, Brecht claimed not only that he alone could license the work, but also that he had Lenya's power-of-attorney, which came as a surprise to her. Eventually compromises effected solutions to most of these problems, but some of the contractual disputes have never been resolved.

At the urging of Edward Cole, director of its classical division, MGM Records decided to risk making a cast album of the off-Broadway production during its initial twelve-week run. But MGM's chief executive officer subsequently attended a performance, and then appeared at the recording session with a list of musical numbers to be deleted and a longer list of objectionable lyrics to be changed. After much debate, Blitzstein and Lenya succeeded in salvaging all the musical numbers (with some cuts) only by acquiescing to the record company's demand for censored lyrics. Blitzstein drafted dummy lyrics on the spot to eliminate all 'hell's' and 'damn's', as well as all references to drunkenness, whores, pimps and cat-houses. Innocuous, nearly meaningless verses replaced those chronicling Sloppy Sadie's knife-wound and Little Susie's rape in 'Mack the Knife'. Clever scissors-work removed the 'offensive' imagery of the 'he steps on your face' sequence from the first finale. New lyrics converted 'Tango Ballad' into an antiseptic domestic 'sit-com'. Even 'Get off your ass' had to be changed to 'Stand on your feet' in 'Call from the Grave'. Because Blitzstein's adaptation has never been published, it is still erroneously assumed by those without access to the rented performance materials that the cast album accurately documents what was presented at the Theatre de Lys.

The album sold far better than MGM's marketing department thought possible: 30,000 copies in the first three months, 150,000 in the next two years, and after five years, more than any original cast album except *My Fair Lady*. The recording's unexpected success allowed Cole to expand MGM's Weill series to a dozen records, which it advertised in the programme books of the production. Indeed, one measure of the range of the 'Weill renaissance' is a discography gleaned from record companies' advertisements in the programmes from 1955 to 1961. In addition to the expected ads for the cast album and various popular spin-offs of single songs, the programmes included displays for reissues or new recordings of *Der Jasager*, *Kleine Dreigroschenmusik*, the Violin Concerto, Peter Sandloff's *Kurt Weill in Berlin*, *Tryout* (Weill playing and both he and Ira Gershwin singing), and the Vienna State Opera's recording of *Die Dreigroschenoper*. While *The Threepenny Opera* was running, Lenya recorded *Berlin Theatre Songs*, *Die sieben Todsünden*, *Mahagonny*, *Johnny Johnson*, *Happy End*, *Die Dreigroschenoper*, and *American Theatre Songs*. As a result, by the end of the decade, at least the major Weill–Brecht works were no longer foreign to many English-speaking listeners.

Before the New York production closed in December 1961, there were two attempts to launch national touring companies, both unsuccessful. The first opened in September 1960 in San Francisco with several New York alumni in leading roles and the original musical director, Samuel Matlovsky. After just four weeks, it moved to Los Angeles where Lenya joined the company; the show was no better received there and quickly closed. A year later, a second company, headlined this time by Gypsy Rose Lee as Jenny, set out on what was to be a 35-week tour. But after its first two-week stop in Toronto, this ill-received troupe also disbanded. Clearly, *The Threepenny Opera* could not be circulated in the same manner as a typical Broadway musical; it needed a certain intimacy and cultural ambience that the Theatre de Lys and Greenwich Village provided.

Nonetheless, *The Threepenny Opera* had been widely acculturated beyond any expectation Weill might have had. *Threepenny*-fever in New York nearly equalled the *Dreigroschenoper*-craze that had swept Berlin in 1928–29. Louis Armstrong and Bobby Darin made the names of Lucy Brown and Lotte Lenya familiar to those who had never even heard of Brecht and Weill. The show inspired several visual artists (including Arbit Blatas, who created a series of *Threepenny* watercolours and sculptures) and even an article in the *American Journal of Psychotherapy* on the implications for psychoanalytic technique of the socially determined behavioural patterns of *Threepenny*'s characters. The impact of 'Mack the Knife' was such that WCBS-Radio in New York suspended airings of the song during a spate of teenage gang knifings that had been linked to its popularity. Other cautious stations played only instrumental renditions. In 1962

Tams-Witmark Music Library acquired the exclusive right to license all stock and amateur productions of the work in the United States and Canada. Conforming to standard Broadway practice, the rental materials preserved faithfully all of the musical compromises dictated by the original cast of the Theater de Lys and the exigencies of that production. Since then, hundreds of regional theatres, summer stock companies, and college drama departments in America have presented the show in this version. As Blitzstein observed in his promotional piece for Tams-Witmark, 'What began as a labor of love has blossomed into a nationwide accolade ... *The Threepenny Opera* will no longer be just a name on everybody's tongue, but a part of everybody's theatre experience.'[40]

What accounted for the success of *The Threepenny Opera* in America? Brecht's answer in the epigraph for this essay is as valid for New York in the fifties as it was for Berlin in the twenties. When asked a similar question in 1959, Capalbo and Chase responded: 'Neither of us did the show because we liked Brecht's social criticism. We did it because we thought it was a great show.' Like their counterpart in Berlin, Ernst Josef Aufricht, who called the piece a 'literary operetta with flashes of social criticism', the American producers recognized that despite Brecht's *post facto* theorizing and Marxist interpretations, *The Threepenny Opera* is essentially a comedy. For all its political and philosophical underpinnings, its theatrical success depends on not taking itself too seriously.

It is a simplistic but irrefutable fact that the off-Broadway production also 'came at the right time'. The reopening of the show in 1955 coincided with the date of James Dean's car crash; that year Brando won an Academy Award for *On the Waterfront*; the rebellious beat generation could identify with certain anti-Establishment aspects of *The Threepenny Opera* as well. McCarthyism was finally precipitating an inevitable cultural backlash, even in middle-class America. Brecht had belatedly achieved overdue recognition in America as a major playwright, at least within certain intellectual and political circles. The American musical had reached maturity and could now embrace works that stretched its boundaries and challenged its formulas. A post-war nostalgic view of the perceived decadence of the Weimar Republic, personified in Lenya, may have undercut Brecht's social criticism, but it still enlivened the doldrums of the fifties. Language, themes and situations that had both shocked and titillated an audience in Philadelphia in 1933 now seemed deliciously exotic — at least in the theatre. Without minimizing Blitzstein's own unique contribution, America had come of age; it could accept the form, understand (if not endorse) the message, and appropriate as its own the music of *The Threepenny Opera*.

Lenya herself was also responsible for its success. Her appearance in *The Threepenny Opera* launched a revival of an international recording, stage, and concert career that had seemed unlikely after her retirement from the stage, precipitated by the disastrous *Firebrand of Florence* in 1945. By the time she left the cast at the Theatre de Lys for the last time (after several leaves of absence for various projects in Europe), she commanded a loyal New York following which called for periodic concert appearances, always with the songs from *The Threepenny Opera* as the core of her programmes: in July 1958 at Lewisohn Stadium, in February of 1959 and 1960 and January 1965 at Carnegie Hall.[41] Shortly after her last Carnegie Hall concert (at age 67), the New York City Opera finally realized its intention to present *Die Dreigroschenoper* – but in German with Kurt Kasznar, Martha Schlamme, Stefan Schnabel, George S. Irving, and Anita Hoefer among the cast. Julius Rudel conducted, and Lenya sat in the audience, content that *The Threepenny Opera* had now fulfilled Virgil Thomson's prophetic dictum in 1951 that the work belonged in the repertory at City Center.

Subsequent productions are too numerous to consider here, and the drama of *Threepenny*'s struggles is no longer suspenseful, since it has become a permanent and (for better or worse) thoroughly respectable citizen. However, in 1976, Joseph Papp's New York Shakespeare Festival challenged the near-classic status Blitzstein's adaptation had achieved by producing Richard Foreman's staging of a new translation by Ralph Manheim and John Willett. (The exclusivity granted Blitzstein's version indirectly by virtue of the licensing agreement with Tams-Witmark exempted such 'first-class' productions.) More faithful to the tone and diction of Brecht's play (the 1931 literary version) than Blitzstein had been, and unencumbered by the theatrical conventions and language-restrictions of the fifties, the translation was trumpeted by Papp as 'the REAL *Threepenny Opera*'. With a cast headed by Raul Julia as Macheath and Ellen Greene as Jenny, the controversial production elicited sharply divided reviews. Douglas Watt called it a 'fantastic and sensationally theatrical production' that 'will mesmerize, thrill, blind and perhaps blister you', but noted that the translation 'is often more difficult to sing' than Blitzstein's.[42]

Writing one of the three reviews published in the 10 May 1976

17 Ellen Greene (Jenny) reads the fortune of Raul Julia (Mac the
    Knife) in the American première of the Manheim/Willett
    translation. Richard Foreman directed for Joseph Papp's New
    York Shakespeare Festival, 1976

issue of *The Village Voice*, Julius Novick doubted any assertion that
this 'new' *Threepenny Opera* was preferable to the 'old':

Most of the singing in this production, like most of the acting, is loud, cold,
dead. The prevailing refusal to communicate is clearly not accidental; it is
done with considerable authority. But why should it be done at all in the
Threepenny Opera? '*Threepenny* audiences roar with laughter,' says Eric
Bentley. Not at the Beaumont they don't. Mr. Foreman has sowed salt on 'The
Threepenny Opera' so that nothing can grow. Comedy, satire, poignancy,
all wither. The play's implications for our real lives can hardly be seen or
felt: the tough *Threepenny* of 1976 has less to say to us than the jolly *Threepenny* of 1954.

Michael Feingold, a noted translator of Brecht himself, devoted his space in the *Voice* almost exclusively to an appraisal of the Manheim—Willett translation:

> In the midst of all this toughness and accuracy, only one artist has been scanted: the composer ... The question is one of whom *Threepenny Opera* belongs to. Theatre people may see it as a work by Bertolt Brecht, but musicians see it as one by Kurt Weill. When lyrics are written with the intention of being set to music, and are set by one of the century's master composers (which Weill was), then there are obligations to the composer as well as to the librettist ... Manheim and Willett have taken pains to fit the words note for note and phrase for phrase, but this is no guarantee of either comprehensibility or naturalness in song ... Anyone who has ever wrestled with one of these monsters will feel complete sympathy with Manheim and Willett in their dilemma to make songs that are both Brecht and singable, but the assumption that Blitzstein didn't share this dilemma (refracted through the sensibility of 20 years ago) is a piece of unwarranted snobbery ... We have no right to suppose that Blitzstein was out to clean up Brecht, anymore than we have to insist that Manheim and Willett, having the exact words, have had the final one. [At the time of this article's going to press, Feingold was completing a new translation based on the 1928 libretto, which was to be given its Broadway première in October 1989, with Sting cast as Macheath.]

Threepenny Opera ran for 306 performances at the Vivian Beaumont Theater, and Columbia released a cast album which preserves Stanley Silverman's vocal arrangements (including a choral setting of 'Mack the Knife' in four-part harmony!) and new orchestration for a larger ensemble. (There is no surviving correspondence that explains why Lenya allowed the extensive musical changes; previously she had adhered to Weill's demand that only his orchestrations and arrangements could be used in major theatrical productions.) With the expiration of the contract with Tams-Witmark in 1984 and the subsequent reassignment of American stock and amateur rights of the Blitzstein adaptation to Rodgers and Hammerstein Theatre Library, it became legally possible to license the Manheim—Willett version in the United States and Canada, but to date the copyright owners have declined to do so.

To trace the influence of *The Threepenny Opera* on the form, performance practice, subject matter and style of the American musical theatre after 1954 would require a lengthy essay of its own. Initially its success confirmed off-Broadway as a viable alternative to Broadway for legitimate theatre in New York. During its run, the number of off-Broadway theatres increased from seven to thirty-eight. However, few of the ventures fared as well; in his article in the *Herald Tribune* commemorating the fifth anniversary of the Theatre de Lys production, John Allen estimated that 'as a result of *Threepenny*'s success, eager angels have been prodded into the loss of something close to $1,500,000 over the last four years'. No sooner had *The Three-penny Opera* vacated the Theatre de Lys than Cheryl Crawford's production of *Brecht on Brecht*, starring Lenya, moved in for a run of 424 performances. In 1972, when *Berlin to Broadway With Kurt Weill* opened — at the Theatre de Lys — Christopher Street closed and was renamed 'Kurt Weill-Strasse' for an hour of homage to his posthumous contributions to the off-Broadway theatre and the part they had played in the transformation of the neighbourhood.

Threepenny's impact has revealed itself in many less ostentatious and more far-reaching ways. Although non-linear 'concept' musicals utilizing commentary numbers have now become so commonplace that a given show's descendancy from the precedent of *The Three-penny Opera* cannot be conclusively demonstrated, it seems unlikely that *Cabaret*, *Company* or *Chicago*, for example, could deny direct links to *The Threepenny Opera*. Not all of its influence has been propitious: although the show prompted new interest in other Weill–Brecht works, producers and directors have been tempted to recast them in *Threepenny*'s mould. Capalbo himself mounted a now legendary, disastrous production of *Mahagonny* in New York in 1970, cast with singing actors and rescored for a smaller orchestra and rock band; Lenya and Stefan Brecht filed suit to stop performances. The distorting effect of a 'threepenny' lens may account even now for some critics' myopic views of the remainder of Weill's *oeuvre*.

In 1928 Weill wrote that he and Brecht were addressing an audience 'which either did not know us at all or, at any rate, never considered us capable of interesting a circle of listeners much wider than the average concert- and opera-going public'.[43] In Europe, *Die Drei-groschenoper* achieved that goal almost instantaneously, whereas in America it struggled for many years before finding a wide audience and achieving sustained popularity. But the tale of *The Threepenny Opera* in America is not simply that of *Die Dreigroschenoper* in the English language. The interaction between the work and its American cultural setting has left neither unchanged, and the latter will un-doubtedly continue to alter both the substance and the perception of the former. The Americanization, or perhaps de-Germanization, of *Die Dreigroschenoper* has required adaptation no less profound than production of Weill's American theatrical works in present-day Germany would require. In 1987 McDonald's, whose golden arches symbolize to the world the enterprise of American capitalism, supplied the 'Moritat vom Mackie Messer' with new lyrics to promote the culinary delights of a 'Big Mac Tonite' — fully cooked hamburger instead of the Kanonensong's Beefsteak Tartar. The slick television commercial served as an ironic reminder of Brecht's interview with himself: 'And what would have mattered to you? The critique of society.'

ANALYSIS AND CRITICISM

5 'The Threepenny Opera'

BERTOLT BRECHT (1928)
Translated by Stephen Hinton

The Threepenny Opera, which has been performed in theatres throughout England under the title *The Beggar's Opera* for the past two hundred years, takes us into the milieu of London's criminal districts, Soho and Whitechapel, which are still, as they were two hundred years ago, the refuge of the poorest and not always most transparent strata of London's population. Mr Jonathan Peachum has a novel way of capitalizing on human misery by artificially fitting out healthy human beings as cripples and sending them out to beg, thereby making a profit from the sympathy of the prosperous classes. He does not do this because he is in any way innately bad. 'My position in the world is one of self-defence' − that is his principle which continually forces him to act with the utmost decisiveness. In London's criminal underworld he has only one serious rival, and that is Macheath, a gentleman idolized by all the girls. Macheath has abducted Peachum's daughter Polly and married her in a completely bizarre fashion, in a stable. When Peachum learns of his daughter's marriage − which causes him pain not so much for moral as for social reasons − he starts an all-out war with Macheath and his gang of rogues. The vicissitudes of that war form the plot of *The Threepenny Opera*. It ends with Mac being literally saved from the gallows and the whole affair is happily resolved in a grand, somewhat parodistic operatic finale.

The Beggar's Opera was first performed in 1728 at the Lincolns Inn Theatre in London. The title does not mean, as a number of German translators have assumed, *Die Bettleroper*, that is, an opera in which beggars appear, but rather *Des Bettlers Oper*, that is, an opera for beggars. Written at the instigation of the great Jonathan Swift, *The Beggar's Opera* was a travesty of Handel, and reportedly so successful that Handel's theatre went bankrupt. Since the situation today does not call for parody as it did with Handelian opera, we have abandoned

121

any attempt at such: the music is a completely new composition. What we do still have, however, is the same sociological situation as *The Beggar's Opera*: just like two hundred years ago, we have a social order in which virtually all strata of the population, albeit in extremely varied ways, follow moral principles − not, of course, by living *within* a moral code but *off* it. Formally speaking, *The Threepenny Opera* represents the prototype of opera: it contains elements of opera and elements of spoken theatre.

Translator's note: The second paragraph was first published under the title 'Autoren des Monats: Brecht: The Beggar[']s Opera' in the house journal of the Theater am Schiffbauerdamm, *Das Stichwort*, ed. Heinrich Fischer (September, 1928), No. 1, p. 1. The complete article first appeared in the programme booklet of the 'Volksbühne' as an unsigned introduction (*Einführung*) to the Schiffbauerdamm production on 8 September 1928.

6 Correspondence concerning 'Threepenny Opera'

**between Hans Heinsheimer, editor of *Anbruch*,
and Kurt Weill (1928)[1]**
Translated by Stephen Hinton

Dear Mr Weill,

The sensational success of the *Threepenny Opera*, whereby a work
with a thoroughly new, forward-looking style has suddenly been
turned into a box-office hit, gratifyingly confirms the prophecies
repeatedly made in this journal. The new, popular opera-operetta,
drawing as it does the right conclusion from the artistic and social
premisses of the present, has succeeded in splendid and exemplary
fashion.

Your practical achievement and proven success gives you an evident
advantage over our sociological and aesthetic ratiocinations. May we
now ask you to give our journal your theoretical opinions about the
path you have chosen?

Dear Anbruch,

I thank you for your letter and am pleased to let you have a few words
about the path that Brecht and I have chosen to take with this work
and which we intend to pursue.

You refer in your letter to the *Threepenny Opera*'s sociological
significance. The success of our piece does indeed prove that the
creation and realization of this new genre not only came at the right
moment for the situation of art but that the audience seemed actually
to be waiting for the renewal of a favourite type of theatre. I'm not
so sure that our type of theatre will replace operetta. With Goethe
having reappeared on earth through the medium of an operetta tenor,
why shouldn't another series of historical or at least aristocratic
personalities utter their tragic outcry at the end of the second act?[2]
That will take care of itself, so I don't believe any niche worth
occupying is opening up here. More important for all of us is the fact
that for the first time a breakthrough has been achieved in a consumer

industry previously reserved for a completely different kind of
musician and writer. With *The Threepenny Opera* we are reaching
an audience which either did not know us at all or, at any rate, never
considered us capable of interesting a circle of listeners much wider
than the average concert- and opera-going public.

Seen in this way, *The Threepenny Opera* aligns itself with a
movement that involves nearly all of today's young musicians. The
abandonment of the *l'art pour l'art* standpoint, the turning away from
an individualistic principle of art, the ideas on film music, the contact with the youth music movement, the simplification of the musical
means of expression connected with all these things – these are all
steps along the same path.

Only opera still persists in its 'splendid isolation'. The opera-going
public still represents a closed group seemingly removed from the large
theatre-going public. 'Opera' and 'theatre' are still treated as two
completely separate concepts. In recent operas the dramaturgical style
employed, the language spoken, and the subjects treated would all
be quite unthinkable in contemporary theatre. And one still hears:
'That might work in the theatre, but not in opera!' Opera was established as an artistic genre of the aristocracy, and everything one calls
'operatic tradition' only underlines the class basis of this genre.
Today, however, there is no other artistic form in the entire world
whose bearing is so unabashedly engendered by established society
[*gesellschaftlich*]. The theatre in particular has moved quite decisively
in a direction that can rather be described as socially regenerative
[*gesellschaftsbildend*].[3] If the bounds of opera cannot accommodate
such a rapprochement with the theatre of the times [*Zeittheater*], then
its bounds must be broken.

Only in this way can one understand the fact that nearly all
worthwhile operatic experiments in recent years have been basically
destructive in character. With *The Threepenny Opera* reconstruction
became possible, since it allowed us to start again from scratch. What
we were aiming to create was the prototype of opera [*Urform der
Oper*]. With every musical work for the stage the question arises: how
is music, particularly song, at all possible in the theatre? Here the
question was resolved in the most primitive way possible. I had a
realistic plot, so I had to set the music against it, since I do not consider music capable of realistic effects. Hence the action was either
interrupted, in order to introduce music, or it was deliberately driven
to a point where there was no alternative but to sing. The piece,
furthermore, presented us with the opportunity to make 'opera' the

subject matter for an evening in the theatre. At the very beginning of the piece the audience is told: 'Tonight you are going to see an opera for beggars. Since this opera was intended to be as splendid as only beggars can imagine, and yet cheap enough for beggars to be able to watch, it is called *The Threepenny Opera.*' Thus the last 'Dreigroschenfinale' is in no way a parody. Rather, the idea of opera was directly exploited as a means of resolving a conflict and thus shaping the action. Consequently it had to be presented in its purest, most pristine form.

This return to a primitive form of opera entailed a far-reaching simplification of musical language. The task was to write music that could be sung by actors, that is, by musical amateurs. At first this appeared to be a limitation. As work progressed, however, it proved to be an enormous enrichment. Only the realization of a coherent, identifiable melodic line made possible *The Threepenny Opera*'s real achievement: the creation of a new type of musical theatre. Yours truly,

KURT WEILL

7 'The Threepenny Opera': a Berlin burlesque

The Times' **Berlin correspondent, A.** EBBUTT **(1928)**

There is a piece being played at the Theater am Schiffbauerdamm, in Berlin, called *Die Dreigroschenoper* (The Threepenny Opera). An English visitor who omitted to buy the inadequate programme generally provided in Berlin theatres, or paid very slight attention to it, would wonder, during the first scene, what it was all about. He would conclude that he had blundered into one of those combinations of drama, cinema, jazz, and discord with which the name of the Communistic Herr Piscator is associated. He would, perhaps, have been even more bewildered if he had noticed beforehand in small letters beneath the title, '*The Beggar's Opera*, a piece of music, in a prologue and eight scenes, after the English of John Gay, with ballads by François Villon and Rudyard Kipling inserted.'

Gradually something familiar would strike him, rather in general than in detail; then he would learn, from cinematograph captions flashed on the wings in the best Piscatorial manner, that the formal name of Mackie Messer, the bandit chief in the bowler hat, was Captain Macheath, and other well-known names, such as Peachum, Polly, and Lucy, would become distinguishable. At first, like the loyal Savoyard at last year's German production of *The Mikado* as a *revue*, he might feel indignant; at the close he might well conclude that, although what he had seen was not *The Beggar's Opera*, it retained in some unaccountable way the spirit in which John Gay burlesqued the manners, the morals, and grand opera of his day, and provided a good evening's entertainment. He might even, like the enthusiasts of the last London revival, want to go again.

What Herr Kurt [sic] Brecht and his associates have done may be indefensible to many minds, but it is an interesting example of the more earnest efforts now being made to break new ground on the German stage. Herr Brecht, in his adaptation, starts from the standpoint that *The Beggar's Opera* is a bright idea, with a good story pervaded with fun and satire. But, as it was written partly as a skit

126

on a form of grand opera that no longer cries for drastic chastise-
ment, he decided to reduce that element, which only remains in its
full original absurdity in the last scene. As, too, Gay made use only
of popular airs of the day, it was decided to provide entirely new
music. The absence of any of the Old English airs is regrettable, but
the music composed by Herr Kurt Weill for the Lewis Ruth Jazz Band
is by no means unattractive.

The band is composed of players of the saxophone and the rather
more startling of present-day dance music instruments, perched at
various levels behind and beside the pipes of a large organ situated
at the back of the stage and illuminated from time to time by coloured
electric lights. Herr Weill can compose a slow, sweet melody as easily
as a jazz dance or one of those queer, monotonous syncopated
rhythms with which the more 'advanced' composers of other than
dance music seem to be experimenting. A skilful combination of them
all produces a quaint and often haunting effect. An evening of the
music composed for some of the recent Piscator productions left one
with a bursting head and jangling nerves; one retains after *Die
Dreigroschenoper* snatches of song and rhythm.

Having discarded much of the opera burlesque and all of the music,
there apparently seemed no reason for retaining the eighteenth-
century atmosphere, so Herr Brecht put the scene forward, not 200
years, but about 170. It is vaguely about the end of the nineteenth
century, a period which provides picturesque and convincing costumes
and make-ups for Peachum and his beggars, though it has led to a
temptation to present Macheath's 'street bandits' as music-hall tramps
of the present day. Macheath himself wears a bowler hat of old style,
a large white pointed collar, a double-breasted blue lounge suit with
black silk lapels and tight trousers. He carries a yellow cane and
generally gives the impression of a fourth-rate professional boxer.
Herr Harald Paulsen, however, almost succeeds in giving him the
devil-may-care personality of Macheath. Herr Erich Ponto's
Jonathan Peachum is an excellent performance.

The production of the piece is deliberately crude. Adopting the idea
that it should be a 'Threepenny Opera', which fits in well with tendencies now in the dramatic air, the producers have provided a dirty
cream-coloured curtain about 10ft high, worked by a primitive
arrangement of strings, such as might be used in amateur theatricals.
Across the curtain is painted in crooked, badly formed letters 'Die
Dreigroschenoper'. For the stable scene, in which Macheath and Polly
celebrate their wedding breakfast, there is provided only a wooden

wall a few feet high and a door. The rest of the stable is indicated by means of the cinematograph. There is an occasional expressionistic touch, such as the sudden letting-down of a placard by ropes from above.

There are regrettable omissions, such as the appearance at the execution of Macheath's former lovers with their babies, and some doubt may be expressed as to whether such *revue*-like additions as the brothel scene, in which Macheath is arrested, are really in the spirit of John Gay. The ballads after Villon and − so it is said, though one failed to identify them − Mr Kipling, sung by Peachum and Macheath almost give the piece at times the air, deliberately fostered by music and effects, of a morality play. But *Die Dreigroschenoper* is not, of course, a morality play, it is not a *revue*, it is not a conventional burlesque, and it is not *The Beggar's Opera*; but it is an interesting combination of them illustrating the progress of a movement towards freeing music, acting, and the cinematograph from the ruts of Italian opera, Wagnerian music-drama, drawing-room comedy, and Hollywood, and creating something new with them.

8 *'The Threepenny Opera'*

THEODOR WIESENGRUND-ADORNO (1929)
Translated by Stephen Hinton

The success of *The Threepenny Opera*, comparable only to that of operetta, entices one into believing that here, with simple means, with utter comprehensibility, operetta has quite simply been exalted and made palatable for the requirements of the cognoscenti, who need neither get bored nor be ashamed of entertainment. On society's flat dining-table, one might aver, something had been dished up that was satisfying in itself or had, as it is called, class and which, at the same time, could be consumed by society at large. Anyone who mistrusts, in sociological terms, such congruous harmony initially finds himself contradicted by the very fact of the success − a success supported by the innocent and legitimized by the most progressive intellectuals. Hence one finds oneself having to bear out doubts concerning the purportedly exalted operetta form and, with reference to the work itself, to reveal its success to be a misunderstanding; ultimately − provided the work stands up − to defend it against that success. The success of significant works at their first appearance is invariably a misunderstanding. It is only behind the exterior of the known and commonplace that the original substance of something new can come into contact with those who hear it − so long as, that is, it was not veiled in the darkness of the work beforehand; talk of Mahler's banality, of the Romantic and, later, Impressionist Schoenberg is evidence of this. Perhaps the tension between the work and the listener resides wholly, as the history of any work reveals, in a misunderstanding, and it would be making no improbable claim on behalf of *The Threepenny Opera* to look for such a misunderstanding in it. For its surface structure easily accommodates the interpretation of it as new operetta. Everyone can sing the new melodies, which are written for actors; the rhythm, simpler than that of jazz, from which much colour is borrowed, is hammered home in sequences; the thoroughly homophonic framework is quite audible to amateur ears; the harmony keeps house with tonality, at least with tonal chords. All this sounds,

129

initially, as though the road to the paradise of comprehensibility were paved with all the achievements of the modern age and were blithely being driven along; the functional links between the chords may, to use Westphal's expression, be severed, because that's what one likes doing in the New Objectivity [*neue Sachlichkeit*], juxtaposing those chords as it does barely and expediently; they may be spiced with grotesquerie, loosened up with jazz; yet they themselves, the chords, ultimately remain what they are. In short, it begins to look as though the comfortably educated man had been supplied with a pretext to like in public what he had hitherto secretly played to himself on the gramophone.

But a second look at the work reveals that all is not so. *The Threepenny Opera* may at first appear like a parody of opera or, even more, operetta; in retaining the means of opera and operetta it distorts them. Yet precisely the fact that it adopts those forms so bluntly, leaving them so thoroughly intact, as is possible only with an attitude that has nothing to do with freely chosen forms, whereas proper jazz composers nimbly modernize and fluently refine such elements — that, in other words, opera and operetta appear here with, as it were, a fixed grin should make one wary of the fortuitous popularity. For nothing of what's at work, being so nakedly drawn from things past, can be taken that literally. And even the notion of parody, which might help to explain this superficially simple method of quotation, does not lead far. What is the point, the relevance, of parodying opera, which is dead, or even operetta, about whose sphere so little deception is possible that it scarcely needs to be unmasked in order to show its empty face?

What is really at work will rather be perceived in what happens at some remove from immediate actuality and any parodistic intention — not jaunty and snappy, not suitable for bars, but old-fashioned, dusty, anachronistic and stale, 1890 or even 1880. One knows the love duet of Mackie and Polly, in the stable; a *valse lente*, not, it should be noted, a boston; as emotionally hackneyed and whimperingly consoling as only otherwise appears on the barrel organ; even the wheezing caesuras remind us that there are holes in the roll; and a pathos of love thrives as though from the first great electrical exhibition; a woman ought to have a high bosom and big, prudishly displayed calves; at the back perhaps a bustle, a *Cul de Paris*. The cavalier carries in the one hand an opera hat [*Chapeau claque*] and in the other an artificial bouquet; he does not do it himself, since he is after all in the stable of New Objectivity; the music does it for him.

They sing of the marriage certificate they don't possess, and would like to know who married us, like the good old gypsy baron, who always uses the cathedral shaveling for such purposes; doleful libertinism from bygone years, when grandmother had a relationship and no one dreamed of it. That just has to be dreamt and not parodied, just in the way that dead things do not give themselves to parody. Yet it does return as a *ghost*. One is aware from photos, fashion pictures, and also from such melodies how much surface property from the second half of the nineteenth century has intrinsically become ghostlike to us. The surface of a life, which was apparently self-contained and then declined, has become transparent, all life having fled from it; the festering coziness of that bourgeoisie haunts our dreams as angst; the shreds of a dream, all we have left, can be appropriated by art; art may disclose their demonic root, which still lacks a name; to aim at that root as its object, and to capture it, nameless, in an image, is at once to interpret it and destroy it. This is what *The Threepenny Opera* is about, even if it was not the conscious intention of the authors, who thought within the model and demonstrated insight into it. On the surface of its form, composed from opera and operetta, the work captures the little ghosts of the bourgeois world and reduces them to ashes by exposing them to the harsh light of active memory. The cracks in the music of 1890, through which all content has drained away; the falsity of emotion therein; whatever fractures time metes out on the past surface – Weill, who sees things from here and now, from the other side and from a three-dimensional perspective, against the background of things past, must, as it were, composer out in full what time has sketched on the face of those things in our consciousness. The bygone melodies are broken, and we hear their metrical regimentation as the piecing-together of fragments; in order to interpret old melodies, Weill composes his new ones, fragmentarily pieces together the debris of the empty phrases shattered by time. The harmonies, the fatal diminished-seventh chords, the chromatic alterations of diatonic melodic steps, the espressivo that expresses nothing, they sound false to us – in which case, Weill must make the chords he draws on false, add to the triads a tone that sounds just as false as the basic triads in the light music of 1890; must distort the melodic steps because the simple ones as we remember them are distorted; must construct the stupidity of those modulations by not modulating at all but instead allowing successions of chords that do not belong together, nor did they when there was a modulation in between; or, in the most artful passages of the score, must shift the modulatory balance to such an extent that the harmonic proportions become overturned and fall into the demonic abyss of the inanity attending a composition that modulates from nothing to nothing. A quite clear path leads from such a technique to the best, radical Stravinsky; that of the *Soldier's Tale* or the pieces for piano duet, which to a large extent begin as parodies. Except that Stravinsky is in a hurry to abandon such forms, to surpass them with capricious vituperations, rapidly seeking salvation somewhere other than here, where there is little room left between madness and triviality; whereas Weill's approach penetrates all the further into the ghostly region, the more closely he feels his way along its sundered walls; the more faithfully, that is, he appears to take what the old operetta presents to him. That is how the musical structure is understood; the strange, unrelated juxtaposition of the banal sonorities, their alteration with wrong notes, the photographic, almost pornographic glibness of the rhythmic motion; the incessant mobilization of a musical expression that would like nothing better than to gush into complete inanity. It may have a great and enlightening force when, alongside what is nineteenth century, jazz formulas are introduced which here, under the moon of Soho, already sound as resigned as this 'Who married us'. It is completely a part of the interpreting form of the opera that it takes its material from another opera, and equally, that it keeps that material in the *lumpenproletariat,* which itself, in a concave mirror, reflects the entire questionable order of the bourgeois overworld; rags and ruins, that's all that's left for enlightened consciousness of that thoroughly demystified overworld; perhaps it is only rags and ruins that it can redeem in an image. The operetta of the past reveals itself to *The Threepenny Opera* as satanic; that is the only way it is feasible as contemporary operetta. A sudden end is put to practical operetta, to sprightly *Gebrauchsmusik.*[1]

This, however, does not happen with a clear purpose, nor wholly unequivocally. It would seem to be the fate of any artist who interprets the world and who seriously dares to enter that demonic realm of decay that he all the more perilously succumbs to it, the deeper he goes. For Stravinsky it was no different. In forming and capturing in an image the light music of 1890, *The Threepenny Opera* has to pay the price of becoming, over long stretches, the light music of 1930. It contains a wealth of unbroken vitality from the region of jazz which excites those who really ought to confront themselves on the stage as corpses; the parodistic surface is hermetic enough, sparkling and brightly coloured, to make those believe in fun who observe a little better, though not too closely. And the melodies – people really can sing them. The little children like to know when the pimps, too, have their morality, which one laughs at because it's comforting; they like to know, too, when the criminals, whom they at the same time envy because of their liberality, are revealed to be just as philistine as the decent people in the stalls. Nor should the erotic attraction of dashing Mackie Messer be underrated. After all, the audience which creates the success comes from the Kurfürstendamm and not from the Weidendamm-Brücke, the venerable property of poor man's poetry where the piece is playing.[2] That, however, is no proof against *The Threepenny Opera*'s rebellious nature – a rebelliousness which extends beyond the subject matter of the work. Society has many ways of coping with uncomfortable works. It can ignore them; it can critically demolish them; it can swallow them in such a way that nothing is left. *The Threepenny Opera* has given it a limitless appetite. Meanwhile, it's a question of how the meal goes down. For, even when consumed purely for pleasure, *The Threepenny Opera* remains menacing: no community ideology is present, neither in terms of subject matter nor musically, since nothing noble or transfigured is postulated as a collective art, but rather the dregs of art are salvaged to find the right tone for the dregs of society. And whoever interprets here the discarded collective content is thoroughly alone, only with himself; perhaps that's why they like it so much, because they can laugh at his loneliness like a clown's. Not with a single melody from *The Threepenny Opera* can one play reconstruction; its subverted simplicity is anything but classic. It could, after all, be performed better in bars, where the semi-darkness sharply illuminates it, than in the open air. *The Threepenny Opera* is meant for the collective – and which art of truth, even the loneliest, were not that – yet not the given, non-existent collective, which it serves, but the not-given, existent one which it wishes to mobilize. The successful interpretation of what is past becomes for it a signal of something in the future, which is visible because the old can now be interpreted. In this and in no more banal a sense can *The Threepenny Opera* be seen, despite its singability and box-office, as *Gebrauchsmusik*. It is *Gebrauchsmusik* which, because one is safe, may be enjoyed today as an enzyme, but which cannot be used to cover up what exists. Where it switches from interpretation to direct language it demands quite openly: '... for it is cold: Consider the darkness and the great coldness'.

Silhouette by Lotte Reininger

9 'The Threepenny Opera'

ERNST BLOCH (1935)
Translated by Stephen Hinton

It appealed to many in an especially light-hearted way. It was a pleasant lark, something they could take home with them. Hit tunes to boot, both bitter and sweet, curiously double-edged, yet not offensive. This harmlessness occurs, above all, where the burgher laughs. The hit tunes seem like those he dances to elsewhere, though better concocted. And the beggars seem to be content with a situation that still allows them to sing and play so merrily. A cheerful sound can induce many to dance who in reality have no such need.

So far, so good; but the bit about the cheerful sound doesn't really stand up. Rather, Weill succeeded, in a very lively way, in draining the foul waters, especially those of the hit tune. 'Instead of staying at home, they need amusement': the wrong notes, the transposed rhythms of this amusement are composed out and laid bare, thus betraying and perfidiously transforming the gratification of urges which the audience normally enjoys from hit tunes; that is to say, the *commodity* as a hit tune no longer exists; instead the hit appears as the hampered surrogate for a *good*. Weill, wearing a popular, even vulgar mask, managed to affect those whom progressive music couldn't even reach. Even though the smallest proportion of these many are proletarians, Weill transforms that better mix of classes that does listen not so much into '*Volk*', whose praises are to be sung, as into subversion, which strikes at the very root of popular music. Weill is not radically monotonous like Eisler, and certainly not merely playful [*musikantisch*], that is, falsely direct, like the born, instinctive social democrat Hindemith; even less does he adopt the hit tune in the form of a song as if it were a new folksong. After all, the hit tune has long been an industrialized commodity; the new one, above all, containing as it does poor Negroes and the more elegant basic instincts, has become standardized and set apart, particularly anonymous and abstract in its gratification of urges. Yet the hit tune equally contains a touch of hanky-panky, of the red-light district and

135

fun house adjacent to the boulevard; if the hit tune — as rhythm, melody and text — faithfully follows the standardized course of the times, then it also conceals a crooked, even trashy face which removes with the greatest superficiality any surface appearances. The shabbiness of the hit tune not only succeeds in remaining longer in the memory than the middle-of-the-road material of its time (even very early hit tunes, such as *Fischerin, du kleine, Die Holzauktion im Grunewald, Male, Male, lebt denn meine Male noch, Der Rixdorfer*, stick in the related subconscious). Thanks to the ferment of the period, *The Threepenny Opera* was able to latch on to this shabbiness with particular precision; its beggars and rogues are no longer those of the opera buffa, or even of cheap charity balls, but of subverted society in person. Hence, oh false friends, these tones, hence Brecht's mocking sweetness, once again his double-edged levity, hence the tunes of Mack the Knife, hence this Tiger Brown. Hence the voice of Lotte Lenya, sweet, high, light, dangerous, cool, with the radiance of the crescent moon; hence Pirate Jenny and the demonic ballad for which she finally plucks up courage. *The Threepenny Opera* would not exist without the boldly construed disintegration in Stravinsky's *Soldier's Tale*; even less so, however, without the general disintegration, without the post-1880 hit tunes. The 'tingle' and slush no longer have any better music above them than that in which they are quoted; the sickly beauty of the trumpet melody at Polly's farewell from the robbers turns into the quotation of a life that has yet to find space for itself. The experiment of *The Threepenny Opera* put the worst music at the service of today's most advanced music; and this appears menacing. The whore on bourgeois street duty turned into nothing less than an anarchistic smuggler. Various traits intermingle, creating friction. The angular tone and the bad air, the closed number and the rebellious content. The simplified means of expression and the extremely polyphonic dream of Pirate Jenny, the cheerful melodies and the burgeoning desperation; lastly, an explosive chorale. The song doesn't act, it reports conditions, just as the old aria did; yet without exception it reports a condition that is blighted (and the 'infernal "d'you feel my heart beating?" line'). An old cellar is set up here as a house; occasionally, too, a new roof is set up down on the ground; admittedly, a society's future cannot be predicted, let alone generated, from the cross-section of the two. If the actual pleasure that music of this kind affords does not obstruct the path of society's transformation, then it does not always lie on that path either; only on occasions does its tone bear its sword. General limits are imposed here, even on things stronger than the experiment of *The Threepenny Opera* and its liberated hit tune ammunition. The nail hit on the head by the politically most focussed music and literature is only in a very indirect way one in the coffin of existing reality. Yet if music cannot change society, then it can, as Wiesengrund [Theodor Wiesengrund-Adorno] rightly says, signify its change in advance by 'absorbing' it and proclaiming what is dissolving and what forming under the surface. Above all, it illuminates the impetus of those who march into the future even without music, though with it all the more easily. Weill's is the only music today with any socio-polemical impact, and the wind blows through, the honest wind, which is where no buildings can impede it, where all around the times have not yet become reality. Weill has put a spanner in the appealing works of the playful [*musikantisch*] singers and their own 'Volk'. The Cannon Song showed that soldiers also live on the left, but the right ones. And Pirate Jenny came for a few moments as near to the heart of the people as Queen Luise once did.[1] Nothing can demonstrate more clearly what hit tunes and the joy of alloying extemporization are currently capable of.

10 *Three-groats opera*

ERIC BLOM (1931)

This has nothing to do with 'opera at 2d. a week'. It is simply an English equivalent of the title of the *Dreigroschenoper*, the German adaptation of the *Beggar's Opera*. A good deal has been heard here of the success of this piece at its production in Berlin in the summer of 1928 and of its victorious progress throughout Central Europe ever since. Many people over here having felt inordinately gratified by what they fondly deem to be an irrefutable proof that what Hammersmith thinks to-day the world thinks to-morrow, it may be as well to say quite plainly in an English musical journal that we have no cause whatever to be proud.[1] For the distressing fact is that the *Dreigroschenoper* is not the *Beggar's Opera* at all. We have, indeed, some reason to be alarmed lest its patrons should be under the impression that it has more than a very superficial connection with John Gay's satirical ballad opera.

They must know, of course, that the music by Kurt Weill was not written for 1728, but for 1928. Its Imperial Palace Hotel idiom and the prevalent tone of the saxophone must have made this obvious enough even to those who had never heard the composer's name and who possess but the slightest faculty of listening historically. But it may not have been quite so obvious that the distance between Gay's book and the German version is not one of centuries alone, in spite of some amusing anachronisms that hint at the modernity of the latter broadly enough for those who know their London. (The wedding of Macheath and Polly is celebrated − in an empty stable − with a picnic for which the plates have been stolen from the Savoy Hotel and the egg mayonnaise from Selfridge's.)

On the German title-page we read that the *Beggar's Opera* is translated by Elisabeth Hauptmann, and the 'German adaptation' made by Bert Brecht.[2] What 'adaptation' means in this case it is not easy to decide. Except for the names of some of the characters, there is precious little left of the original. If the translation was faithfully

made there can thus be next to nothing left of that either, and it
follows that it was not a case of an adaptation so much as of a new
play. Why it should have been thought advisable to launch it under
an English flag it is hard to imagine.

The piece is described as 'after John Gay'. It is − a long way after.
Satire has yielded to coarse invective, pointed dialogue to blunt
twaddle, polished verse to lamentable doggerel. There are a few neat
points, either in the dialogue or in the songs: foulness and silliness
alternate where they do not happen to combine. I will give a sample
or two, translated as closely as possible, and with no attempt at
making them appear worse than they are in the original.

The quarrelling duet between Polly and Lucy, 'Why, how now,
Madam Flirt?', runs thus in the German version:

'Come along, you beauty of Soho, and let's have a look at your pretty legs!
I'd like to see something nice for a change. For there's nobody as handsome
as you. They say you make such an impression on my Mac!' 'Do they, really?'
'Well, I must say it makes me laugh.' 'Does it, really?' 'Ah, it is truly funny!'
'Oh, it is really funny?' 'That Mac should think anything of you!' 'That Mac
should think anything of me?' 'Ha, ha, ha, a creature like you doesn't appeal
to a man, anyhow.' 'Well, we shall see about that.' 'Yes, we shall see about
that.' 'Mackie and I lived like turtledoves; he loves me alone, there's no getting
away from that. By your leave, it can't be all over just because such mucky
cattle has turned up. Ridiculous!'

So much for Brecht's dialogue.[3] To this specimen of brilliant
repartee I will add a translation of his verse that is faithful to the
original, at any rate in spirit − if the word may pass:

> Man, alas! is very bad,
> So just hit him on his hat.
> When you've hit him on his hat,
> Perhaps he won't be quite so bad.

And lest the reader should suspect me of having made the worst of
the case, I will submit a verse in the original to the judgment of those
who know German:

> Die Welt ist arm, der Mensch ist schlecht,
> Da hab' ich eben leider recht!
> Und das ist eben schade,
> Das ist das riesig Fade.
> Und darum ist es nichts damit,
> Und darum ist [das] alles Kitt.

This extraordinary cheapness and slanginess is characteristic of almost
the whole piece, dialogue and verse, though I confess that I did not
set out to choose the noblest and most inspired passages.

It would be priggish and unfair to suggest that the author and the composer are not perfectly aware that the libretto is poor. No doubt they would argue that the poverty is intended to match the title and contents of their play, just as its grossness is meant to reflect the low personages who appear in it. That Messrs Brecht and Weill had a definite purpose in view is not to be denied. In fact, they put themselves in the company of Gluck and Wagner: they are out to reform the opera – once again. Let the composer speak for himself for a moment (I translate from a letter addressed by him to the *Musikblätter des Anbruch*):

Opera alone still persists in its splendid isolation. The operatic public remains an exclusive set of people which appears to stand outside the general play-going public. 'Opera' and 'Theatre' are still treated as two entirely different concepts. New operas continue to make use of dramatic means, of a language and of subjects which are wholly unthinkable in contemporary drama. And we hear it said again and again: 'That may be all very well in drama, but it will not do for opera.' Opera came into being as an aristocratic species of art, and what is called the 'operatic tradition' emphasizes the exclusive character which is the basis of that species. But nowhere in the whole world is there another art form so completely devoted to 'society' to-day, and the theatre especially has turned with great decision in a direction that may rather be called sociological. The conclusion is that if the framework of the opera does not permit of any approach towards the theatre of our time, that framework had better be burst.[4]

Provided that Messrs Brecht and Weill have correctly diagnosed the artistic needs of the present day, which it would be beside the purpose of this article either to assert or deny, this argument is perfectly sound. But it does not follow from their theoretical solution of the problem that they have succeeded in practice. One cannot help suspecting that the very public to whom they wish to appeal will prefer *Figaro*, *Meistersinger*, and *Aïda* to the *Dreigroschenoper*, once they have come to see the difference. How is it that two people who are anxious to bring art to the proletariat so underestimate the intelligence of that section of the public as to provide it with a form of art that can only appeal to simpletons and – what is far worse from their point of view – to snobs? For it must be confessed that both words and music of the *Dreigroschenoper* look suspiciously as if they had been deliberately written for cretins.

It is, of course, possible to take the favourable reception of the play for an indisputable proof of its validity as a new form of art. Indeed, Kurt Weill says in his letter, complacently enough: 'As a matter of fact the success of the piece not only proves that the creation and assertion of a new species saved the situation for art at the right moment, but that the public actually seemed to wait for the renewal of a favoured theatrical entertainment.' One wonders what public he is referring to. The operatic public? If so, he and his associate failed to attract the crowd whom they set out to capture and to captivate. Or does he mean that crowd? In that case it would be nonsense to talk of their waiting for the renewal of an entertainment which they had scarcely known at all in its old forms and certainly never favoured. Or the playgoing public in general? Then his labour was superfluous, since, on his own showing, the drama already provides them amply with the novelty they seek.

Can Messrs Brecht and Weill seriously fancy that it was the sociological tendency of their work which made its success? Did they ever study their audiences? Did they find the stalls occupied night after night by the poor? Was the price of admittance the modern equivalent of three groats, and was evening dress *strengstens verboten*? Did they, perhaps, insist that what dress there was should be hired for the night from the beggar's wardrobe of their 'Herr' Peachum?

No, it must be taken for granted — heartrending thought! — that the bulk of the eager audience who flocked to see the *Dreigroschenoper* was composed of snobs, and its long run can only lead one to the distressing conclusion that snobbery is as prevalent in the centre of Europe as on its periphery. One cannot help feeling that the authors ought to have foreseen that the very people who would care to see the goings-on among thieves and harlots, the wedding breakfast in a stable and the scene in a low brothel — let us put it bluntly to show how crude it all is — and all the rest of the bedraggled show would be those for whom that sort of thing has the charm of actual as well as artistic novelty. They might have known that those who live among the squalor of a big city want to see all the splendours of a full-blown operatic production, to listen to the largest orchestra that money can produce, and to admire singers whose salary for one night would mean comfort for life for them. That supremely democratic institution, the cinema, has surely shown conclusively enough that what the great public like is prettiness, the magnificent life of the idle rich, and sugary sentiment.

The *Dreigroschenoper*, to be sure, is neither pretty nor magnificent, nor by any means sugary, and the ingenuousness and freshness of an art calculated to attract a public innocent of aesthetic experience is the least of its qualities. It is a morbid entertainment for those who are sated, not only with all that is sublime, but with everything that is any way artistically agreeable. For them it has a spice of novelty, though it is quite evidently not a new departure, but a decadent offshoot of socialism, dramatic realism, and utility music. Thus one condemns it not for its much-advertised newness, but for the extraordinary effect of staleness and weariness it produces. Were it a genuine attempt at novelty, it would have to be at least theoretically welcomed as such, even though one would have to disbelieve that it could possibly attract a new audience merely for that reason. It is the public that has tasted of everything which craves unaccustomed experiences. There is no point in going out of one's way to create them for those who have never known the forms of art already in existence.

If our esoteric Sunday stage productions ever ran to anything like opera − and this is not much of an opera, forsooth, needing but a few instruments and no highly trained singers − it would be worth while giving a private performance of this super-beggarly version of the *Beggar's Opera* in London. It would be no costly venture, for the shabbier and dingier the staging and dressing the better would it suit the piece, which, in fact, ought to look the complete antithesis to Sir Nigel Playfair's prettification of Gay's acid little masterpiece. Everything in the Brecht−Weill concoction indicates soilure and decay, the music no less than the play. Having already given some indication of the quality of the latter, I will endeavour, in conclusion, to characterize the score briefly.

The composer appears to have begun with some idea of harking back to the period of the *Beggar's Opera*. His overture has a kind of debased Handelian stateliness and contains an abortive fugue. Then, too, he lets Peachum sing a 'morning hymn' at the opening of the first act which is actually based on the tune of the original character's song, 'Through all the employments of life'. This looks the more hopeful, if only for the reputation of the *Beggar's Opera* abroad, because the setting is quite admirably done − as well in its way, in fact, as Mr Frederic Austin's version. But Weill at once abandons the method of quotation, which he has clearly adopted only because the plot here provides for Peachum's actually singing a familiar tune. The rest of the music is frankly modern, based on jazz and the rest of the world's current dance and popular song stuff. Unfortunately it is song and dance of the dismallest sort. One thinks of the moonlit tenement backyards in the slums of Berlin, where a consumptive cornet player, trying to snatch some fresh air, practises among the dustbins, while a lovelorn saxophonist utters his puling notes from an upper window: a vertical *Katzenjammer* atmosphere. It must be said, though, that it is all rather fascinating in an unpleasant sort of way. These slimy tunes and false basses and wry harmonies somehow fit the whole 'assoiléd show' extremely well. Still, a doubt is left in one's mind whether it is a show worth fitting.

The song in the prologue concerning the murky deeds of Macheath (who rejoices in the odd nickname Mackie Messer) is played in the manner of a barrel organ and marked 'blues-tempo'. It is rather a striking tune ending on an added sixth, with a curiously uncomfortable, creepy feeling about it. The Peachums' and Polly's first songs are indifferent, but a fox-trot (no. 7) for Macheath and Brown (*alias* Lockit) has swing and vigour. The best thing of the kind, however, is a slashing shimmy for Macheath (no. 13 [now 14]). The quarrelling duet (no. 14 [now 15]), on the other hand, musically matches its verbal inanity to perfection. So the music goes on, up and down between flashes of swaggering tunefulness, a kind of tarnished prettiness and a distressing insipidity. The fluctuation is at any rate something more than what is achieved by the almost unrelieved poverty of the libretto.

11 'L'Opéra de Quat'Sous'[1]

WALTER BENJAMIN (?1937)

Translated by Stephen Hinton

When the ruling classes put in circulation a hypocritical morality, then, according to the socialist Charles Fourier, a 'counter-morality' comes into being by virtue of which those on the side of the oppressed join together in opposition to their oppressors. The English poet John Gay (1688 [*recte* 1685] – 1732), who had his *Beggar's Opera* staged in 1729 [*recte* 1728], was a particular connoisseur of the counter-morality that prevailed in the London underworld. It had not been easy for him to peddle his knowledge. No theatre had dared to take on his piece. Eventually private funds were made available; they sufficed to fit out a barn in such a way that the piece could be presented in it. The success was enormous. In 1750 the opera was translated by A. Hallam into French. Just 50 years later, however, the work was already forgotten on the Continent, and little more was known of Gay except that he had been a friend of the great satirist Pope as well as an author of well-crafted idylls, and that he had been a peace-loving citizen.

Exactly 200 years had elapsed since the première when, on 31 August 1928, *The Threepenny Opera* began its progress into the world from Ernst Aufricht's Berlin theatre. On his voyage into immortality, Gay had chanced upon the German poet BERT BRECHT who, from a disposition of Elective Affinity,[2] had grasped the Englishman's tremendous audacity and recklessness. Brecht grasped, furthermore, that 200 years had not been able to loosen the alliance that poverty had sealed with vice, but rather that this alliance is as enduring as a social order whose consequence is poverty. For this reason, it becomes perhaps even clearer in Brecht's *Threepenny Opera* than it does in Gay how intimately the counter-morality of the beggars and rogues is bound up with the official morality or, as the English say, cant.

Thus *The Threepenny Opera*, which on account of its picturesque setting appeared distant, became at a stroke something of considerable

144

relevance. One should not lose sight of this fact if one wishes to comprehend its enduring success over the last ten years. It has been translated into almost all European languages, it has entered the repertoire of innumerable theatres, and reached as far as America, Russia and Japan. In 1930 one could catch it in Tokyo in three separate theatres – that is, in three separate conceptions – at once. In France, it was Gaston Baty who first presented it, in 1928 [*recte* 1930]. The total number of performances around the world is estimated at 40,000.

It follows from this that the news item [*fait divers*] from the eighteenth century, as depicted by Brecht, is an occurrence that we too can make sense of. The choruses and songs of *The Threepenny Opera* offer several humble suggestions as to how this can be done. Moreover, these songs perform the function of making us better acquainted with the main characters.

First, there is Mack the Knife. He is the *patron* for whom the members of his gang work. His master morality[3] is as at home with the sentimentality of the petit bourgeois ('Vois-tu la Lune') as it is with the less sentimental practices of the pimp ('Dans le bordel').

In his own way, Mack the Knife's friend, Tiger Brown, is also a moralist. He finds a way out of the tragic conflict between official duty and loyalty to a friend in the form of corruptibility. But the enterprise does him no good. He runs around, as Mack the Knife says, like bad conscience personified, and blossoms out only when he thinks of the old days ('Song des Canons').

Peachum, Mack the Knife's father-in-law, to a certain extent represents the intellect of the opera. He has made the Bible his *vade mecum* – not so much for the sake of its wisdom but rather for the sake of the afflictions it relates and also the human insufficiency one can attest from it. Peachum always keeps his hat on because at any moment he expects the roof to cave in on his head. He is convinced that we live in the worst of all possible worlds. He confides to the audience, in the first finale ('Premier Finale'), the conclusions that are to be drawn from this fact. As for the women – Peachum's wife and their daughter, Polly – their cheerful disposition shields them from the ethical problems with which their men have to concern themselves.

William Hogarth, the moralist among English artists, was the first illustrator of *The Beggar's Opera*. The theatre illustrates it in its own way. Brecht has provided the sets with dictums such as one can find for the clarification of stories on old illustrated broadsheets.

12   'The Threepenny Opera'

HANS KELLER (1956)

At the Aldwych Theatre at the time of writing, and possibly for many weeks to come, a work is being produced that represents the freshest, healthiest, most imaginative and inspired musical entertainment of the season, a Third-Light Programme piece which is the weightiest possible lowbrow opera for highbrows and the most full-blooded highbrow musical for lowbrows. But while those responsible for the staging of Weill's *Dreigroschenoper*, *i.e.* Oscar Lewenstein, Wolf Mankowitz and Helen Arnold, deserve our thanks and encouragement, it must be realized that they are, to a surprising extent, the instruments of a torrential revival that has swept right across our musical world, both European and American: through the mediums of actual performance, film, gramophone record and even the barrel-organ, not to speak of the efforts of popular American arrangers like 'Satchmo' Armstrong, Les Paul, or Tito Puente, the *Dreigroschenoper* seems to have come back to stay. In London, the 'Peachum Production' has proved so successful that it had to move to the West End, after the music (as distinct from the dramatic) critics had written it off as a flop, *The Times* opining that most of the music 'could have been turned out by a hack in Charing Cross Road'.

As distinct from Bert Brecht's text, which is brilliant but uneven (and of whose translation Marc Blitzstein has made an excellent job), Weill's music is, throughout, a demonstrable masterpiece, only inasmuch a product of the twenties as this decade happens to have laid the foundations for much of our century's art and science. The 'sordidity' of Weill's inventions is very much in the ear of the listener who, in fact, contributes to the work: Weill grimly ironizes, amongst other things, our own conception of decadence.

Like Gershwin's, Weill's songs create new forms out of eclectic material whose elements of jazz, Blues and cabaret idiom make it easy for the insensitive listener to mistake the style for the stuff. As soon

146

as the stuff is understood, however, the style itself discloses its originality and homogeneity.

Thematically, there is strict organization behind what may seem the free and easy succession of numbers. The basic motif of the motto tune (mediant-dominant-submediant) proves not only the melodic, but also the harmonic cell of much of the work. The harmony itself, with its progressive tonalities, sundry modulatory dislocations, and polytonal implications, shows complex developments which Frank Howes' West End hack could never as much as hear, since not even Mr Howes can. The chief harmonic principle is that of inhibition, of interrupted cadences in the widest sense of the term. The eternally repeatable motto tune is the prototype: avoiding Aeolian insinuations, its submediant obsession creates an extended *appoggiatura*, a suspense by prolonged suspension, enhanced by the tonic-dominant bass as well as by the alternation of tonic chord and dominant seventh. The sixth is, of course, the inhibitory degree *par excellence*, because its opposition to the tonic is based on the strongest possible measure of agreement or *tertium comparationis*, including as only the submediant triad does the tonic third: hence the arch-inhibition, the interrupted cadence V–VI. Hence, too, the added sixth – a familiar jazz device – is the rightest 'wrong' note. The harmonic inhibitions of the opera's ensuing structures are, of course, far more sophisticated, but however paradoxical, for the moment, a surprise turn of chordal events may seem, it never proves unfunctional within the wider whole – a sharp contrast, here, to some of Bert Brecht's own paradoxes that do not appear to worry about anything but their momentary effect which, admittedly, is invariably striking.

As a logical counterpart to what, I suppose, the composer would have liked us to call the dialectic harmony, the rhythmic structures move between symmetry and anti-symmetry (as distinct from asymmetry), both formally and, where counterpoint or homophonic imitations come into play, texturally: in the shimmy 'Ballad of the Easy Life', for example, the orchestral echoing motif, in itself syncopated and cross-accented, undergoes a diminution which creates a most original texture, *i.e.* that of a *quasi*-linear *stretto*. The actual rhythmic thought is extremely virile and, as such, not sufficiently realized by the current production's conductor-pianist Berthold Goldschmidt.

Altogether, the stage direction by Sam Wanamaker is enthusiastic, yet conspires with the musical direction to emasculate the work. For those of us – the present writer included – who have not heard and seen any previous production, the present one is certainly more than worth while, but I can imagine that an older generation must be disappointed by the fact that the spirit of operatic parody, which should properly be reserved for the third *finale*, permeates the entire show. It so happens that the prettification of the work is epitomized by the new English title for the great E minor tango duet between Macheath and Jenny, the 'Ballad of the Fancy Man', which should really be called the 'Pimp's Ballad' (*Zuhälterballade*). The best single feature is the *décor* by Caspar Neher, who wrote the libretto for Weill's opera *Die Bürgschaft* which was first produced in Berlin the year before the Nazis came in and the composer got out.

'With Kurt Weill', wrote Hans F. Redlich at the end of his obituary (*Music Review*, 11:3, August 1950, p.208), '... one of the few composers to succeed in bridging the gap between artist and audience has vanished from the contemporary scene.' That depends on what you understand by 'audience'. To the music critics of *The Times* or *The Daily Telegraph* the jazzy Weill is as sealed a book as the twelve-tonal Schönberg, and they would be unable to explain the popular musical success of either the *Dreigroschenoper* or *Moses und Aron*. The isolation of our age's masters is indeed diminishing fast. It is the music critics that are becoming isolated. Socially, they are well on the way towards forming a characteristically modern unit – the psychotic group.

13 *Motifs, tags and related matters*

DAVID DREW (1965/87)

Despite notable advances in recent times, the idea of considering
Weill's music from other than literary, ideological, or broadly
journalistic points of view is still unfamiliar enough for there to be
pitfalls in every approach to topics such as the present one. To remark
that an understanding of Weill's thematic-motivic processes in any
of his European works is inseparable not only from the other formal
aspects of the work in question but also from a proper study of those
same processes in at least a representative selection of the preceding
works is to risk stating the obvious in a context that lends it a spurious
air of originality.

Weill's early creative development became decisive for the future
at the point where his essentially harmonic intuitions began to be
modified by his first apprehension of contrapuntal possibilities.
Between 1918 and 1922 — that is, between the inception of the B
minor String Quartet and the completion of the *Sinfonia Sacra*
(Fantasia, Passacaglia, Hymnus) — he absorbed lessons from his
counterpoint teachers (and also from his informal encounters with
the polyphonic thinking of Bach, Reger, and Busoni) that were to
remain influential throughout his European music, not least, or indeed
especially, where the textures are homophonic.

The intensification of Weill's motivic thinking in the works of
1921—23 was seemingly brought about by a fusion between his
contrapuntal preoccupations during that period and his discovery
through Busoni of Lisztian transformation-processes. The latter were
to assume a strictly dramatic significance in his first post-Busoni
opera, *Der Protagonist*, where the very concept of 'Verwandlungen'
is already fundamental to the drama explicit in the text. *Der Protagonist* is the key work in relation to Weill's methods of dramatic composition and to the critically interesting but practically insignificant
question of whether, and if so how far, his methods were deliberate
rather than intuitive. In *Der Protagonist* the dissociation of rhythm

149

from pitch — in one case by means of a relatively complex prose rhythm — and the transformation of intervallic structures by registral and other means achieves foreground effects which are foreign to *Royal Palace* (the intended companion piece for *Der Protagonist*) but not to its successor, *Der Zar lässt sich photographieren*.

It should go without saying that it is the character of any given work rather than its quality that is determined by the relative density of thematic and motivic working. *Der Protagonist*, for example, is motivically much more active and integrated than *Royal Palace*, yet the latter work is in every musical respect the richer and more confident. Whereas in *Royal Palace* the function of companion piece to *Der Protagonist* is fulfilled by way of reversing the compositional as well as the characteristic priorities, in *Der Zar* the same function is fulfilled by ironic variation of the methods of *Der Protagonist*. On the motivic level this process results in a more or less overt parody of *leitmotiv* techniques as presented in the popular opera-guides of yesteryear. Both the dramatic function and the musical effect are in complete contrast to the types of integration characteristic of the next major work, *Aufstieg und Fall der Stadt Mahagonny*, in which the underlying structure consistently contradicts the parodistic intentions ascribed to the work by Brecht's celebrated notes on it.

Though first performed long before the completion of the *Mahagonny* opera, *Die Dreigroschenoper* must be heard as one of that work's several consequences, compositionally no less than historically. In the systematic structure of relationships which the *Threepenny Opera* music erects above and across those defined by the libretto, there are three levels, of which the first — the base level so to speak — is one that had no structural function in the two Kaiser operas: tonality. The second level — the idiomatic or characteristic — is dependent upon tonality. The third is the subject of this present survey.[1]

The motivic procedures in the *Threepenny Opera* score owe less to Weill's previous experience in non-tonal fields than do those of later and less overtly popular works. With one notable exception, the intervallic content of each motif or tag is defined in terms of a diatonic hierarchy which, like the intervals themselves, remains unchanged at each recurrence.

The present fame of *Die Dreigroschenoper* owes much to the necromantic conjurations of the three-note motif (ex. 1a) with which, after the neo-classical overture, the 'Moritat' singer introduces Macheath; but since the 'Moritat' was apparently the last number Weill composed (which helps explain his subconscious and painfully ironic memory of the farewell cadences of *Das Lied von der Erde*!), the motif actually derives from, though in effect it prepares for, Macheath's 'Ballade vom angenehmen Leben' (ex. 1b). In Peachum's C major 'Lied von der Unzulänglichkeit menschlichen Strebens', Macheath's identity card is appropriately turned back to front (ex. 1c).

Ex. 1a

(♩=66)

Und   der Hai - fisch   der   hat Zäh - ne

Ex. 1b

(♩=96)

p   (Und   der Hai - fisch)

Macheath: Da   preist man   uns   das   Le - ben   gro - sser   Gei - ster

Ex. 1c

Peachum: Der Mensch lebt   durch   den   Kopf

Ex. 1a, b, c: Weill. *Die Dreigroschenoper*. Copyright 1928 by Universal Edition A.G., Wien. Copyright renewed. Copyright assigned to European American Music Corporation. All rights reserved. Used by permission of European American Music Corporation.

Vertically expressed, the *Moritat*-motif becomes the harmonic *idée fixe* of the entire song − the chord of the added sixth. In its minor form, that chord acquires, during the course of the score, a signalling function so prominent that one may well describe it as the *Dreigroschenoper* chord, if only to distinguish it in principle from the mere mannerism it threatened to become during Weill's first post-German period (up to and including *Knickerbocker Holiday*). At this early stage the influence of his non-tonal procedures is still clearly apparent: in Act I the chord (exx. 2a−c) is identified by its pitch components rather than by its tonal function − a device for which there is an exact precedent in the second act of Krenek's *Jonny spielt auf*. In Act II the motto chord is identified by rhythm rather than pitch (exx. 2d−f) − a tango rhythm (R¹) related, by the elision of one term, to Seeräuberjenny's whispered warnings (ex. 2a) and their explosively *fortissimo* fulfilment at the very close of the Act I finale.

Ex. 2a

Ex. 2b

Ex. 2c

Ex. 2d

Ex. 2e

Ex. 2f

Whereas the motto chord has no dramatic connotations, its melodic counterpart is entirely concerned with the pretences and realities of Macheath's love life. It is first heard at the start of the Polly–Macheath 'Liebeslied' (see ex. 3).

Ex. 3

Since Weill, like Busoni, tended to view the passions of love and war with the same sceptical eye, it is characteristic that the 'love motif' arises from the immediately preceding 'Kanonen-Song'. Its salient feature (A) is a compression of the decisive elements in the 'Kanonen-Song's' introduction (ex. 4a), while its cadential complement (B) echoes the song's 'Soldaten wohnen' refrain (ex. 4b).

154   *David Drew*

Ex. 4a

Ex. 4b

Sol - da - ten   woh - nen   auf den Ka - no - nen

Ex. 4a, b: Weill. *Die Dreigroschenoper.* Copyright 1928 by Universal Edition A.G., Wien. Copyright renewed. Copyright assigned to European American Music Corporation. All rights reserved. Used by permission of European American Music Corporation.

After the 'Liebeslied', the 'love motif' comes into its own as the basis for the refrain of Polly's 'Barbara-Song' (ex. 5a); and just as the 'Liebeslied' began with it, so does its dramatic counterpart, the 'Pimp's Ballad', end with it (ex. 5b) – at the very point where the policeman hailed by Jenny lays his hand on her lover's shoulder.

In the 'Salomon-Song', Jenny comments on Macheath's downfall as if she, and not Polly, had been the singer of the 'Barbara-Song'. Solomon had been a prey to his own wisdom, and Caesar to his own audacity. And according to Jenny in the 'Salomon-Song' (ex. 5c) the fatal flaw in Macheath (and herself) was passion – *Leidenschaft.* How enviable, she concludes, are those who are free from passion.

Ex. 5a

Polly: Ja   da   kann   man   sich doch nicht nur   hin - le - gen

Ex. 5b

Ex. 5c

Ex. 5a, b, c: Weill. *Die Dreigroschenoper.* Copyright 1928 by Universal Edition A.G., Wien. Copyright renewed. Copyright assigned to European American Music Corporation. All rights reserved. Used by permission of European American Music Corporation.

The connotations of 'Leidenschaft' are not necessarily erotic. But thanks to an etymology peculiar to the German language and conveniently amenable to the psychology of German romanticism, the semantics are inseparable from the word's root, which is 'Leid', denoting pain or suffering. The connotations of the Ex. 5 nexus certainly include that root, and as far as Weill was concerned harked back to some of his earliest *Lieder*, such as the Eichendorff song of 1916, 'Sehnsucht'.

Macheath's suffering is the wholly serious subject of the two numbers which follow the 'Salomon-Song' – the 'Ruf aus der Gruft' and the 'Epistel'. Weill's superb setting of the 'Epistel' culminates in a furiously denunciatory passage whose melodic and harmonic constituents recall the principal motive of his first 'revolutionary' work, the 1921 symphony. Macheath is no longer the engaging rogue of the previous scenes, indeed, is no longer Macheath. He has become a tragic figure who speaks with the voice of all whom the world, justly or unjustly, has condemned. It is a voice that cries for vengeance as loudly as for forgiveness.

So frank an exposure of the work's inner seriousness at so late a stage created a structural problem which Brecht solved by parodying the conventional happy end (an idea borrowed from Gay but more closely related in satirical function to the epilogue of F. W. Murnau's famous film *The Last Laugh*). Although it was essentially a literary device, Weill might have able to adapt it to his musical purposes had he not already ensured that his settings of Macheath's two valedictions were the culmination of every serious element he had previously introduced. His conception of the finale could therefore be related to Brecht's only in the sense that it was complementary to it. 'The last finale', he wrote, 'is in no way a parody. Rather, the idea of opera was directly exploited as a means of resolving a conflict and thus shaping the action.'[2]

A lively chorus in 6/8 time introduces the Riding Messenger (Tiger

Brown) and his *recitativo* proclamation of the Queen's pardon.
Musically, Macheath's response to the good news ignores the
deliberate bathos of words and situation, for its hypothesis is still the
authentic anguish of the previous scene. Weill was not exaggerating
when he claimed for the finale a relationship to opera in its 'purest,
most pristine form'.[3] Macheath begins his lyrical yet inwardly
troubled C minor arietta as if he were Mozart's Belmonte and the
Queen were Selim. And what of Polly, Macheath's Constanza? Her
conclusion to the arietta is a Weillian masterstroke (see ex. 6).

Ex. 6

Weill. *Die Dreigroschenoper.* Copyright 1928 by Universal Edition A.G., Wien.
Copyright renewed. Copyright assigned to European American Music Corporation.
All rights reserved. Used by permission of European American Music Corporation.

Polly may consider herself 'fortunate' (*glücklich*); for her darling
Macheath is indeed 'saved'. But the orchestral coda with its quotation
from the 'Barbara-Song' belongs, like Macheath, to Jenny as much
as to Polly. Moreover, the setting of Polly's 'Ich bin sehr glücklich'
is an exact transposition of the phrase with which Macheath, in the
'Zuhälterballade', had remarked upon the plurality of amorous
relationships and the irrelevance of wedding rings (see ex. 7).

Ex. 7

Macheath: Es geht auch an - ders

So much for the illusory happy end. But the Peachums have still to make their grimly realistic comment. The anapaestic rhythm of the ensuing C minor Allegro moderato echoes that of Macheath's 'Ruf aus der Gruft' and Polly's 'Seeräuberjenny', while the continued commitment to the minor mode reinforces the idea that in truth nobody has been saved – for the world remains poor and man remains evil. It seems as if the furious fatalism of the Act I finale is about to re-emerge as the parting message of the whole work. But a sudden burst of dominant-seventh harmony – rare in *Die Drei-groschenoper* – announces the confident C major of the chorale. Apparently the tension has been resolved just as had been promised in the Overture – which began in a C minor resembling that of Peachum's final warnings, but ended cheerfully in the tonic major. However, the chorale moves away from C major, and its return path is blocked by the minor chord on the dominant – an inhibitory harmony characteristic of Weill's tonal thinking since his first discovery of Mozart. The chorale, like Jenny's C major 'Salomon-Song', closes in the subdominant.

About half the numbers in *The Threepenny Opera* are tonally open-ended. Within the Lutheran tradition from which the *Threepenny Opera* chorale descends, tonal concentricity is naturally identified with theocentricity. Weill's agnostic rather than atheistic chorale proceeds accordingly: while the loss of its tonal centre corresponds to the loss of the absolute faith implicit in its traditional models, the very choice of model still conveys some sense of continuity. 'Rob not the poor, neither oppress the afflicted', says the Book of Proverbs, and in effect the *Threepenny Opera* chorale says the same. The difference lies in the corrolary. While Proverbs maintains that 'the Lord' will 'plead the cause' of the poor and afflicted, and will 'despoil those that despoil them', Brecht postulates a natural rather than a divine order by proclaiming that in the dark and cold 'vale of tribulation' injustice will freeze to death of its own accord.

Although the chorale is tonally inconclusive just as the drama is ideologically inconclusive, it does not leave the impression that anything remains to be said within the work's terms of reference.[4] So far from being a mere epilogue to the score, the melody is a synthesis of disparate elements. Like the finale as a whole, it 'resolves a conflict'.

Busoni had been a lifelong devotee of Bach's chorale-preludes, and had doubtless shown his pupils that many of the old Lutheran melodies derived from popular and secular songs. In that respect, Weill's chorale-melody is a *tour de force*. No fewer than six of the *Threepenny Opera* songs have contributed to it (exx. 8a–g). For convenient reference, the parent-phrases in example 8 have, where necessary, been transposed to the tonally appropriate pitch.

Ex. 8a

Moderato (♩ =85)

Peachum: Denn für die-ses   Le - ben   ist der Mensch nicht schlau ge - nug

Ex. 8b

Ihr   saht____   den   wei - sen   Sa - lo - mo____

Ex. 8c

(♩ =58)

Macheath: Ich schüt -zte   Sie   und   sie   er - nähr - te   mich

Ex. 8d

Andante quasi largo

Mrs Peachum: Da ist nun   ei - ner schon der Sa - tan sel - ber

Ex. 8e

Macheath: le - bten wir   schon zu - sam - men,   sie   und   ich

Ex. 8f

Macheath: Mac - heath liegt   hier nicht un - ter'm Ha - ge - dorn

Ex. 8g

f Ver - folgt   das   Un - recht   nicht   zu   sehr,   in   Bäl -

de   er - friert   es   schon von   selbst, denn   es   ist   kalt.

Be - denkt das   Dun - kel   und   die   gro - sse   käl -

te   in   die - sem   Ta - le   das   von   Jam - mer schallt.

Despite its tonally interrogative close, the chorale creates the effect
of a homecoming. The 6/4 metre and, in more general terms, the
orchestral counter-figure, hark back to the chorale-like arrangement
of the folk tune with which Peachum begins the first act. It is the only
tune Weill has borrowed from *The Beggar's Opera* (where it is
introduced by the same character at the same point). A beginning
which suggests that the score is merely to be a modern arrangement
of the original airs seems no more than a playful trick in the light of
the subsequent numbers; yet the tension it creates is in the end shown
to be functional. Peachum's 'Morgenchoral' opens a classical gate-
way which remains open until the final chorale closes it. Thus the
intervening explorations of nineteenth and twentieth-century idioms
are delimited by the classicism they themselves ignore.

The closing chorale underlines the meaning of the text 'clearly and
intelligibly' while solving the musical problem posed by the dynamics
of the entire score: the problem, that is, of how to formulate a
structurally binding conclusion to a score in which the digressive
tendencies have not yet been overcome by the incursive motivicism.
A chorale-type statement was uniquely capable of fulfilling the
requirements. In a general historical sense it harmonized with the
popular conventions of the score and yet in a musical sense it allowed
for a more thorough motivicism than they did. Weill's chorale is not
only an inspired induction from the foregoing material, but also a
masterly demonstration of the truth in Schoenberg's axiom that 'style
arises spontaneously out of the exigencies of form'.

In the *Threepenny Opera,* as in *Happy End*, every number,
however small, is a memorable and indeed inspired composition. But
what distinguishes the *Threepenny Opera* score from its successor are
the interacting relationships and tensions that combine to create a
music-dramatic form. It is the total form, and not the quality of the
individual numbers, that ultimately raises the score to the level of a
minor masterpiece.

Demonstrably, the score is not the *chef d'oeuvre* it was once
mistaken for. Heard with the right ears, it cannot even be mistaken
for a representative work by a light-weight composer. It has all the
marks of an inspired occasional piece by a substantial composer who
is necessarily holding his main forces in reserve. Already in 1928,
Weill's more perceptive admirers welcomed it as such and looked
forward to the major works which they rightly felt were sure to follow.

14   The 'Dreigroschen' sound

GEOFFREY ABBOTT

My initial interest in the 'Dreigroschen' sound was purely practical. Having been appointed musical director for a production of *Die Dreigroschenoper* at the Stadttheater Giessen in 1983, I was curious to listen to recordings other than the 1950s one starring Lotte Lenya and conducted by Wilhelm Brückner-Rüggeberg, which I already knew well. A colleague lent me the recording of excerpts made in 1930 by members of the original cast, with the original band under the original musical director, Theo Mackeben. I was at once astounded and inspired. This brilliant music suddenly came alive (an impression one does not get from the Brückner-Rüggeberg recording), and I was immediately convinced that this was how *Die Dreigroschenoper* should be performed. At the same time, I was hearing notes, even instruments, that were not in the score, and not hearing things that were! I began to investigate this unexpected turn, already biased as I was in favour of Mackeben's interpretations and thus eager to discover additional, objective reasons for taking them seriously. My interest had become both historical and philological.

'Authentic performance practice' is a term predominantly used in connection with Early Music; in recent times, the search for authenticity has also extended to later, Classical music. With music written this century, however, one would think there could be no doubt about a work's authentic or original sound, particularly with one of the most prolifically performed works in the repertory. Just this is the case with *Die Dreigroschenoper*, however, as my experience with those early recordings confirmed.

There are two principal reasons for this neglect. First, there is the matter of tradition. The popular musical style drawn on by Weill in *Die Dreigroschenoper* – dance music from Berlin of the 1920s – has now been virtually forgotten. This is partly because sound recordings from the period are rare. But it is also because the style itself was continually changing, evolving under Anglo-American influence until

161

it was eventually superseded by swing, a quite different style. An even more decisive factor was the suppression of the work under National Socialism. From 1933 until the end of the war *Die Dreigroschenoper* was officially denounced in Germany as 'degenerate art'; the establishment of a performing tradition was thus brutally and abruptly obstructed. Second, as the 'authenticity movement' has amply demonstrated, there are always aspects of performance practice – the 'power which fills the space between the notes with music', to use Weill's phrase[1] – that cannot be notated. In this case, there are manifest discrepancies between what was played at the first production and what subsequently appeared in print, although these discrepancies seem less surprising when one looks in detail at the events surrounding the genesis of the work and its ultimate publication. (For a full account of the work's genesis, see chapter 2).

The music used for the first production was all handwritten, Weill having completed both the vocal score and the full score too late for the material to be printed. The singers learned their songs from manuscript copies or, for certain numbers, from lithographed handwritten parts hastily prepared by Universal Edition. The orchestra played from parts copied by hand in the Held-Werkstätte in Charlottenburg, Berlin, only hours before the first rehearsal. There were six musicians in the band for whom parts had to be written out; Theo Mackeben, who conducted from the piano (and harmonium), presumably played from a copy of Weill's manuscript vocal score.

Fortunately, the band parts have survived. Kept by Theo Mackeben, they are now in the possession of his widow, Frau Loni Mackeben, who kindly granted me access to them. The paper is well thumbed, the set of parts having been used not only for the run of the original production but also for various recordings, including that for the film. The distribution of the instruments is the same as in the manuscript score, except that the percussionist is allotted the second trumpet part – an indication that the drummer who played in the original production happened also to play the trumpet. The scheme is as follows:

1   alto saxophone in E flat, baritone saxophone, clarinet and flute
2   tenor saxophone in B flat, soprano saxophone, bassoon and clarinet
3   trumpet
4   trombone and double-bass

5   banjo, guitar, bandoneon and cello
6   percussion and second trumpet
7   piano-conductor, including harmonium

The material was evidently copied in great haste directly from Weill's hurriedly completed full score, and includes several curious anomalies: for example, passages for soprano saxophone in the 'Overture' are written too high for the instrument, and insufficient time is allowed for players to change instruments. Since, however, the players engaged by Mackeben were all professional studio musicians used to rectifying mistakes or difficulties at sight, such anomalies in the parts could be of little account. The musicians performed under the name of 'The Lewis Ruth Band', after Ludwig Rüth, a classical flautist and conductor turned saxophonist and bandleader, who led the group.[2] Other members of the band might have included Frank Goebel (banjo), Max Neuf, George Hearst or Kurt Hohenberger (trumpet), Billy Barton or Curt Hasenpflug (tenor saxophone), Kai Michelsen or Josef Hadrawa (trombone), Dick Stauff or Leon Collier (drums), all of whom were either still playing with Rüth in 1937 or were familiar names along with Mackeben's in the Berlin recording studios in 1928 (see figure 18).[3]

18   Theo Mackeben (centre) and the Lewis Ruth Band at the Theater am Schiffbauerdamm, 1928

It was not until 7 September, eight days after the première, that Weill wrote to Universal Edition: 'The earliest I can send the complete score is tomorrow ... together with the missing sections of the vocal score. I'm still busy at the moment completing the full score following the experiences of the current production ... It is quite a big job, which I must do as thoroughly as possible in order to avoid problems when provincial theatres tackle the work.' However, he did enclose the full score of three 'hit numbers' − the 'Kanonensong', the 'Zuhälter-ballade' and the 'Liebeslied' − so that danceband arrangements could be made.

The extent of Weill's post-première adjustments is impossible to discern exactly, even where the relevant materials have survived. What we do know, thanks to the surviving recordings and the band parts, is that the infidelity was reciprocal: just as Weill didn't faithfully follow the first production when completing the final version of his full score, so the Lewis Ruth Band hadn't followed Weill's score to the letter either.

When they received the score, the publishers commissioned Norbert Gingold to prepare a piano reduction as quickly as possible. As letters of 14 and 19 September reveal, UE were bothered by discrepancies in the sequence of the numbers between the score, the vocal score material already in their possession and the libretto. The confusion, which principally concerned the placing of the 'Barbara-song', was eventually cleared up with Weill's help.[4] Nonetheless, the publishers didn't always heed the composer's advice. On 10 September he wrote that the following should be printed in the vocal score before the 'Moritat': 'At Macheath's various entrances the orchestra can start playing this piece softly. At the beginning of the eighth scene it is played in a slow tempo as a funeral march.' This note appears in none of the editions of the music. Nor was the following instruction, dispatched two days later, carried out:

The orchestral parts are to be arranged in the following way:

1	piano and harmonium (also conductor)
2	soprano, alto and baritone saxophone, clarinet, possibly flute
3	soprano and tenor saxophone, clarinet, possibly bassoon
4	trumpet in B flat
5	trombone
6	banjo, bandoneon, guitar
7	percussion, possibly 2nd trumpet

To judge by the comprehensive description of woodwind instruments, Weill has carefully listed here all the instruments he considers necessary based on his experience of the première. The flute, bassoon and second trumpet are evidently only optional, not indispensable (Weill uses the German abbreviation *ev.* [*eventuell*]), while the double-bass, cello, celesta and piccolo are not listed at all. I am convinced that this list gives us the instrumentation used by the Lewis Ruth Band at the première. Certainly, Mackeben directed from the piano and harmonium; Ludwig Rüth was a trained flautist, as mentioned; the Mackeben parts reveal that the drummer also played the second trumpet. There are also a couple of 'ad lib.' passages for bassoon in the second woodwind part, though there is otherwise no evidence that the Lewis Ruth Band included a bassoonist. On the other hand, even though Weill omits the double-bass in his list, what are we to make of the 'pizz.' markings in the trombone part? Could the Lewis Ruth Band's trombonist also play the double-bass? Did the banjoist happen to be a cellist as well? Or was Weill (and hence the copyist of the band parts) indicating instrumentation that he didn't necessarily expect to be played at Schiffbauerdamm? This must certainly be the case with the final version of the score (later edited by Karl Heinz Füssl and published by UE in 1972 as Philharmonia No. 400), which specifies the full gamut of 24 instruments (not counting the half dozen or so untuned percussion instruments). At the same time, Weill does make some practical suggestions for reducing the number of instruments. The following are typical examples: in the 'Anstatt dass-Song' the composer supplies a hypothetical bass line for the harmonium 'in case the cello and double bass are missing'. In the 'Kanonensong' the piccolo is marked 'ad. lib.', in the 'Zuhälterballade' the Hawaiian guitar can be replaced by a mandoline, and in the first finale an option is indicated between flute and clarinet.

The vocal score (UE 8851) came off the presses on 22 October, the orchestral parts on the 25th, and the piano-conductor score (UE 8849) on 6 November. By this time *Die Dreigroschenoper* was a box-office hit, and even if he had wanted to, Weill could no longer have altered details in the printed material. Besides, he was busy with other matters: composing the Berliner Requiem, writing his regular articles again for the radio journal *Der deutsche Rundfunk*, working on the opera *Aufstieg und Fall der Stadt Mahagonny*, and promoting other compositions. Nonetheless, on 28 November, three weeks after the publication of the piano-conductor score of *Die Dreigroschenoper*, he wrote to UE with the following complaint:

In the piano-conductor score there are loads [*eine Unmenge*] of mistakes which could make my music sound very different. It would therefore be worth considering whether one ought to include an errata list to correct at least the worst errors. I shall prepare a short note for theatres about the performance of the music ... and send it on to you in a few days time.

On 11 December he still hadn't attended to these tasks: 'Unfortunately I still haven't got round to checking through the score of *Die Dreigroschenoper*, but I hope to be able to do so in the next few days.' Weill also expressed his intention to produce a simplified version of the score for the provinces. But despite a reminder from UE sent on 14 December, neither the errata list, the note for theatres, nor the simplified version ever materialized — or if they did, there is now no trace of them.

In addition to the handwritten orchestral parts mentioned above, Theo Mackeben's piano-conductor score has also survived. Not having appeared in print until 6 November, this is obviously not what Mackeben played from at the première, but he may well have transferred some of his original markings to it. Of the other materials that may have been used by the singers for the première, the only surviving items are copies of the 'Barbarasong' and 'Pollys Lied' (both in Weill's handwriting), a lithographed copy of the 'Eifersuchtsduett' in vocal score, and a female chorus part, all of which are in the estate of Kate Kühl (the original Lucy).[5] Although all these written sources contain a lot of interesting information, they cannot be taken as incontrovertible evidence of what was played at the première, for two reasons. First, in the case of the Mackeben material, it is difficult to decipher which markings refer to which occasion of the material's being used, be it for Schiffbauerdamm, for the recording studio, or the film soundtrack. Second, certain changes were made during the course of rehearsals, either by Weill or Mackeben, which were not necessarily written down, as Weill himself testified. On 12 September, in a letter to UE, he explained that 'there are certain things I had to write down ... which I only needed to pass on to the musicians here by word of mouth'.

When, in March 1929, Weill published the following tribute in his 'Notiz zum Jazz' he doubtless had in mind, among others, the Lewis Ruth Band, with whom he had worked during those rehearsals six months before:

Anyone who has ever worked with a good jazz-band will have been pleasantly surprised by the eagerness, self-abandon and enthusiasm for work which one seeks in vain in many concert and theatre orchestras. A good jazz musician has a complete mastery of three or four instruments, he plays by heart, and is used to a kind of ensemble-playing where each player contributes individually to the overall sound; above all, however, he can improvise, and has a free, uninhibited way of playing, in which the interpreter plays the most productive part possible.[6]

This brings us to our second main source: the recordings made by the Lewis Ruth Band with members of the original cast under Theo Mackeben. The earliest recording was the purely instrumental version of the 'Zuhälterballade' and the 'Kanonensong' made on 22 November 1928 by the Lewis Ruth Band under Theo Mackeben. The most comprehensive of the early vocal recordings to have survived is that of excerpts made on 11 December 1930 with Kurt Gerron, Erich Ponto, Willy Trenk-Trebitsch, Lotte Lenja and Erika Helmke; it consists of fourteen numbers, though not always in full. All of the singers took part in the première except for Trenk-Trebitsch, who had replaced Harald Paulsen as Macheath. Erika Helmke originally played one of the whores and Lotte Lenja played Jenny, but on this recording they cover between them all the female roles. The soundtracks to the German and French films of *Die Dreigroschenoper* were also recorded by Mackeben and the Lewis Ruth Band.

Of the other extant recordings, the most interesting are:

1   Four numbers sung by Harald Paulsen (the original Macheath) with an unidentified orchestra.
2   Two numbers by Carola Neher (the original Polly, who was replaced a week before the première, but who later played the role, both on stage and in the Pabst film) with the Lewis Ruth Band and Mackeben.
3   Two songs sung by Brecht with the Lewis Ruth Band and Mackeben.

(For full details, see discography.)

A certain amount of caution must be exercised in drawing conclusions about the première from these documents. Sound recording in the late 1920s was still in its infancy, and despite the use of one of the most modern condensor microphones for the excerpts recording (it was used by the Ultraphon company and nicknamed 'the bottle' [*Die Flasche*]), exact details of instrumentation and arrangement are occasionally impossible to discern. Nor should one forget that it was common practice to make adjustments to the arrangement especially for recordings. The bass-line of the excerpts, for instance, is reinforced throughout by a tuba, a frequent extra in recordings from this period, used to correct poor bass response as well as being the typical bass instrument of the twenties dance band. It should also be borne in mind that, as time passed, Mackeben and his musicians would have been inclined to play the score — or at least the hit tunes for the commercial recordings — with more liberty than they had at the première. Nonetheless, by drawing on the recorded evidence in conjunction with the written material, we can learn a great deal about the authentic *Dreigroschen* sound. A note-for-note analysis would go well beyond the scope of this essay. Instead I shall discuss selected aspects of some of the numbers by way of illustrating salient features of the original performance practice.

Overture

The tempo in Mackeben's excerpts recording is ♩ = 96, which is not far removed from the ♩ = 100 in both the full score and the piano-conductor score. ♩ = 84 is given in Gingold's vocal score; it is also the tempo Weill chose for the instrumental suite *Kleine Dreigroschenmusik*. For my taste, this slower tempo makes for a rather plodding opening. Unlike the full score, there is no banjo part in the Mackeben parts. But there is, in Weill's hand, a bandoneon part which plays fortissimo in all tutti sections.

Moritat

The first two verses of the 'Moritat' were accompanied by a barrel organ, the roll having been made specially by the Berlin firm Bacigalupo. It is probable that the same roll was used on Brecht's own recording.

The 'Moritat' theme was used in the original production to accompany Macheath's entrances as a kind of *leitmotiv*, varied according to the mood of the scene. In scene 2, the marking in the first edition of the libretto is simply 'very soft, like a motive'; in scene 8 (later to become scene 9): 'as a funeral march'. For the sixth scene Weill indicated in the proofs of the libretto that 'the orchestra can play the Moritat no. 2 softly as a waltz'. But for some reason the instruction wasn't printed. Some of these interpolations are not only indicated but actually written out in the Mackeben parts. For example, the first trumpet part contains the following cue for the waltz variant (ex. 1).

Ex. 1

[Trumpet in B♭]

Seeräuberjenny

This is one of a number of songs whose texts were added to by Brecht.
Neither the manuscript vocal score, the published scores, nor the first
edition of the libretto contains the verse 'Meine Herren, da wird wohl
ihr Lachen aufhören'. However, both Lotte Lenya and Carola Neher
sing it on their recordings, which means it must have been an early
addition. Annotations in the Mackeben parts indicate that the song
was played at some point with four verses, and that the accompaniment was varied for the third verse, with held chords in the wind
(ex. 2).

Ex. 2

[Clarinets]

[Trpt.]

It is indeed remarkable that in none of the strophic songs in *Die
Dreigroschenoper* does Weill repeat any accompaniment more than
once without variation − in order, as he stated in a letter to Brecht
dated 17 January 1949, to avoid monotony.[7] The variation for the
third verse may well have been Weill's own invention.

It is interesting to note from the autograph vocal score and the
Mackeben trombone part (also in Weill's hand) that the effective and
characteristic repetition of the fifth line of each verse is a later
addition. In the phrase following this repetition both Lotte Lenya and
Carola Neher sing the following melodic variation, which fits the text
much better than the published version (ex. 3).

Ex. 3

ein Ge - schrei   sein am Ha - fen und man   fragt:

In his copy of the piano-conductor score Mackeben has added the
bass in octaves to the accompaniment of this same phrase (ex. 4).

Ex. 4

bar 15

etc.

At the end of each verse – 'und ein Schiff mit acht Segeln und mit
fünfzig Kanonen' – the Mackeben parts allocate the full score's first
clarinet line to the trumpet and vice versa; and in the accompaniment
to the last verse Mackeben's piano part abandons its characteristic
rhythm at the end of the second bar and merely doubles the voice
instead. In my opinion, both of these amendments provide better
support for the voice.

The word 'töten' in the last verse is accompanied the first time,
not by a single tutti quaver, but by two, which correspond to the
word's own rhythm: something particularly effective after eleven bars
of ♪♪♪. The eerie answer in the percussion to the menacing question:
'Welchen sollen wir töten?' is played not by the triangle but by the
cymbal.

Kanonensong

The piccolo called for in the printed score does not feature in any of
Mackeben's recordings, and is heavily crossed out in Ludwig Rüth's
alto saxophone part.

The instrumental recording by the Lewis Ruth Band includes an
extra verse for piano solo – perhaps just to fill the side – affording
a fine example of how freely and stylishly Mackeben plays, particularly the way he does not bind himself to the rather thick textures
of Weill's piano writing. The most distinctive touch is a glissando into
the fermata bar before the final refrain. The fermate, incidentally,
are intended only for the last chorus, not throughout as on Harald
Paulsen's recording, where repetition weakens the effect. In the third
verse Weill gives a short solo to the Hawaiian guitar without allowing
the banjoist enough time to change instruments. On the instrumental
recording the solo is played on the banjo.

Another striking feature of Mackeben's rendition, which may have arisen as an improvisation, occurs in the final refrain. The excerpts recording includes an embellishment (ex. 5) for trombone (a slightly simpler version being pencilled into the Mackeben trombone part).

Ex. 5

etc.

Liebeslied

This number, one of the work's most haunting, may well have been written before it had become clear which instruments were going to be available. More than any other passage in *Die Dreigroschenoper*, the recitative calls out for strings. The accompanying chords were originally scored for cello and double-bass tremoloes, the upper voices consisting of tenor saxophone and clarinet tremoloes, and this version was copied into the Mackeben parts. However, since it is impossible for the clarinetist to play both the tremolo and the important alto saxophone solo, the tremoloes are crossed out. Accordingly the autograph full score was altered, with the tremolo chords being given to the piano. On their recordings, the Lewis Ruth Band use the bandoneon for the chords (possibly with trombone reinforcing the bass line), and the Mackeben parts include this additional material for the bandoneon together with a hastily written banjo part for the boston-tempo. The lilting quaver figure in the ninth bar of the boston-tempo, which Weill gives to the cello, is missing from all the Mackeben recordings.

The instrumentation is not the only anomaly in the recitative. Mackeben's recordings feature an original version whose rhythm perfectly fits that of the spoken text. Weill changed this passage in his autograph score by pasting in new time signatures and scratching out a chord. Although this amendment was made in time for all the printed material to include it, Mackeben continued to play the original version. The change occurs in the seventh bar. In the first six bars the trumpet and alto saxophone solos follow exactly the rhythm and inflection of the spoken text. From the seventh bar onward the revised form is suddenly half the speed of the natural rhythm of the text, whereas the original version goes into allabreve time and thus continues in the natural speech rhythm. In addition, the original version has the change to the B flat chord in the eleventh bar instead of the tenth, thus achieving a smoother, more natural connection between the two last sentences.

Barbarasong

Polly sings this song in front of her parents at home. The frugality of the solo piano accompaniment is dramaturgically motivated: it suggests a parlour song and hence underlines the protagonist's bourgeois upbringing. In his recordings, however, Theo Mackeben introduces some subtle instrumental colouring which enhances the textual turns of the song without upsetting its delicacy.

The only one of Mackeben's recordings to include all three verses is the film soundtrack. Here, however, the 'Barbarasong' fulfils a quite different function: it is sung in the stable in place of 'Seeräuberjenny'. For this reason, it cannot be used as a model. The best sung of the early recordings is that by Carola Neher. She sings just two verses, so one hears two verses of Mackeben's accompaniment which ought really to go with the second and third verses of a complete version, the first being accompanied by solo piano. Neher's recording begins with just piano, played with an attractive syncopation. Then, at 'Ja da kann man', the melody is doubled by the sensuous tones of the Hawaiian guitar. In the last verse, saxophone chords support the piano for the first eight bars and the last six bars before the refrain, where, as written, the whole band enters. Mackeben introduces a few of his own embellishments into the piano part; and he plays the scales in the sixteenth bar with G natural and C natural in the right hand, as in Weill's autograph score.

1. Dreigroschenfinale

The bass line appears to have been played by the trombone, there being no marking in the part to indicate a change of instrument to double-bass. At 'Tempo I' the first clarinet part contains an alternative scoring for flute, though the latter is heavily crossed through. Not so clear is the choice between bassoon and tenor saxophone a few bars later at Frau Peachum's 'Wie gern wär' ich', where both alternatives are written in the second saxophone part with the following variant at the end of the passage:

Ex. 6

poco meno mosso

mf

etc.

In the following 'poco meno mosso' Mackeben's piano-conductor score favours the piano rather than the harmonium. At 'Wir wären gut, anstatt so roh, doch die Verhältnisse, die sind nicht so' the trombone doubles Peachum's vocal line, offering the singing actor added support.

Ballade vom angenehmen Leben

Weill's metronome marking ♩ = 96 (also prescribed in the *Kleine Dreigroschenmusik*) may suit the accompaniment to this song, but the text can become laboured. Harald Paulsen's tempo on his recording is considerably faster: ♩ = 168, but at this speed the accompaniment is nothing more than a hectic stream of undotted semiquavers. Norbert Gingold, who arranged the vocal score for UE and also conducted the Viennese première in 1929, in which Paulsen starred, remembers that Paulsen insisted on a very fast tempo and that Weill let him have his own way. Mackeben's tempo of ♩ = 132 represents for me an ideal compromise.

This song, like the third finale, shows that the role of Macheath was written with a trained singer in mind. The melody of the second half of the verse ('Das simple Leben lebe, wer da mag'), especially the minim d^2, is crucial; without it, the saxophone counterpoint disturbs the rhythm of the text. Indeed, on the excerpts recording, where Macheath is sung by the actor Willy Trenk-Trebitsch, Mackeben has the trombone double the vocal melody for eight bars, which allows the performer to devote more attention to the text.

Eifersuchtsduett

The Mackeben parts are transposed down a whole tone lower than the published scores; and there is a marking to the effect that the opening bar should be played twice, thus lengthening the otherwise rather perfunctory introduction. In the tenth bar a 'stop' on the third beat throws into the foreground the subsequent text, and the ladies' excitement is accentuated by the fact that the clarinet and saxophone's semiquaver figure on the first beats of bars 11 and 13 is transposed up an octave.

The clarinet is deleted from bars 19 and 20, and in bars 20 and 21 the alto saxophone merely doubles Lucy's part, which, together with Polly's, has the following variant:

Ex. 7

(Transposed)

Lucy: Ja, das wer- den wir schon seh'n!

Polly: Na, das wer-den wir   ja seh'n!

This variant also appears in the study material used by Kate Kühl, and is still visible in the autograph vocal score, where it has been scratched out in favour of the published version. The Mackeben material has the following variant in the last five bars of the trumpet and tenor saxophone parts:

Ex. 8

(Transposed)

Two further, rather questionable variants can be heard on the excerpts recording of 1930: wrong notes from Lucy in bar 2, and (transposed) E naturals instead of E flats in bar 6, the latter appearing in the trombone, trumpet and tenor saxophone parts as an alteration. It seems to me, however, that Lucy's mistake weakens the irony of Weill's setting, and that the altered harmony is not as strong as Weill's original progression.

2. Dreigroschenfinale

The manuscript full score, vocal score and first edition of the vocal score have the following in the twenty-second and twenty-third bars:

Ex. 9

Soon after the publication of the vocal score, however, Weill changed the bass of this characteristically bold progression to the more straightforward, chromatically ascending figure: B flat–B natural–C, and pasted the new version into the manuscript score, in time for it to appear in the piano-conductor score just a few weeks later; it appears in all subsequent editions of the vocal score too. Mackeben evidently didn't consider this revision an improvement: he changed the bass line in his piano-conductor score back to the original and played it on both the film soundtrack and the excerpts recording.

Ruf aus der Gruft

In the Mackeben material the alto saxophone part is given to the clarinet and transposed accordingly. This was presumably for the sake of the instrumental blend, making for more homogeneous pianissimo chords. Weill's piano part is difficult to play at once pianissimo and rhythmically. Mackeben accordingly reduces the texture in his piano-conductor score by playing just one quaver chord in the left hand at the beginning of each bar and leaving the anapaest rhythm to the tom-tom alone.

3.   Dreigroschenfinale

It can be seen from the autograph vocal score that the whole of Macheath's 'Gerettet' solo was a later addition. Weill's first draft has Frau Peachum's 'So wendet alles sich am End' zum Glück' following on immediately from the King's Messenger – which explains the thematic similarity between the two bars marked 'solemnly' (*festlich*) in the recitative and Frau Peachum's music.

The piano part in the opening chorus 'Horch! Wer kommt?' is remarkable for its virtuosity. Similarly, the clarinet part is extremely high; in the Mackeben parts it is marked down an octave from bar 21 onwards. Although Macheath's solo was conceived for a trained singer, the Mackeben parts have the trombone double the vocal line for eleven bars. Perhaps this was a later addition to assist Paulsen's successor, Willy Trenk-Trebitsch. At Polly's entry 'Gerettet' Mackeben has written 'broader' (*breiter*) into his score; the trumpet part at this point has the marking 'calmer' (*ruhiger*) added.

The above-mentioned details are just one aspect of the score's original realization. An equally, if not more, crucial facet of the 'authentic' sound is the nature of the instruments used. Consideration must also be paid to how these were played and, not least, to the appropriate vocal style.

Of the instruments called for in *Die Dreigroschenoper* only one is not widely known these days: the bandoneon. It is like a concertina but somewhat larger and squarer. Although of German origin, it is better known in South American tango orchestras than in Europe. Its sound can be closely imitated by a mild-toned accordion. In an article on Weill's *Kleine Dreigroschenmusik* (which also features the instrument), Theodor Wiesengrund-Adorno goes even further when he writes: 'Bandoneon, let it be said, [is] a classier name for concertina or accordion [*Ziehharmonika*] which is what is meant'.[8]

The piano's role is central. In several numbers, such as the 'Kanonensong' and the 'Moritat', it bears sole responsibility for providing the bass line, thus making desirable the use of an instrument with a rich bass, preferably a grand piano.

It is apparent from the early recordings how smoothly and elegantly the saxophone was played. The 1920s were a heyday for the instrument – in Berlin there was, for example, a well-known dance band called the 'Saxophon-Orchester-Dobbri' – and it was used as much as an ensemble instrument as it was in a solo capacity. For this reason, the contemporary style of playing tended to blend better than the overt solo sound one encounters in today's popular music.

The trumpeter and trombonist used a variety of mutes, including the hat and the cup mute. The Lewis Ruth Band's trumpeter used the latter to exotic effect in the 'Zuhälterballade'. Suitable occasions for using a trombone mute would be the 'Anstatt dass-Song' or the 'Ballade von der sexuellen Hörigkeit'.

The banjo in the dance music of the 1920s was an important member of the rhythm section. In recordings one often hears subtle syncopations, which require a loose wrist action. In the fourth verse of the 'Moritat', for piano and banjo only, the banjoist of the Lewis Ruth Band departs from Weill's full score with his lively syncopated strumming.

The guitar has two passages where it has to hold its own against several other instruments – in the second 'Dreigroschenfinale' and the third finale at 'Wenn die Not am höchsten'. The type of guitar used in order to produce sufficient volume would have been an acoustic guitar with steel strings, possibly an arch-bodied guitar like the Gibson L5 which was introduced in 1924 and quickly became popular with jazzbands and dance orchestras. Although the score calls, ideally, for an Hawaiian guitar in the 'Kanonensong', the Lewis Ruth Band give the solo to the banjo instead. However, the Hawaiian guitar is used in the 'Zuhälterballade' and the 'Barbarasong'. In the absence of a proper instrument the effect can be achieved with a 'bottle neck' on the fingerboard of a steel-strung guitar. It is likely, in fact, that this was the method employed by the Lewis Ruth Band.

Turning lastly to the drums, we find in the 1920s a much more subtle sound than is common today. The typical drum set comprised a fairly large bass drum, a snare drum, two or more Chinese tom-toms of different sizes, and at least one suspended cymbal with a raised centre, producing a hollower sound than its modern counterpart. There were various smaller instruments or 'traps', including wood block and triangle. One instrument that was certainly *not* present was the 'hi-hat' cymbal, an instrument associated with Swing and first patented in America in 1927. The 1920s drummer was both inventive and versatile, often being called on for special effects in variety and cabaret. As mentioned above, the Lewis Ruth Band's drummer appears to have played trumpet as well.

The Threepenny Opera, as its title brazenly announces, is a provocative challenge to the operatic genre. If it seems less provocative today, then that is because we have lost sight not only of *why* but also of *how* that challenge was delivered. This goes as much for the vocal as it does for the instrumental sound. It is not just a matter of finding singers who can act or actors who can sing, although that is difficult enough. Weill's text-setting requires a style of delivery which, although common in the 1920s, is no longer part of modern performance practices, as my encounter with the early recordings immediately made clear. The formidable task facing both singers and actors has been succinctly formulated by Egon Voss: 'On the one hand the notes must be hit clearly and precisely; yet on the other hand the

diction must remain that of speech.'[9] Such a succinct statement of
course requires amplification and qualification. When enunciating
Brecht's texts the singer should not distort his or her singing voice
for the sake of it, despite many examples to the contrary. But there
are occasions where he or she should also not be afraid of sacrificing
musical nuance in order to focus due attention on the text and its
meaning. One very simple example is the famous refrain from
'Seeräuberjenny' – 'und ein Schiff mit acht Segeln'. Polly should
not sing 'Schiff' if her resulting exertion destroys the eerie effect. In
this case a quaver would be better. There are many other occasions,
however, where for the sake of musical (as opposed to mere verbal)
meaning the singer must hold a note longer than the bare minimum
(and the right note at that), possibly without accompaniment. A good
example is Lucy's high F sharp in the 'Eifersuchtsduett'. For instruction in individual instances we can usefully turn to the old recordings.

During the composition of *Die Dreigroschenoper* Weill informed
his publishers that 'it is being written in a very easily singable style
since it is supposed to be performed by actors'. This, however, is not
the same as saying that any actor can perform it. The vocal ranges
of the various parts are surprisingly demanding – a fact which is not
clear from the many recordings which have little to do with how the
work was originally performed. We must even include here recordings
with Lotte Lenya. To be sure, her prewar recordings set an almost
perfect example. Later on, however, her famous renditions – whether
of the songs of Polly, Jenny or roles from other works by Weill –
were invariably transposed down at least by a fifth; and in doing so
she perpetrated a thoroughly misleading image of the Brecht–Weill
heroine who automatically sings with a dark, worldly-wise and husky
voice.

Vocal range is an important means of characterization, and Weill
intended that Polly and Lucy should sing high, that Jenny should sing
not quite so high, and that Mrs Peachum should sing low. A contralto Polly is as absurd as a contralto Susanna or Gilda. Macheath's
part was written for an operetta tenor, that is, a high, heroic, musically
trained voice, while Peachum's was intended for a mature actor's
baritone. The 1930 edition of *Reclams Opernführer*, for example, still
respected these distinctions, allotting each part to a particular vocal
range, whereas more recent guides, such as Kloiber's *Handbuch der
Oper*, first published in 1951 and reprinted several times since, simply
lists various 'spoken roles with song'.[10]

The question of transposition is therefore a sensitive one. On

Mackeben's excerpts-recording both the 'Barbarasong' and the 'Eifersuchtsduett' are transposed down a tone. The music still sounds 'high', while being a little less strenuous for the singers. Macheath's very high and demanding solo in the third finale, however, does not lend itself so readily to transposition, since the finale is through-composed.[11] Mrs Peachum's music, on the other hand, may require to be transposed up, since it was intended to be sung an octave lower than written. Although there is no marking to this effect in Weill's score, the evidence is compelling. First, the role was created by the deep-voiced cabaret artist Rosa Valetti (later to be seen and heard in Joseph von Sternberg's film *Der blaue Engel*). Second, on Mackeben's excerpts recording Erika Helmke sings Frau Peachum's part in the first finale an octave lower than written, despite its being, for Helmke, an uncomfortably low tessitura. Third, the pitch of the instruments that double Mrs Peachum's solos suggests the lower octave. And finally, were the role to be sung as written, its overall tessitura would be higher than Polly's − a situation without parallel in musical mother−daughter relationships![12]

Weill himself was naturally sensitive to his score's being tampered with, particularly the instrumentation. Just six weeks after the première, on 11 October 1928, he protested to UE: 'I hear from Frankfurt that they want to start making all kinds of orchestral reductions in *Die Dreigroschenoper*. I consider this very dangerous and ask that director Hellmer be strictly forbidden from making any changes whatsoever to the music or the instrumentation without my consent.' Not only could Weill not oversee the production, but the score was not yet published. As the work's popularity increased, so did Weill's sensitivity. True, he himself encouraged arrangements of individual 'hit' numbers. But when it came to the work as a whole he was unswerving about the inviolability of his own orchestrations, as he later was on Broadway, too. Faced with the prospect of the American première of *The Threepenny Opera* in 1933, he wrote to UE on 14 March of that year:

Perhaps it would be helpful if you would send him [Francesco von Mendelssohn] my original full score of *Die Dreigroschenoper*. The printed score is really full of errors and gives rise to many false impressions on account of its being a reduced piano-conductor version. We must do everything to assure a first-class performance of the music. I also ask that you write Mr Dreyfus, the head of Harms ... Give him a description of the musical idiosyncrasies of the piece − that it is not jazz-music in the American sense but rather a quite special, new sound, which can be achieved only by a meticulous realization of the original full score.

What, then, was Weill's opinion of Mackeben's interpretation? Mackeben's interpretation had resulted from close collaboration with the composer himself and, ultimately, provided a partial basis of that original full score. As the score shows with the various alternative versions it proposes, Weill was certainly aware of the need to adapt to circumstances.[13] Norbert Gingold recalls from the preparations for the Viennese première in 1929, which Weill attended, that he was very accommodating when, for example, a singer wanted a faster or slower tempo, or when Gingold himself wanted to orchestrate a piano reminiscence of the 'Moritat'. Weill, he said, was not a composer to state categorically, 'That is how I want it!'[14] Yet it should not be forgotten that Weill was a composer of serious music, not of light music, which traditionally gives arrangers a free hand. Weill's full score represents the composer's 'ideal' sonic intentions, the *Urtext*, which the Schiffbauerdamm production had only partially realized.

When asked in an interview, given in Paris in 1934, what he thought of the gramophone recordings of his music, he praised only those which adhered to his instrumentation, among which he included the Odeon records of numbers from *Die Dreigroschenoper* and the selections from *Mahagonny*:

The rest were made using 'arrangements' which have nothing to do with my instrumentation! It is regarded as cranky, since it is widely held to be superfluous, when one gives thought to the extent to which the composer's instrumentation is respected or not — and yet it is exclusively thereon that the *original* piece of music depends.[15]

The temptation to modernize *The Threepenny Opera* by updating the slang expressions, the costumes, and the décor will never go away. Good music, however, does not lend itself so readily to such adjustment. The best and most authentic example we have for how Weill's music should sound is provided by those early performances. For it is not just a matter of following the letter of the *Urtext* (or rather the version one chooses from Weill's alternatives) but also of invoking the music's original spirit, its *Urgeist*.

15 *Misunderstanding 'The Threepenny Opera'*

STEPHEN HINTON

The notion that *The Threepenny Opera* owes its success to a misunderstanding is as enduring as that success itself. So persistently has it informed commentaries since the time of the première that one might well talk of a 'misunderstanding thesis'. The thesis itself arises from the nagging question: how could a work of subversive tendency and high artistic merit attract such widespread public acclaim? The question, of course, begs further ones. On what sort of understanding was the work's public acclaim based? In what respects can *The Threepenny Opera* be defined as subversive? What is a misunderstanding anyway? How does one determine it? The task of resolving such broad and controversial issues may seem dauntingly abstract, if not impossible. In the first instance, however, the following discussion concerns itself less with proving or refuting the thesis per se than with examining the assumptions behind it; what counts is less the final critical judgment than how it was arrived at. Readers are left to draw their own conclusions.

The 'misunderstanding thesis' can appear as the expression of irritated disbelief, such as in the letter written by the philosopher Ernst Bloch to fellow intellectual and critical theorist 'Herr Wiesengrund' (Theodor Wiesengrund-Adorno) shortly after the première. 'Curious', Bloch commented, 'how the "gaiety" masks what is *épatant*. No-one boos, the house is sold out every night, and even the *Friederike* audience is happy.'[1] By *'Friederike* audience' he means the patrons of light, innocuous shows such as Franz Lehár's operetta about Friederike Brion, one of the young Goethe's inamoratas, which opened in Berlin a month after *Die Dreigroschenoper*. By way of providing a counter-example Bloch goes on to report the scandal provoked by Otto Klemperer's performance of Stravinsky's *L'histoire du soldat* at the Krolloper in the same month. Such an audience reaction, he insinuates, would have been far more appropriate to the Weill–Brecht work than unrestrained approval, adding that 'without the Soldier's Tale there could scarcely be any Threepenny Opera'. Weill himself acknowledged the debt even before he composed *Die Dreigroschenoper*. 'What Stravinsky attempts in his *Soldier's Tale*', he declared in January 1926, 'can count as the mixed genre [*Zwischengattung*] most assured of a future ... perhaps it can form the basis of a certain type of new opera.'² There is much in the Weill–Brecht work – the economy of forces, the visibility of the instrumentalists, the use of modern dance idioms, the epic structure, the separation of elements, the ironic humour – that can be traced back to Stravinsky's pioneering piece of music-theatre. Yet why should public acceptance of Weill's Stravinsky-influenced new opera constitute a misunderstanding? It is this question that Bloch and especially Adorno were at pains to address in their essays on *The Threepenny Opera* – essays which rate among the most celebrated pieces of critical writing on the work (and two of which are reprinted here in translation as chapters 8 and 9).

Adorno's attempt to 'defend the work against its success' rested on the premiss that art cannot be 'significant' and 'satisfying in itself' at the same time as being 'consumed by society at large'. Popular success and artistic quality, for Adorno, are necessarily mutually exclusive. If the popularity of *The Threepenny Opera* seemed to contradict his premiss, he reasoned, then either the work in question will not tolerate closer analytical scrutiny or, alternatively, it must have become the object of a misunderstanding. The sentiment may put one in mind of Schoenberg's dictum: 'If it is art, it is not for all, and if it is for all, it is not art.'³ For Adorno and Bloch, however, the critique contains a socio-political dimension which would have been quite anathema to the Viennese master. It is not just a matter of significant art being technically beyond the reach of the masses; the masses are also hampered by a pervasive false consciousness, a kind of ideological brain-washing. 'A cheerful sound', wrote Bloch, 'can induce many to dance who in reality have no such need.' In 'misunderstanding' *Die Dreigroschenoper* the public at large was attracted by the similarities to – rather than the differences from – popular music, which has the ideological function of diverting consumers and thereby blinding them to objectionable social conditions. Adorno asserted in his 1932 tract on 'The Social Situation of Music': 'Weill's is unquestionably the only music nowadays with a genuine socio-polemical impact'.⁴ If it failed to achieve this impact, as the critical theorists thought, then that was less the composer's fault than the audience's, ultimately society's. The music of *Die Dreigroschenoper* 'contains a

wealth of unbroken vitality from the region of jazz', Adorno wrote
in his 1929 essay, 'which excites those who really ought to confront
themselves on the stage as corpses'. Those with a deeper understanding, he deemed, should penetrate beyond the superficial aesthetic
appearance just as Weill had done in his music. They should perceive
the work's critical, rebellious nature, not just the false image of social
harmony reflected by the jazz-influenced surface. Bloch's apologia
eventually went so far as to dismiss the validity of the general public's
response altogether. 'The unforgettable *Dreigroschenoper* music', he
wrote in 1937, 'succumbs to the danger of being applauded by a public
for which it was not written.'[5] For whom, one may well wonder, was
it then written?

Following Bloch and Adorno's critical appropriation of *The
Threepenny Opera*, the distinction between a 'proper' understanding
and the general public's purported 'misunderstanding' has found
frequent echoes in commentaries on the work. In his Weill monograph
of 1962, for example, Hellmut Kotschenreuther thought it 'questionable whether the public that attended the première and provided the
impresario Ernst Josef Aufricht with a full house for months on end
understood in the slightest either what was happening on stage or what
constituted the essence of Weill's music ... the huge success of the
Dreigroschenoper was primarily a misunderstanding'.[6] The same
claim surfaced in a recent study of 'Brecht and music': 'It cannot be
maintained', stated the author Albrecht Dümling, 'that the majority
of the public really understood the work.'[7] Nor was the problem
restricted to the first phase of *Threepenny*-fever. Boris Singerman,
to name but one among many, has written of 'a series of misunderstandings that also characterize later productions'.[8]

Against the background of the last quarter of a century or so, in
which literary criticism has grappled with the hermeneutic questions
raised by reader-oriented textual theories, any notion of 'misunderstanding', which posits the existence of a single, definitive reading
of a text, seems not only elitist but also old-fashioned, even naïve.
Critics have increasingly undermined exegetical certainty by drawing
attention to matters such as the fallacy of authorial intention, the gulf
between signifier and signified, the indeterminacies of meaning
lurking in all language use, particularly in literature. That readers
should attempt to resolve these indeterminacies in diverse ways is both
legitimate and inevitable. Yet such critical awareness would itself have
been unthinkable without an aesthetic revolution reflected in the
works themselves. Formalism, structuralism and poststructuralism,

for instance, are not only modes of criticism but also approaches to artistic production. Every work has its interpretative limits, some more flexible than others. And *The Threepenny Opera*'s chequered stage history suggests that its limits are very flexible indeed. At any rate, it is not to be ruled out that the so-called 'misunderstanding' of *The Threepenny Opera* applies less to the work's success than to the interpretation that posits that misunderstanding in the first place. It is possible, in other words, that the 'misunderstanding thesis' itself constitutes a misunderstanding.

Apologists may be no less guilty of imposing inapplicable categories than detractors. Was, for example, Cäcilie Tolksdorf in her 1932 doctoral dissertation in which she compared *Die Dreigroschenoper* with Gay's *Beggar's Opera* wider of the mark than Wiesengrund-Adorno? The differences – and similarities – in their approach are certainly striking. Tolksdorf's perspective in assessing Brecht and Weill's achievement was that of nineteenth-century idealist philosophy, in particular the work of Theodor Lipps. When measured against the aesthetic principles of such a mentor's work, it is hardly surprising that *Die Dreigroschenoper* is found wanting. Quoting Lipps, Tolksdorf writes that 'philosophy, any kind of thoughts or ideas one cannot carve or paint. One cannot even create them as poetry or music. One can only capture life, as experienced, in tangible forms. And therein rests the meaning of art.' From this vantage point she bemoans the fact 'that Brecht distorts his "idea" in the sense of "tendentiousness", that the work of art becomes for him a vehicle for ideas and beliefs, destroys what is artistic; what remains is mere "word-mongering" [*Schriftstellerei*]'.[9] In general she holds that 'if the form is a problem for the writer himself, if he himself constructs it intentionally, then it can no longer be an artistic structure, since this alone is the organically developed, living contour of material infused by the content'.[10] 'The parts of [*Die Dreigroschenoper*]', on the other hand, 'are merely related to one another artificially in such a way that the thesis, the problem understood as fact, can be expanded as skilfully as possible and brought to an effective end. It is no longer an organic whole but a logical one that is in evidence ... One is merely expected to witness a mechanically construed sequence of events.'[11]

Classicist principles, which prescribe the unity of organically derived diversity, are assuredly violated by Brecht and Weill at every turn. It is not that Tolksdorf fails to register the authors' intention. She does so quite perceptively. It is that her negative definitions inform her negative aesthetic judgment. She can find nothing positive in the work.

For the dialecticians Adorno and Bloch, the negative is the positive. Adorno wrote specifically and approvingly about the *Dreigroschenoper*'s 'false' harmonies, Bloch about 'boldly construed disintegration'. The simplicity of the work, which Adorno found 'anything but classic', is also 'subverted'. As for organicism, Adorno remarked how 'the experimenter Weill has so little belief in the unconsciously organic that one can safely assume he will not succumb to the danger of harmlessness'.[12] The critical theorists would have thought it fitting if the masses had instinctively responded more like Tolksdorf. In not doing so, the masses were 'misunderstanding'. From Bloch and Adorno's point of view Tolksdorf's dismissal is not so wide of the mark after all.

The fact remains, irrespective of any value judgment, that *The Threepenny Opera* has widely been understood in terms of its sub-version of traditional categories. On this point Tolksdorf was at one with Bloch and Adorno. An episode of litigation, reported in October 1929 in the right-wing *Zeitschrift für Musik*, offers further, judicial support. It began in the Lübeck Stadttheater 'where a series of performances of *Die Dreigroschenoper* was given with a cast of actors employed for spoken theatre'.

At the end of the production the actors claimed that, according to their contract, they were not required to perform in an opera and demanded increased fees. The management refused to comply, whereupon legal action was taken. The theatres' court of arbitration in Hamburg ruled that *Die Dreigroschenoper* was *not an opera* but a play with rhythmically spoken song interludes and dismissed the case with costs.

Not content with merely reporting the incident, the journal glee-fully seized upon the court's decision as confirmation of its own cultural-political convictions.

On the basis of the operas produced by our 'new' generation of artists there is much written about opera's demise. Here, too, the sound verdict of a German judge seems to have been necessary to establish order at last. Let us rid ourselves of these fashionable revue and operetta operas and clean up our temples of art! What is rare but good will then have light and air to flourish and we shall once again take joy in our opera.[13]

Both the judge, who was obliged to decide either way, and the proto-National Socialist commentator, with his rhetoric of 'purity' and 'order', failed to grasp the crucial point. It is that the

Dreigroschenoper brazenly resists categorization. The detractors no less than the apologists tend to favour negative definitions. What, however, positively informs the work at every level, from the overall generic designation to more local matters such as word-setting, is ambiguity.

Weill conceived *Die Dreigroschenoper* as a work of experiment and reform. To use his term, it is a *Zwischengattung*, an 'in-between genre': systematically between existing genres, historically a stepping-stone in a development towards a new type of musical theatre. The neutral description 'play with music' (*Stück mit Musik*) obscures the fact that many different genres have been assimilated. When Weill initially talked in terms of a 'farce' (*Posse*), for example, he may well have had in mind the work of the nineteenth-century satirical playwright Johann Nestroy. The critic Heinrich Strobel certainly did, drawing attention in his review of the première to 'an unbuttoned performance with Nestroyesque traits'.[14] Other, indisputable influences are cabaret and variety. In his short epistolary article on the work (reprinted here as chapter 6) Weill noted that the piece 'presented us with the opportunity to make "opera" the subject matter for an evening in the theatre'. It is not so much opera as opera about opera. Macheath may declare during the wedding scene 'I'm not exactly asking for an opera', but the resemblances, the ironic references, nonetheless remain. For Adorno and many other contemporaries the principal point of reference was operetta. If the original entr'actes had been printed in the vocal score, as they originally were in the libretto, it would certainly bear a formal resemblance to that genre, the intention behind the resemblance being of course double-edged. It was suggested in chapter 2, for example, that the 'Barbara-Song' could have been an allusion to 'Ich bin nur ein armer Wandergesell' from Eduard Künneke's *Der Vetter aus Dingsda*. In the same way Polly and Mac's 'Melodrama' ('Do you see the moon over Soho') picks up the clichéd theme of moonlight's romantic influence such as can be found in *Der Vetter von Dingsda* at the point in that work where the heroine, Julia, attempts to explain away, over the instrumental epilogue to 'Ich bin nur ein armer Wandergesell', her scarcely concealed susceptibility to the 'poor wayfarer': a familiar stereotype is given a parodistic, 'alienating' twist. The statements are ambiguous. Polly and Macheath sing to a melody that could have been lifted straight out of a Künneke operetta: 'Love lasts, or it doesn't last.'

In the context of the various 'temples of art' – the shrines of operetta, opera and music-drama – both Weill and Brecht commit irreverences. A parallel can be drawn to Gay, who openly parodied the form and content of conventional opera. Yet the irreverence can rest as much in the absence as in the presence of convention. Thus Weill stated in an interview in 1929 that *The Threepenny Opera* could be seen as 'the most consistent reaction to Wagner'. One may detect occasional instances of Wagnerian harmony such as the use of the 'Tristan chord' in 'Die Ballade von der sexuellen Hörigkeit'. By and large, however, the reaction to Wagner consists in Weill's implicit flouting of the traditions of nineteenth-century opera and music-drama. This is not full-scale, grand opera but a cheap 'threepenny' version. 'The old grand operatic form is suppressed by Lied, cabaret song and ballad.'[15] For a so-called serious composer to have made such a move was unsettling enough for Alban Berg to remark, two months after the première, that 'even the likes of us cannot make up their minds in favour of a "Drei-Groschen-Oper" or a "Zehntausend-Dollar-Symphonie"'.[16]

The most striking irreverences in the text concern the Bible. Sacred means are used to profane ends. 'Wake up, you corrupt Christian', sings Mr Peachum in his opening 'Morgenchoral'. The alert listener will indeed stumble across a whole host of biblical quotations and allusions. For example: Polly's 'Wo du hingehst, da will ich auch hingehen' in the 'Liebeslied' is lifted verbatim from Ruth 1, 16 ('Whither thou goest' etc.). It is first of all quoted by Mr and Mrs Peachum with a blasphemous 'Jonny' tacked on the end in their 'Anstatt Dass-Song' and twice parodied by Polly when she becomes 'poetic' before the first finale, quoting the exchanges between Macheath and Brown: 'If you down another [cocktail], then I want to down another one, too' and, with lavatorial euphemism, 'If you go somewhere, then I want to go somewhere, too.' Peachum's 'Zum Essen Brot zu kriegen und nicht ein Stein' in the first finale is a paraphrase of Matthew 7, 9 ('Being given bread to eat and not a stone'). Macheath's fate may even be seen to parallel in its broad contours the fate of Jesus Christ. The marriage to Polly, the beginning of the story, takes place in a stable. Presents are brought, not by kings but by gangsters. Mac, like Christ, is betrayed on a Thursday and is to be executed on a Friday. Peachum bribes Jenny, just as the Caiaphas paid Judas. Brown, like Peter, disowns his friend (in scene vi Mac borrows from Luke 22, 61–2: 'I looked at him and he wept bitterly', adding 'I learnt the trick from the Bible'). Jesus begs forgiveness for the sins of others; Macheath for his own. Jesus is raised from the dead; Macheath reprieved by the King's Messenger.[17] When asked by the magazine *Die Dame* in October 1928 about 'the strongest influence' on his work, Brecht replied: 'You'll laugh: the Bible.' He was probably being serious.

Not necessarily identified as such by the audience, the biblical quotations and innuendoes nonetheless strike a familiar chord as common clichés. That alone would justify Felix Salten's observation, cited in chapter 3, about 'the perfect unity of Brecht-Weill'. Reviewing the Viennese première in 1929, Salten sensed 'that the young Weill's music is as characteristic as Brecht's language, as electrifying in its rhythm as the lines of the poems, as deliberately and triumphantly trivial and full of allusions as the popularizing rhymes, as witty in the jazz treatment of the instruments, as contemporary, high-spirited and full of mood and aggression, as the text.'[18]

Sacred and profane, high and low, aristocratic opera and popular music, bitter and sweet – the ambiguity is often also a product of an intentional disunity between text and music. Weill himself illustrated the point during a brief episode of dissension with his publishers. When, for reasons of decency, Universal Edition wanted to publish the music of Mac and Jenny's tango without the words, the composer protested.

As far as the 'Zuhälterballade' is concerned, I request that you leave the text of the two verses in. [The third verse was not published until 1931.] The charm of the piece rests precisely in the fact that a rather risqué text (not, by the way, as offensive as a lot of operetta texts) is set to music in a gentle, pleasant way.[19]

He presumably meant just the cantilena of the vocal line, which itself sharply contrasts in an inimitably Weillian way with the jaunty tango rhythm of the accompaniment. As a whole the music is equivocal, its effects thoroughly ironic.

In 1982 the distinguished literary critic Helen Vendler, discussing the work of Sylvia Plath, employed the term 'Threepenny Opera style'. 'Self-consciously theatrical poems like "Daddy" and "Lady Lazarus"', Vendler observed,

are in one sense demonically intelligent, in their wanton play with concepts, myths and language, and in another, and more important, sense not intelligent at all, in that they willfully refuse, for the sake of a cacophony of styles (a tantrum of style), the steady, centripetal effect of thought. Indeed, they display a wild dispersal, a centrifugal spin to further and further reaches of outrage.

'The Threepenny Opera style', she says, is a 'jeering style'.

'Lady Lazarus' is a mélange of incompatible styles, as though in a meaning-less world every style could have its heyday: bravado ('I have done it again'), slang ('A sort of walking miracle'), perverse fashion commentary ('my skin/Bright as a Nazi lampshade'), melodrama ('Do I terrify?'), wit ('like the cat I have nine times to die'), boast ('This is number Three'), self-disgust ('What a trash/To annihilate each decade'). The poem moves on through reductive dismissal ('The big strip tease') to public announcement, with a blasphemous swipe at the *ecce homo* ('Gentlemen, ladies/These are my hands/My knees'), and comes to its single lyrical moment.[20]

Bravado, slang, perverse fashion commentary, melodrama, wit, boast, self-disgust, blasphemous swipes and lyrical moments — these are all intermittently present in *The Threepenny Opera*, either in the text or the music or both, as an array of effects that makes up the multi-layered irony. It is a style of wilful and relentless equivocation on absolutely every level, which stamps the work as 'modern' in a quintessentially twentieth-century sense.

Any message the work might contain at once undermines, even deconstructs itself. 'Love lasts, or it doesn't.' The tone of delivery is tongue-in-cheek *épater le bourgeois*. The meaning moves away from — rather than towards — any centre. If the work exerts any socio-polemical impact, which Bloch and Adorno claimed, it is at best indirect. Unlike in *The Beggar's Opera*, the outrage expressed in *The Threepenny Opera* is general, not particular. Werner Hecht has reduced the differences between the two works to a pair of neat and beguiling formulations: '1728: veiled critique of an open state of affairs', '1928: open critique of a veiled state of affairs'.[21] Gay's satire contains scarcely camouflaged barbs against the Walpole administration, whereas Weill and Brecht's satire lampoons conven-tional bourgeois morality, both in and out of the theatre.[22] Yet the nature of this latter critique has often been genuinely misunderstood insofar as *The Threepenny Opera* has been the object of exegetical anachronism, as outlined in chapter 2. In revising the work for the 1931 *Versuche* edition Brecht seemed to be heeding the criticism of the work published in the communist *Rote Fahne*. 'Not a trace of modern social or political satire' was the verdict of that newspaper's critic. Brecht's revisions sought to introduce a critique of capitalism and big business not contained in the 1928 version. It is by no means insignificant, for example, that proponents of the 'misunderstanding thesis' tend to clinch their reading of the work by citing a manifesto-like passage that was not added until 1931, namely Macheath's pseudo-Marxist valediction.[23] Arguably a more appropriate way of capturing the original spirit of the piece would be to cite some of the material intended for the first version but ultimately suppressed. A good example is the play-within-a-play passage in which the actors step out of their roles to quarrel with the author over the happy ending (see chapter 2, p. 24). This, I believe, gives a far more faithful impression of the sort of playful subversion that the authors originally intended and which the première audience quite readily understood and appreciated. As John Willett has written, 'the work as Brecht and Weill conceived it is still something of a bomb planted not so much beneath our society (because I don't really believe it blew all that much of a hole even in the flimsy Weimar structure) as beneath its more outmoded art forms and the snobberies which these reflect'.[24]

When *Die Dreigroschenoper* had run continuously for 250 performances at Schiffbauerdamm, whereupon it transferred to the Komödienhaus, the critic Alfred Kerr attempted an assessment of the work's appeal.

What, after all, does the dear old *Beggar's Opera* have to do with the present? Oh God. Because the slightly threatening gait of the beggars' battalion and a bit of pseudo-communism have shamefully been grafted on? Bunkum!

Without the music, by the splendidly economical Weill, it's a dud. A washout. An old volume from the Everyman Library [*ein alter Tauchnitz*]. Run of the mill.

Don't try and make out of it any theoretical drivel and platitudes about achievement. That lies somewhere else … in what is expected. In what is truly to come …

Rather, believe (if you have a clue about the fantastic nature of the stage) in uneven, free thought: the theatre is not a load of theoretical nonsense. It is dynamic and full of variety, of life. It is laughter in all kinds of weather. It is the bustle of humanity. As it was stated here quite recently. *Die Dreigroschenoper* was appealing. Not a programme.[25]

If *The Threepenny Opera* did not contain the unequivocally political message that Brecht's 'Notes' and other commentaries would have us wish, a considerable component of satire is nonetheless present. Far from misunderstanding it, claims the writer Elias Canetti, who was living in Berlin at the time of the première, the audience understood it all too well. They may have been forced to confront on stage their own unchristian, villainous traits. They were not repelled, however. They liked it.

It was a stylish production, coolly calculated. It was the most precise expression of Berlin. The people cheered themselves, they saw themselves, and were pleased. First came *their* food, then came their morality, no-one

19 Watercolour sketch of the 3rd *Dreigroschen*-Finale by Caspar Neher, stage designer of the première at the Theater am Schiffbauerdamm (31 August 1928). Reproduced by permission of the Theatermuseum der Universität zu Köln.

could have put it better, they took it literally. Now it had been said, no bug in a rug could have felt snugger. The abolition of the death penalty had been taken care of: the mounted messenger with a real horse. Only those who experienced it can believe the grating and bare self-satisfaction that emanated from this production.

If it is the job of satire to castigate people for the injustice they represent and commit, for the misdeeds which turn into predators and multiply, then here, on the contrary, everything was glorified that one would otherwise shamefully conceal. Most fittingly and effectively derided was sympathy. To be sure, everything had merely been taken from elsewhere and spiced with a few new indelicacies. Yet these indelicacies were precisely what was genuine. An opera it was not, nor a send-up of opera, as it had originally been; it was, and this was the one unadulterated thing about it, an operetta. What one had done was to take the saccharine form of Viennese operetta, in which people found their wishes undisturbed, and oppose it with a Berlin form, with its hardness, meanness and banal justifications, which people wanted no less, probably even more, than all that sweetness.[26]

More recently, in *A European Past*, the émigré historian Felix Gilbert described his experience of 'the greatest and most unforgettable production ... in which art and politics [were] beautifully combined'.[27] However much the audience may have shared the authors' bleak picture of a society controlled by corruption, he felt they also shared an irrational belief that the cosmopolitan and energizing Weimar world on which they had pinned their hopes would be rescued from execution, like Macheath. For Gilbert, open cynicism about the existing system by no means precludes an ultimate fidelity to it: operatic parody serves here as a device for the expression of positive political hopes and fears. The argument echoes earlier ones from the late 1940s and early 50s when Brecht was still regarded in some circles as a taboo author. When *The Threepenny Opera* was first performed in West German cities after the war aficionados greeted it as 'a former loved one', 'the expression of an epoch ... the most wonderful time of our life'.[28] There were critics, it is true, who continued to censure that cynicism. With the benefit of hindsight, however, the apologists could also read it as 'a work full of prophecy, which meanwhile has been confirmed, even surpassed, by reality'.[29]

The Threepenny Opera's pervasive ambiguity at every level seems positively to encourage contrary readings. In the postwar period in Germany, for example, it could at once prompt nostalgic memories of a bygone era as well as issue concrete political warnings, shamefully unheeded. Sentimentality and critical bite hang in the balance. There have been countless productions that tend more to the one side than the other. The challenge — often underestimated or entirely misunderstood — is to capture both.

Notes

2 The sources and genesis of *Die Dreigroschenoper*

1 *Berliner Börsen-Courier*, 6 May 1929.
2 Karl Kraus, 'Kerrs Enthüllung', *Die Fackel*, 31 (1929), pp. 129–32; reprinted in Kraus, *Widerschein der Fackel: Glossen, Werke*, ed. Heinrich Fischer, vol. 4 (Munich, 1956), p. 404.
3 See Otto F. Beer, 'In Grinzing wächst der Dreigroschentropfen', *Der Monat* (April 1958), No. 115, pp. 75–7; Reinhold Grimm, 'Werk und Wirkung des Übersetzers Karl Klammer', *Neophilogus*, 44 (1960), pp. 20–36; 'Ein Buch aus Erlangen und Brechts Dreigroschenoper', *Erlanger Tagblatt*, 9 January 1986, signed by 'w.g.'.
4 Translation from John Willett, *The Theatre of Bertolt Brecht* (London, 1959; rpt. 1967), p. 93.
5 See Joel Hunt, 'Bert Brecht's "Dreigroschenoper" and Villon's "Testament"', *Monatshefte*, 44:5 (1957), pp. 273–8; Reinhold Grimm, 'Werk und Wirkung'; Daniel Frey 'Les ballades des François Villon et le Dreigroschenoper', *Etudes des Lettres*, 4 (1961), pp. 114–36; Anthony J. Harper, 'Brecht and Villon: Further thoughts on some *Dreigroschenoper* songs', *Forum of Modern Language Studies*, 1 (1965), pp. 191–4; Sara Zimmermann, 'The Influence of John Gay, François Villon and Rudyard Kipling on the Songs in Bertolt Brecht's *Dreigroschenoper*' (MA Thesis, Indiana University, 1968).
6 See Fritz Hennenberg, ed., *Brecht-Liederbuch* (Frankfurt/Main, 1985), pp. 375f. The 'Kanonensong', written *c.* 1924, was first published as 'Lied der drei Soldaten' in Brecht's *Hauspostille* (Berlin, 1927).
7 Ernst Josef Aufricht, *Erzähle, damit du dein Recht erweist* (West Berlin, 1966), p. 73.
8 The latest edition of Brecht's works is the *Grosse kommentierte Berliner und Frankfurter Ausgabe*, projected to comprise 30 volumes. It differs from all previous editions in that it claims to present 'as a matter of principle the authorized and established [*wirksam gewordene*] first editions'. In the case of *Die Dreigroschenoper*, however, which is included in volume 2 (Frankfurt/Main and Berlin, GDR, 1988), the editors elected to reprint the 1931 *Versuche* text, which meets none of the above stipulations. It is not the first edition. It is not the version in which the work became established. Nor was it ever authorized by Weill. The edition that meets all three stipulations is

the libretto published jointly by Felix Bloch Erben and Universal Edition in 1928.

9 Werner Hecht, '*Die Dreigroschenoper* und ihr Urbild', in *Brechts Drei-groschenoper* (Frankfurt/Main, 1985), p. 222; also published in Hecht's *Sieben Studien über Brecht* (Frankfurt/Main, 1972).

10 Bertolt Brecht, 'Über die Verwendung von Musik für ein episches Theater', *Gesammelte Werke*, 15 (Frankfurt/Main, 1967), p. 473.

11 Having opened at Lincoln's Inn Fields on 29 January 1728, *The Beggar's Opera* received a total of sixty-two performances in one season. See John Gay, *Dramatic Works*, ed. John Fuller (Oxford, 1984), p. 46.

12 William Edward Yuill, *The Art of Vandalism: Bertolt Brecht and the English Drama*, Inaugural Lecture (Bedford College, London, 1977). Yuill formulates his general thesis thus: 'The point of adapting plays from earlier times ... is to illustrate the historical dialectic by creating an instructive contrast between the original in its historical context and the contemporary version' (p. 7).

13 Quoted in Giselher Schubert, *Paul Hindemith in Selbstzeugnissen und Bilddokumenten* (Reinbek, 1981), p. 47. Hindemith's correspondence with Schott also shows that he twice approached Brecht, in 1924 and 1925, with the idea of collaborating on an opera, though without success.

14 'Willy Haas berichtet über die *Dreigroschenoper*', *Lingener Tagespost*, 14 July 1963.

15 Ernst Josef Aufricht, *Erzähle, damit du dein Recht erweist* (Berlin, 1966); section on *Threepenny Opera* excerpted as 'Die Moritat vom Mackie Messer', *Melos*, 33 (1966), 'Die Uraufführung von Brechts "Drei-groschenoper"', *Neue Zürcher Zeitung*, 31 July 1966, and 'Gesindel zur Uraufführung', *Stuttgarter Zeitung*, 13 Aug. 1966. Lotte Lenya, 'That was a Time!', *Theatre Arts* (May 1956); reprinted as 'August 28, 1928', in *The Threepenny Opera*, trans. Eric Bentley and Desmond Vesey (New York, 1964), pp. v–xiv. Davis's protocol of the interview is held in the Weill–Lenya Research Center, New York.

16 Heinrich Fischer, 'Die Geburt der Dreigroschenoper über Premiere', *Südwest-Merkur*, Stuttgart, 9 May 1958; reprinted in Kurt Fassmann, *Brecht: eine Bildbiographie* (Munich, 1958).

17 Aufricht, *Erzähle*, pp. 60–5.

18 Letter dated 1 December 1986 from Lee Baxandall of The Naturist Society of America to the Kurt Weill Foundation. Now in Weill–Lenya Research Center, New York.

19 See John Fuegi, 'Most Unpleasant Things with *The Threepenny Opera*: Weill, Brecht, and Money', in Kim Kowalke, ed., *A New Orpheus: Essays on Kurt Weill* (New Haven, 1986), pp. 157–82.

20 Lotte Lenya, 'That was a Time!', p. xii.

21 Elias Canetti, *Die Fackel im Ohr: Lebensgeschichte 1921–1931* (Frankfurt, 1985) p. 259.

22 *The Threepenny Opera*, trans. and ed. Ralph Manheim and John Willett, *Bertolt Brecht, Collected Plays*, vol. 2, ii (London, 1979), pp. 106f.

23 Lotte Lenya, 'That was a Time!', pp. xif. Lenya's etymology of *Moritat* is dubious; the word probably derives from *Moralität*. Her recollection of the organ builder's name is also fanciful; it was Bacigalupo. See 'Das

Orchestrion war nur mit einem Kahn erreichbar', *Die neue Ärtzliche*, 26 March 1986. According to his own testament, Dacigalupo also made a creative contribution to *Die Dreigroschenoper*: he had to simplify Weill's music in order to fit it on to the organ's barrel.

24 Aufricht, *Erzähle*, p. 72.
25 See James K. Lyon, *Bertolt Brecht and Rudyard Kipling* (The Hague, 1975).
26 Kurt Weill, ['Zu der "Unterdrückten Arie" der Lucy], *Die Musik*, 25:2 (November 1932), p. 128.
27 Cited in *The Threepenny Opera*, trans. and ed. Ralph Manheim and John Willett (London, 1979), p. 121f. Original quoted in Hecht, ed., *Brechts Dreigroschenoper* (Frankfurt/Main, 1985), pp. 26f.
28 UE Archive: L1 UE 548. The printed libretto or *Regiebuch* (UE 8850) was first published in October 1928 in a print run of 300 copies. There were two reprintings: 500 copies in November 1928 and another 500 in December 1929 (Gerhard Seidel, *Bibliographie Bertolt Brecht*, Berlin, GDR, 1975, p. 211). Although the cover states that the libretto is printed as a manuscript for theatres, the register of Weill's printed works made available to Weill's attorneys in 1950 by Universal Edition includes the 'Regie- und Textbuch' as having been sold at a price of 5 Marks.
29 See Fritz Hennenberg, 'Weill, Brecht und die "Dreigroschenoper": Neue Materialien zur Entstehung und Uraufführung', *Österreichische Musik-zeitschrift*, 40 (1985), p. 285. Hennenberg also draws attention to an autograph copy of the 'Barbarasong' in Kate Kühl's *Nachlass* in the Berlin Akademie der Künste.
30 See Kim H. Kowalke, 'In Trivial [?] Pursuit: Who sings the "Barbara-song"?', *Kurt Weill Newsletter*, 6:2 (1988), pp. 8–11.
31 See Geoffrey Abbott's essay on the '*Dreigroschen* Sound'.
32 'Kurt Weill, der Komponist der *Dreigroschenoper*, will den Begriff des Musikdramas zerstören', interview, *Wiener Allgemeine Zeitung*, 9 March 1929. The opera critic Oskar Bie described the 'Moritat' as 'developing out of the barrel organ into a leitmotif' ('Die Musik zur Dreigroschenoper', *Berliner Börsen-Courier*, 2 September 1928). The term 'leitmotif' also crops up in the same connection in Erich Urban's review of the music (*B.Z. am Mittag*, 1 September 1928).
33 *Melos*, 7 (1928), p. 498.
34 Ronald Speirs, 'A Note on the First Published Version of *Die Drei-groschenoper* and its Relation to the Standard Text', *Forum for Modern Language Studies*, 13 (1977), p. 25. The differences are readily observable in a heavily marked copy of the 1928 edition, held in the Brecht Archive (BBA 1783/01–80), which Brecht used as the basis for his *Versuche*. The new material consists of typed intercalations on separate sheets of paper.
35 A complete list of the differences between *FE*, *V* and *GW* compiled in collaboration with the present author has been published as an appendix to Steve Giles, 'Rewriting Brecht: *Die Dreigroschenoper* 1928–31', *Literaturwissenschaftliches Jahrbuch 1989* (Berlin, 1989), pp. 249–79.
36 Translation adapted from Bertolt Brecht, 'Notes to *The Threepenny Opera*', in *Collected Plays*, 2, ii (London, 1979), p. 92.

37 Theodor Wiesengrund-Adorno, 'Zur Dreigroschenoper', *Die Musik*, 22 (1929), pp. 424—8; reprinted here as chapter 8.

38 Walter Benjamin, 'L'Opéra de Quat' Sous', unpublished MS; published as 'Nachtrag zu den Brecht-Kommentaren' in Walter Benjamin, *Schriften: Supplementband*, ed. Rolf Tiedemann, 7 (Frankfurt/Main, 1989), pp. 347—9; reprinted here as chapter 11.

39 *Musik für alle*, 274, (Berlin, 1929).

40 Fritz Hennenberg's assertion that one can reconstruct the genesis of the music from the way the various types of manuscript paper are collated is flawed on two counts ('Weill, Brecht und die "Dreigroschenoper"': Neue Materialien zur Entstehung und Uraufführung', *Österreichische Musikzeitschrift*, 40 (1985), pp. 287f.). First he infers a particular stage in the work's composition from the composer's choice of paper, without offering proof of a necessary connection. Second, the songs submitted after the première, although all written on the same type of paper — K.U.V. Beethoven Papier Nr. 39 (30 Linien) — are revisions, not new compositions.

41 I am indebted to Wolfgang Ruf for drawing attention to this connection in his unpublished Habilitationsschrift: *Modernes Musiktheater: Studien zu seiner Geschichte und Typologie* (University of Freiburg, 1983), p. 192.

42 Wll. [Kurt Weill], 'Berliner Übertragungen und Sendespiele', *Der deutsche Rundfunk*, 4:31 (1926), pp. 2138f.

43 Both songs are included in both versions in Fritz Hennenberg, ed., *Brecht-Liederbuch* (Frankfurt/Main, 1985). For a transcription of the Brecht–Bruinier 'Barbara-Song' and a comparison with Weill's setting of the same song, see Michael Morley, '"Suiting the Action to the Word"': Some Observations on *Gestus* and *Gestische Musik*', *A New Orpheus: Essays on Kurt Weill*, ed. K. Kowalke (New Haven, 1986), pp. 183—201.

44 Wll. [Kurt Weill], 'Vom Berliner Sender', *Der deutsche Rundfunk*, 5:2 (1927), p. 86.

45 Albrecht Dümling, *Lasst euch nicht verführen: Brecht und die Musik* (Munich, 1985), p. 134.

46 David Drew, *Kurt Weill: A Handbook* (London, 1987), p. 203.

47 Ruf, *Modernes Musiktheater*, p. 191.

48 Theodor Wiesengrund-Adorno, 'Kompositionskritik. Kurt Weill: Kleine Dreigroschenmusik für Blasorchester', *Musikblätter des Anbruch*, 11 (1929), pp. 316—17; reprinted in *Über Kurt Weill*, ed. D. Drew (Frankfurt/Main, 1975), pp. 49—51.

49 Peter Epstein, 'Die Kleine Dreigroschen-Musik', *Pult und Taktstock*, 6 (March—April 1929), p. 36. Cf. David Drew's chapter on 'Motifs, Tags and Related Matters', p. 151.

50 See letter to *The Times Literary Supplement*, 29 April 1988, from Berthold Goldschmidt, who was present on the occasion. According to Goldschmidt, the performance of Weill's *Kleine Dreigroschenmusik* was preceded by Berlioz's *Rákóczy March* (conducted by Erich Kleiber) and Strauss's *Emperor Waltz* (conducted by Wilhelm Furtwängler).

51 Quoted in *Casparius*, ed. Stiftung Deutsche Kinemathek (Berlin, 1978), pp. 211f.

52 Bertolt Brecht, 'Der Dreigroschenprozess: ein soziologisches Experiment', *Gesammelte Werke*, 18 (Frankfurt/Main, 1967), p. 149.

53 Werner Mittenzwei, *Das Leben des Bertolt Brecht oder Der Umgang mit den Welträtseln*, 1 (Berlin, GDR, 1986), p. 420.
54 'Die andere Seite: Kurt Weill zum "Dreigroschenoper"-Vergleich', *LichtBildBühne*, 13 February 1931.
55 Brecht, 'Der Dreigroschenprozess', p. 149.
56 *Casparius*, p. 180.
57 For a comprehensive study of the *Dreigroschenroman*, see Klaus-Detlef Müller, *Brecht-Kommentar zur erzählenden Prosa* (Munich, 1980).
58 Drew, *Kurt Weill: A Handbook*, p. 293.
59 Letter from Weill to Aufricht dated 18 August 1937.
60 Letter from Weill to Alfred Schlee of Universal Edition dated 11 December 1948.
61 The new material is reprinted in Werner Hecht, ed., *Brechts Dreigroschenoper* (Frankfurt, 1985), pp. 38–48; and in volume 2 of the new Brecht complete edition, ed. Jürgen Schebera (Berlin, GDR and Frankfurt/Main, 1988), pp. 309–22. English translations of the new verses are appended to the Manheim and Willett version (London, 1979), pp. 85–9. Brecht included the new verses in his edition of *Songs aus der Dreigroschenoper* (Berlin, 1949) and also in the unpublished concert version printed here in an abridged translation as chapter 1.
62 See letter from Brecht to Weill, dated 28 January 1949, in Bertolt Brecht, *Briefe 1913–56* (Frankfurt/Main, 1981), pp. 551f.

3 The première and after

1 'Werkstatistik 1986/87: Brecht auf dem Vormarsch', *Die Deutsche Bühne*, 12 (1987), pp. 47–50. If it had been included in the music-theatre charts *Die Dreigroschenoper* would have had to concede first position to Lloyd-Webber's *Cats*, which sold 450,000 tickets for the single production it received.
2 Peter Härtling, *Felix Guttmann* (Darmstadt, 1985), pp. 192–5.
3 Ernst Josef Aufricht, *Erzähle, damit du dein Recht erweist* (West Berlin, 1966), pp. 60–74; Lotte Lenya, 'That was a time', *Theatre Arts* (May 1956); H. W. Heinsheimer, *Menagerie in F #* (New Jersey, 1947), pp. 152–62, and *Best Regards to Aida* (New York, 1968), pp. 119–23; Heinrich Fischer, 'Die Geburt der Dreigroschenoper über Premiere', *Südwest-Merkur*, Stuttgart, 9 May 1958, reprinted in Kurt Fassmann, *Brecht: eine Bildbiographie* (Munich, 1958); Willy Haas *Die literarische Welt: Erinnerungen* (Munich, 1960), pp. 143–51; Felix Jackson, *Portrait of a Quiet Man: Kurt Weill, his Life and Times* (unpublished MS), pp. 54–80.
4 Lotte Lenya, 'That was a Time!', *Theatre Arts* (May 1956); reprinted as 'August 28, 1928', in *The Threepenny Opera*, trans. Eric Bentley and Desmond Vesey (New York, 1964), p. xiv.
5 Ibid., p. xiii.
6 The programme is kept in the Weill–Lenya Research Center, New York.
7 Aufricht, *Erzähle*, p. 73.
8 Bertolt Brecht, 'Aufbau der "Dreigroschenoper"-Bühne', *Gesammelte Werke*, 18 (Frankfurt/Main, 1967), pp. 1000f.

9 For the Brecht–Weill–Neher collaboration on *Aufstieg und Fall der Stadt Mahagonny* plans were discussed for Neher's projections as well as a production booklet to be loaned to theatres in the same way that other performance materials are. Although the production booklet, begun by Neher and Weill, never appeared, its preface was published as Kurt Weill, 'Vorwort zum Regiebuch der Oper *Aufstieg und Fall der Stadt Mahagonny*', *Anbruch*, 12 (1930), pp. 5–7.

10 See John Willett, *Caspar Neher: Brecht's Designer* (London, 1986); Walter Bohaumilitzky, *Caspar Nehers Bühnenbild in den 20er Jahren: Sein Frühwerk* (diss., University of Vienna, 1968).

11 Paul Wiegler, 'Die Dreigroschenoper: Einst und Jetzt', *Musik für alle*, 274 (Berlin, 1929). Revised reprint of the same critic's review first published in *B.Z. am Mittag*, 1 September 1928.

12 Ernst Heilborn, 'Zur Psychologie des Bühnenbildes', *Die Literatur*, 31 (1928/29), p. 184. The article is accompanied, on the facing page, by B. F. Dolbin's drawing of the set (fig. 6).

13 Harry Kessler, *Tagebücher 1918–37*, ed. Wolfgang Pfeiffer-Belli (Frankfurt/Main, 1961), p. 569.

14 A selection of notices can be found in Hugo Fetting, ed., *Von der Freien Bühne zum Politischen Theater: Drama und Theater im Spiegel der Kritik*, vol. 2, 1919–1933 (Leipzig, 1987), pp. 383–95; see also Monika Wyss, *Brecht in der Kritik: Rezensionen aller Brecht-Uraufführungen* (Munich, 1977), pp. 79–87.

15 See Theo Lingen, *Ich über mich: Interviews eines Schauspielers mit sich selbst*, Reihe Theater heute, 9 (Hanover, 1963), pp. 37f. Lingen first played Macheath in the production of *Die Dreigroschenoper* that opened at the Neues Theater Frankfurt on 20 October 1928.

16 Partly unidentified newspaper cuttings from the 'Theaterwissenschaftliches Archiv Dr. Steinfeld' held at the Theatermuseum der Universität zu Köln.

17 Werner Egk, *Die Zeit wartet nicht* (Percha am Starnbergersee, 1973), p. 168. Egk goes on to relate how Peter Pfitzner was expelled from the parental home for playing Puccini on his father's piano.

18 Franz Jung, *Der Weg nach Unten* (Neuwied and Berlin, 1961), p. 355. The pattern of the *Dreigroschen* wallpaper has been reprinted in *Kurt Weill Newsletter*, 6:2 (1988), pp. 4–5.

19 The cast included Kate Kühl (the original Lucy) as Mrs Peachum. See Walter Karsch, *Was war – was blieb: Berliner Theater 1945–46* (West Berlin, 1947), p. 11.

20 Kim H. Kowalke, 'Accounting for Success: Misunderstanding *Die Dreigroschenoper*', *The Opera Quarterly*, 6:3 (1989), pp. 18–38.

21 Martin Linzer, 'Rostock 1959', *Theater der Zeit*, 14:8 (1959), p. 55.

22 Reprinted in Werner Hecht, ed., *Brechts Dreigroschenoper* (Frankfurt/Main, 1985), p. 170f.

23 André Müller, ' "Neues vom Tage": Theaterbrief aus Westdeutschland (V)', *Theater der Zeit*, 16:11 (1961), p. 58.

24 G. Strehler, 'Brecht e Strehler: L'opera da tre soldi', *Gala*, 5 (1973), pp. 30–4.

25 The text of Weill's broadcast has not survived. It is evident from a letter

to his publisher (dated 26 February 1929) that Weill intended to include an excerpt from his 'Korrespondenz über Dreigroschenoper' (reprinted here as chapter 6). The press interview was published as 'Kurt Weill, der Komponist der *Dreigroschenoper*, will den Begriff des Musikdramas zerstören', *Wiener Allgemeine Zeitung*, 9 March 1929.

26 Among the critics to publish extensive reviews of the Viennese première were: Friedrich Lorenz and Elsa Bienenfeld, *Neues Wiener Journal*, 10 March 1929; Ludwig Ullmann, *Wiener Allgemeine Zeitung*, 12 March 1929; Lothar Ring, *Volks-Zeitung*, 10 March 1929; Walther Schneider, *Wiener Mittags-Zeitung*, 11 March 1929; Ernst Decfey, *Neues Wiener Tagblatt*, 10 March 1929; Ferdinand Scherder, *Wiener Zeitung*, 12 March 1929. A survey of postwar Brecht reception in Austria can be found in Kurt Palm, *Vom Boykott zur Anerkennung: Brecht und Österreich* (Vienna, 1983). Palm records a total of 21 Austrian productions of *Die Dreigroschenoper* between 1945 and 1982.

27 Quoted in Werner Wüthrich, *Bertolt Brechts Aufnahme in der Schweiz 1923–69* (diss., University of Vienna, 1974), p. 91.

28 Carl Niessen, *Brecht auf der Bühne* (Cologne, 1959), p. 22. The most exhaustive account of Brecht reception in France is Agnes Hüfner's *Brecht in Frankreich: 1930–1963. Verbreitung, Aufnahme, Wirkung*, Germanistische Abhandlungen, 22 (Stuttgart, 1968).

29 A. V. Lunačarskij, 'Na tri groša', *Večernaja*, 24 September 1928; quoted in Eva Kreilisheim, *Bertolt Brecht und die Sowjetunion* (diss., University of Vienna, 1969), p. 70.

30 V. Bljumenfel'd, *Sovetskij teatr*, 3–4 (1930), p. 24; quoted in Kreilisheim, p. 71.

31 B. I. Zingerman, 'Opera niščich', *Teatr* (1963), p. 29; quoted in Kreilisheim, *Bertolt Brecht*, p. 75.

32 Kreilisheim, *Bertolt Brecht*, p. 74.

33 Walter Benjamin, 'Bragaglia in Berlin', *Gesammelte Schriften*, 4, i (Frankfurt/Main, 1972), p. 523.

34 Paola Barbon, *Il signor B.B.: Wege und Umwege der italienischen Brecht-Rezeption*, Literatur und Reflexion Neue Folge, vol. 5, ed. Beda Allemann (Bonn, 1987), p. 25. Barbon's study, one of the best of its kind, is both encylopedically thorough and full of sharp analytical insight. Without its tendency towards hagiography, it would probably never have been written.

35 Ibid., p. 46.

36 Ibid., p. 182.

37 'Bertolt Brecht/Giorgio Strehler: Ein Gesprächsprotokoll', in Werner Hecht, ed., *Brechts Dreigroschenoper* (Frankfurt/Main, 1985), pp. 134–43.

38 Bertolt Brecht, *Briefe*, ed. G. Glaeser (Berlin, GDR, 1983), pp. 730f.

39 Giorgio Strehler, *Per un teatro umano* (Milan, 1974), p. 287.

40 Barbon, *Il signor B.B.*, p. 194.

41 For further information on *The Judgement of Paris*, see David Drew, *Kurt Weill: A Handbook* (London, 1987), p. 198; see also ch. 4, p. 95.

42 Constant Lambert, *Music Ho! A Study of Music in Decline* (London, 1934), pp. 224–5. The real victim of Lambert's survey is Hindemith,

on whose reputation in England *Music Ho!* has probably been the single most detrimental influence.

43 See Nicholas Jacobs and Prudence Ohlsen, *Bertolt Brecht in Britain* (London, 1977).

44 *The Times* of 19 July 1933 reported that Norman Marshall had taken over the Gate Theatre and intended to mount a production, but the plan came to nothing.

45 'Three-farthing Opera', *The Musical Times*, 76 (1935), p. 260.

46 Not that Weill himself was innocent of making unfavourable comparisons with *The Beggar's Opera*. In an undated letter to Lenya, also on Park Lane Hotel paper, he reported having seen a production of the John Gay original: 'it is one of the best evenings in the theatre I've ever had, incomparably finer and more aggressive than *Die Dreigroschenoper* and much better performed. Stylized theatre as consummate as I've only ever seen from the Japanese.'

47 See 'Exhibition of 20th Century German Art', *Stationen der Moderne: Die bedeutenden Kunstausstellungen des 20. Jahrhunderts in Deutschland*, Exhibition Catalogue (Berlin, 1988), pp. 315–26.

48 Peter Heyworth, 'Lost on Broadway', *Times Literary Supplement*, 25–31 March 1988.

49 *Wolfgang Staudte*, ed. Eva Orbanz (Berlin, 1977), p. 212. See also Staudte, Heckroth and Raguse, eds., *Die Dreigroschenoper 63: Werkbuch zum Film* (Munich, 1964).

50 Wole Soyinka, *Opera Wonyosi* (Bloomington, 1981).

4 *The Threepenny Opera* in America

Unless otherwise noted, all unpublished documents cited are in the Weill–Lenya Research Center, New York. The correspondence of Weill and Lenya is quoted by permission of the Kurt Weill Foundation for Music. All translations are by the author.

1 The undated document in German is in the Bertolt Brecht Archive (BBA 461/93).

2 Dreyfus's notarized affidavit is dated 20 May 1951. Weill's annual income from ASCAP had averaged just under $5,000 per year for the preceding five-year period. *Die Dreigroschenoper* was produced in Europe several times after Brecht had returned to Germany, but Weill received no income because at first Brecht collected all of it and later Suhrkamp licensed the work as if it were Brecht's alone. See John Fuegi, 'Most Unpleasant Things with *The Threepenny Opera*: Weill, Brecht, and Money' in *A New Orpheus: Essays on Kurt Weill*, ed. Kim H. Kowalke (New Haven, 1986), pp. 157–82. Weill's estate did receive an accounting from Universal Edition in August 1950 for DM 90, 18 for performances of *Die Dreigroschenoper* during the period 1946–49.

3 See Pete Hamill, 'Curtain Falls on *The Threepenny Opera*', *New York Post*, 18 December 1961; and John Allen, 'A Five-Year Hit for Only $10,000', *New York Herald Tribune*, 20 September 1959.

4 The programme is in the Weill–Lenya Research Center.

5 Mordaunt Hall, 'A German *Beggar's Opera*', *New York Times*, 18 May 1931.

6 Edward Jablonski and Lawrence D. Stewart, *The Gershwin Years*, (Garden City, NJ, 1973), p.299. Leonard Bernstein recalls his first encounter with *Die Dreigroschenoper* in college 'via the glorious old recording' in Henry Marx, ed., *Weill—Lenya* (New York, 1976), p.6. The Telefunken recordings from 1930 have been re-released as Telefunken Dokumente 6.41911 AJ.

7 BBA 1183/04. Dated 9 March 1942, the letter was Weill's initial response to Brecht's proposal for an all-black production in California. A version of Desmond Vesey's translation has been misidentified as Cochran's and Krimsky's in the Billy Rose Theatre Collection of the New York Public Library at Lincoln Center (Script RM 2316). The single surviving page from an English translation in folder Z 1/110 in the Bertolt Brecht Archive is probably a fragment from the 1933 script. It follows the text of the libretto published in 1928 by Universal Edition and retains in the first stanzas of the 'Moritat' Macheath's alias as the German 'Mackie Messer', as does the programme for the Empire Theatre.

8 The 'Ballade von der sexuellen Hörigkeit' was omitted from both the libretto and piano-vocal score published by Universal Edition, whereas the 'Salomonsong' appeared in both.

9 Contradictory evidence makes it impossible to determine which character sang the 'Barbarasong' on opening night in Berlin; when Carola Neher rejoined the cast as Polly in 1929, however, she performed the number. All published German editions assigned the song to Polly. In Blitzstein's adaptation, too, Lucy sings the 'Barbarasong', even though all published editions of the German text and score assign the song to Polly in Act I, Scene 3. Convincing evidence for Lucy singing the 'Barbarasong' in the original production can be inferred from Herbert Jhering's review of the new cast of *Die Dreigroschenoper* in the *Berliner Börsen-Courier* of 13 May 1929: 'At the centre is the Polly Peachum of Carola Neher ... A new scene: Polly visits her rival to fight over Macheath. Carola Neher played this scene with a magical mixture of irony and anxiety. The way she dabbed her handkerchief to her eyes and patted her face is dictated by the music and recalls the great acting of Gutheil-Schoder in *Rosenkavalier*. Then she sings the Ballad of Lucy, which now has been given to Polly, with charm and an ability to juggle wit and sentiment that is overpowering.' This account jibes with Jhering's review of the première, published on 1 September 1928, wherein he described Kate Kühl, who played Lucy, as 'impressive in a ballad', which could only have been the 'Barbarasong'. The internal musical evidence provided by the passage in the middle of the third finale, when the orchestra ironically recalls a snippet from the 'Barbarasong' to undercut both the sentiment and meaning of Polly's declaration 'Mein lieber Macheath ist gerettet! Ich bin sehr glücklich', is the strongest argument against converting the 'Barbarasong' into the 'Lucy Song'. See Kim H. Kowalke, 'In Trivial [?] Pursuit: Who sings the "Barbarasong"?', *Kurt Weill Newsletter*, 6:2 (1988), pp.8—11.

10 There may have been a performance in 1937. In the Weill/Lenya Archive at Yale University, there is an old set of orchestral parts (UE 3349) that

had been adapted for an English-speaking production. A pencil marking, 'Braunschweig 1929', indicates that the parts had previously been used in Germany; a diagram (dated June 1929) on the back of one of the parts indicates the placement of fourteen players in the pit. One of the saxophone parts also contains the curious notation, 'Beggers [sic] Consolidated Ltd. Planed [sic] for the Pioner [sic] Theatre, 1937'. No record of such a production has been traced.

11 The undated letter in German was written during May 1937 from Santa Monica (where Weill was working on film projects). Francesco von Mendelssohn had directed Lenya in Valentin Katayev's *Die Quadratur des Kreises* ('Squaring the Circle') at the Theater am Schiffbauerdamm in 1930; that cast also included Peter Lorre and Theo Lingen. Mendelssohn was the son of a banking baron and the grandnephew of Felix Mendelssohn-Bartholdy. At the request of Ernst Aufricht, for the 1937 Paris production Weill composed settings of two texts by Yvette Guilbert, who played Mrs Peachum.

12 Marc Blitzstein, 'Popular Music − An Invasion: 1923−33', *Modern Music*, 10 (January−February 1933), p. 101; and 'Theater-Music in Paris', *Modern Music*, 12 (March−April 1935), pp. 132−3. A photocopy of Weill's letter about Blitzstein to Reinhardt's assistant Dr Kommer, dated 15 January 1935, is in the Weill−Lenya Research Center.

13 Marc Blitzstein, 'New York Medley, Winter, 1935', *Modern Music*, 13 (January−February 1936), pp. 36−7.

14 Marc Blitzstein, 'Coming: The Mass Audience', *Modern Music*, 13 (May−June 1936), p. 28. In contrast to Blitzstein's article, Paul Rosenfeld wrote very perceptively and sympathetically about both *The Threepenny Opera* and *Der Jasager* in 'Gebrauchsmusik', *The New Republic*, 3 October 1934, pp. 214f.

15 Marc Blitzstein, 'Weill Scores for *Johnny Johnson*', *Modern Music*, 14 (November−December 1936), pp. 44−6. Weill's own lecture notes, as well as some taken by Tony Kraber, one of the participants, are in the Weill−Lenya Research Center.

16 See James K. Lyon, *Bertolt Brecht in America* (Princeton, 1980).

17 For an account of the complicated contractual history of *Die Dreigroschenoper* from 1928 to 1950 and a discussion of Brecht's handling of Weill's rights and royalties in Europe, see Fuegi, 'Most Unpleasant Things with *The Threepenny Opera*'.

18 The letter is dated 14 March 1941. Although *Lady in the Dark* conclusively established Weill's place in the American theatre, it also severed his few remaining connections with representatives of 'New Music'. See Virgil Thomson's review in the *New York Herald Tribune*, 23 February 1941. Samuel L. M. Barlow lamented in *Modern Music* that he couldn't find 'three minutes of the true Weill' in the score. 'Something first-rate has gone third-rate, which is a loss for everyone who cares deeply about art.' (*Modern Music*, 18 (March−April 1941), p. 192.)

19 The undated letter in German is in the Weill/Lenya Archive.

20 The original letter is in the Bertolt Brecht Archive, BBA 1183/04. Weill and Paul Green had approved an all-black production of *Johnny Johnson* in Chicago that never materialized. Weill provided incidental music for

Hecht's and MacArthur's pageant, *Fun to be Free*, performed at Madison Square Garden on 5 October 1941 and sponsored by Fight for Freedom, Inc. MacArthur was married to Helen Hayes. In 1943 Weill also supplied incidental music for Hecht's *We Will Never Die*, 'dedicated to the Two Million Jewish Dead in Europe', and *A Flag is Born*, Hecht's pro-Zionist pageant that ran on Broadway during the 1946–47 season.

21 Included with Brecht's letter of 12 March 1942 was the poem, 'Ballade vom Soldatenweib', which Brecht suggested Weill should set for Lenya. Lenya and Weill gave the song its première at Hunter College on 3 April 1943. Copies of all correspondence related to the 'Muse affair' are in the Weill–Lenya Research Center.

22 Adorno's letter to Weill is in the Weill/Lenya Archive. Adorno included with his letter two of his recent publications on jazz; in their light, his argument on Brecht's behalf is curiously incongruous. Adorno shared Weill's reply with Brecht, who mentions it in his journal entry for 15 April 1942:

When Weill created difficulties for a planned Negro production of *Die Dreigroschenoper* by Clarence Muse, I asked Wiesengrund-Adorno to write to him. Weill answered him with an angry letter attacking me and a paean to Broadway, which [he says] will produce anything if it's good and continues the European experiments. The last piece for which he wrote the music is supposed to have run 14 months. It's called *Lady in the Dark*. (It is supposed to be an amusing box office hit.) The letter begins with the remark that he is writing in English: 'it's easier for me and I like it better!'

23 Weill's letter to Brecht of 7 April was the only one written in English. It began: 'I write this letter in English because you probably want to show its content to Clarence Muse and his associates.'

24 Weill's letter to Lenya is dated 16 April 1942. All of the Weill–Lenya correspondence from this period is in English.

25 The letter to Brecht, again written in German, is dated 20 April 1942.

26 Weill's letter to Howard Reinheimer is dated 10 November 1942.

27 The only reliable published account of the *Schwejk* and *Sezuan* projects is in David Drew's *Kurt Weill: A Handbook* (London, 1987), pp. 408–16. Brecht and Weill also authorized Elinor Rice to translate *Die Dreigroschenoper*; Weill sent Brecht a copy of her first draft in April 1944, but nothing further was done with it.

28 Drew, *Kurt Weill*, pp. 198, 327. Drew's entry for the arrangements made for the BOST recording erroneously includes the two *Dreigroschen* songs while omitting 'Lover Man' and 'Lost in the Stars' (from the unfinished *Ulysses Africanus*, 1939), which were released on the three-disc set. See chapter 2, p. 47.

29 See Lyon, *Bertolt Brecht in America*, pp. 310–12, for an account of the circumstances surrounding the production at the Hebbel Theater.

30 Eric Bentley's anecdote appears in a letter to the Kurt Weill Foundation, dated 24 January 1988.

31 William Leonard, 'Non Equity, But Non-Amateur', *Chicago Journal of Commerce*, 5 February 1948. For personal recollections and documents concerning Northwestern's production, I am grateful to Eric Bentley, Claudia Webster Robinson, Thomas Willis (now concert director of

Northwestern University), and David Burge, professor of piano at the Eastman School of Music, who doubled as Wally the Weeper and rehearsal pianist. Mr Willis provided a detailed musical report and a copy of the script used in the production; Mrs Webster-Robinson deposited in the Weill—Lenya Research Center virtually complete documentation of her production, including a tape of the cast recording.

32 Marc Blitzstein, '*Threepenny Opera* is Back', *New York Herald Tribune*, 7 March 1954.

33 *New York Herald Tribune*, 5 February 1951. Thomson's negative review of *Lady in the Dark* had strained personal relations between the two composers. Lenya recalled that after they agreed to mend the fences at a party in the late forties, on the way home Weill quipped that 'he liked Virgil better as an enemy'.

34 Bentley's letter is dated 9 November 1951; I am indebted to Eric Gordon for sharing it with me. Mr Gordon also provided information about Blitzstein's adaptation and valued comments on a draft of this section of my essay.

35 Kurt List, 'A Musical Brief for Gangsterism', *The New Leader*, 35 (4 February 1952), p. 26. The 3 March issue included a letter to the editor from Dwight MacDonald protesting List's views. List included in his column a similar letter of protest from Lewis A. Coser of Brandeis University; List answered Coser's charge of censorship by denying that *Die Dreigroschenoper* was 'an authentic work of art'.

36 Capalbo, quoted by Allen in 'A Five Year Hit'. In several phone interviews during October 1986 and January 1987, Stanley Chase provided the author with much valuable information.

37 Harold Clurman in *The Nation*, 27 March 1954; Olin Downes in the *New York Times*, 4 April 1954.

38 Letter from Lenya to Dr Kalmus, Universal Edition, London, 3 September 1954.

39 Ibid.

40 Marc Blitzstein, 'On The Threepenny Opera', *Musical Show* (October 1962).

41 A privately recorded disc of Lenya's 1965 performance at Carnegie Hall is in the Weill—Lenya Research Center.

42 *New York Daily News*, 3 May 1976.

43 Kurt Weill, 'Korrespondenz über Dreigroschenoper', *Anbruch*, 11 (January 1929), pp. 24—5; reprinted here in translation as chapter 6.

6 Correspondence concerning *Threepenny Opera*

1 The idea to write this essay in epistolary form came not from the editors of *Anbruch* but from Weill himself. He first mentioned it in a letter dated 2 October 1928 to Hans Heinsheimer, head of Universal's opera department and an editor of *Anbruch*. In his reply, Heinsheimer found the idea 'splendid' (*famos*) and immediately drafted the letter to which Weill should respond. Weill, in turn, dispatched his essay on 17 October along with a request: 'I would only ask you to omit from your letter ... the sentence: "Weill as Humperdinck", since I have a quite personal antipathy

towards this composer'. (Humperdinck was one of Weill's teachers in composition.) As an alternative formulation he suggested 'From Offenbach to Weill'. In the event the published version of Heinsheimer's letter omits two passages from the original, without adding Weill's suggested alternative. One is at the end of the first paragraph: 'People's opera [*Volksoper*] 1928. Weill as Humperdinck.' The other is at the end of the second paragraph: 'You are one of the few who are able to apply here the deductive method.'

2 Franz Lehár's operetta *Friederike*, with Richard Tauber as Johann Wolfgang Goethe and Käthe Dorsch as Friederike Brion, was given its première in Berlin on 4 October 1928. It played in the Admiralspalast, on the other side of the river from the Theater am Schiffbauerdamm, where *Die Dreigroschenoper* was playing.

3 Weill's distinction between 'gesellschaftlich' and 'gesellschaftsbildend' is idiosyncratic. The clearest clue to the intended connotation can be found in the biographical note printed in the original programme of the *Mahagonny-Songspiel* (1927). 'In his more recent works,' it says there, 'Weill is moving in the direction of those artists of all art forms who predict the liquidation of arts engendered by established society [*gesellschaftliche Künste*]. The small epic piece *Mahagonny* merely takes the logical step from the inexorable decline of existing social structures. It already addresses an audience that naïvely demands its fun in the theatre.'

8 *The Threepenny Opera*

1 Adorno's article appeared as part of a special issue of *Die Musik* devoted to the idea of *Gebrauchsmusik* (literally 'use music'), a concept with which both critics and composers in the second half of the 1920s sought to develop a new musical aesthetic. Where, in his article on *The Threepenny Opera* (reprinted here as chapter 6), Weill writes of a path which embraces 'the abandonment of the *l'art pour l'art* standpoint, the turning away from an individualistic principle of art, the ideas on film music, the contact with the youth music movement, the simplification of the musical means of expression' he is describing ideals which were all subsumed under the concept of *Gebrauchsmusik*. See Stephen Hinton, *The Idea of Gebrauchsmusik* (New York, 1989).

2 In the 1920s, the Weidendamm-Brücke, adjacent to the Theater am Schiffbauerdamm, was in a rather rundown area, whereas the Kurfürstendamm in Berlin's West End was one of the more exclusive residential areas, as it still is today.

9 *The Threepenny Opera*

1 Queen Luise, wife of Friedrich Wilhelm III, lived from 1776 to 1810.

10 Three-groats opera

1 Sir Nigel Playfair's London revival of the *Beggar's Opera*, which Blom touches on later in his review, opened at the Lyric Theatre, Hammersmith, on 5 June 1920.

2 Blom is referring here to the piano vocal score (UE 8851), first published in 1928.

3 It should be pointed out, in fairness to Brecht, that Blom is quoting from the 'Eifersuchtsduett' and that it is sung — as opposed to spoken — dialogue.

4 A new translation of the complete text of this letter is printed here as chapter 6, including a discussion of Weill's idiosyncratic terminology.

11 *L'Opéra de Quat'Sous*

1 Whether this essay was ever published in Benjamin's lifetime has not been established. A copy of the typescript, in German, is held in the Bertolt Brecht Archive, East Berlin (BBA 1503/05-07); the text has recently been published as 'Nachtrag zu den Brecht-Kommentaren' in Walter Benjamin, *Schriften*, Supplementband, 7, ed. Rolf Tiedemann (Frankfurt/Main, 1989), pp. 347—49. Since Benjamin writes of 'the enduring success over the last ten years', and particularly since he refers to the work and its song titles in French, there is every reason to assume that the essay was written in conjunction with the second French production of *L'Opéra de Quat'Sous*, which received its première at the Théatre de l'Étoile on 28 September 1937. The impresario on that occasion was Ernst Josef Aufricht, who (as Benjamin makes a point of mentioning) was the former director of the theatre in which *Die Dreigroschenoper* was first performed, the Theater am Schiffbauerdamm.

2 'Wahlverwandte Veranlagung': Benjamin is no doubt playing on the title of Goethe's novel *Die Wahlverwandschaften* ('Elective Affinities'), published in 1809.

3 The term is Nietzsche's: see *The Case of Wagner*, trans. by Walter Kaufmann (New York, 1967), p. 190: 'In the narrower sphere of so-called moral values one cannot find a greater contrast than that between a *master morality* and the morality of *Christian* value concepts ... master morality ('Roman', 'pagan', 'classical', 'Renaissance') is ... the sign language of what has turned out well, of *ascending* life, of the will to power as the principle of life. Master morality *affirms* as instinctively as Christian morality *negates* ('God', 'beyond', 'self-denial' — all of them negations).'

13 Motifs, tags and related matters

1 The following notes are adapted from the penultimate section of my essay on *The Threepenny Opera*, written in 1965 for my as yet unpublished critical biography of Weill.

2 Kurt Weill, 'Korrespondenz über Dreigroschenoper', *Musikblätter des Anbruch*, 11 (1929), pp. 24—5; reprinted here in translation as chapter 6.

3 Ibid.

4 In G. W. Pabst's film of the *Threepenny Opera*, the chorale is followed
   by a reprise of the 'Moritat', for which Brecht provided three additional
   verses. The symmetry of C major is thereby restored, at the cost of
   diminishing the formal and expressive significance of the chorale.

14 The *Dreigroschen* sound

1 Kurt Weill, 'Fort vom Durchschnitt! Zur Krise der musikalischen
   Interpretation', *Berliner Börsen-Courier*, 20 Aug. 1925; translated by
   Stephen Hinton as 'Say No to Mediocrity! The Crisis of Musical Interpretation', *Kurt Weill Newsletter*, 5:2 (1987), pp. 6–7.
2 Herbert Connor, 'Lewis Ruth, der jazzende Symphoniker', *Skizzen: Il-
   lustierte Monatsschrift für Kunst, Musik, Tanz, Sport, Mode und Haus*,
   4:10 (1931), p. 17.
3 See Horst Lange, *Die Deutsche '78er' Diskographie der Jazz- und Hot-
   Dance Musik 1903–1958* (Berlin, 1978).
4 The question of the placing of the 'Barbarasong' is discussed by Kim
   Kowalke in chapter 4, note 9. See also the same author's article 'In Trivial
   [?] Pursuit: Who sings the "Barbara-Song"?', *Kurt Weill Newsletter*, 6:2
   (1988), pp. 8–11.
5 Nachlass Kate Kühl, Akademie der Künste, West Berlin.
6 Kurt Weill, 'Notiz zum Jazz', *Musikblätter des Anbruch*, 11 (1929), p. 138.
7 'From the musical point of view, I find that extending the "Ballade vom
   angenehmen Leben" to 5 verses must have a monotonous effect (in the
   original the 3 verses were musically varied).' The letter is kept in the
   Weill–Lenya Research Center, New York.
8 *Über Kurt Weill*, ed. D. Drew (Frankfurt, 1975), p. 50; the article was
   originally published as 'Kompositionskritik. Kurt Weill: Kleine
   Dreigroschenmusik für Blasorchester', *Musikblätter des Anbruch*, 11
   (1929), pp. 316–17.
9 Egon Voss, 'Anmerkungen zur Diskographie', in Attila Csampai and
   Dietmar Holland, eds., *Bertolt Brecht/Kurt Weill, Die Dreigroschenoper.
   Igor Strawinsky, The Rake's Progress: Texte, Materialien, Kommentare*
   (Reinbek, 1987), p. 312.
10 *Reclams Opernführer*, ed. G. R. Kruse (Leipzig, 1930), p. 549; Richard
   Kloiber *Handbuch der Oper* (Regensburg, 1951; Munich, 1978), p. 723.
11 See David Drew's remarks on tonal relationships within the work as a
   whole (chapter 13). If such large-scale relationships are to be respected,
   then no transposition whatsoever is permissible. [Ed.]
12 An analysis of the note values of particular pitches in the solos of Polly
   and Mrs Peachum reveals that the pitches that sound for the largest
   proportion (say, at least 10% in any one song) of the total of sung note
   values range, in Polly's case, from $d\#^1$ to d^2 and, in Mrs Peachum's,
   from g^1 to e^2.
13 Michael Danzi, a virtuoso banjo player who worked in Berlin in the
   twenties and thirties, has related his experience of playing in an early
   production of *Aufstieg und Fall der Stadt Mahagonny*: 'Kurt Weill paid
   extra attention to the banjo during the rehearsal but at the end of the
   number he said, 'Bravo, bravo – this is the first time I have heard the

chords played as written: most banjo players have told me that the part was not written for banjo!' (Michael Danzi, *American Musician in Berlin* (Schmitten, 1986), p. 58).

14 From an interview with Norbert Gingold in San Francisco, September 1986.

15 Ole Winding, 'Kurt Weill i Exil', *Aften-Avisen*, 21 June 1934. Weill went on to remark: 'Besides I'm not, as most musicians certainly aren't, especially in favour of "canned music".'

15 Misunderstanding *The Threepenny Opera*

1 Letter of 4 November 1928 in Ernst Bloch, *Briefe 1903–1975*, vol. 2, ed. Karola Bloch *et al.* (Frankfurt, 1985), p. 412.

2 Kurt Weill, 'Die neue Oper', *Der neue Weg*, 55 (1926), p. 24. Writing to his teacher Busoni from Frankfurt, where the first German performance of *L'histoire du soldat* had taken place in June 1923, Weill described the work as 'a kind of "folk play with song and dance", something in between pantomime, melodrama and farce. As far as this kind of theatre permits, it is masterfully structured, and even the glance towards the taste of the man in the street is bearable in the way it fits the subject matter.' (Unpublished letter from Weill to Busoni, dated 21 June 1923; original held in the Deutsche Staatsbibliothek, East Berlin).

3 Arnold Schoenberg, 'New Music, Outmoded Music, Style and Idea', *Style and Idea* (New York, 1950), p. 51.

4 Theodor Wiesengrund-Adorno, 'Zur gesellschaftlichen Lage der Musik', *Zeitschrift für Sozialforschung*, 1 (1932), p. 122. Adorno's formulation is echoed almost exactly in Bloch's essay on *The Threepenny Opera*: 'Weill's is the only music today with any socio-polemical impact.'

5 Ernst Bloch, 'Eislers "Kantaten" in Prag', *Deutsche Volkszeitung*, Prague, 26 December 1937.

6 Hellmut Kotschenreuther, *Kurt Weill* (Berlin, 1962), p. 48.

7 Albrecht Dümling, *Lasst euch nicht verführen: Brecht und die Musik* (Munich, 1985), p. 176.

8 Boris Singerman, 'Zur Ästhetik der Montage', in W. Hecht, ed., *Brechts Dreigroschenoper* (Frankfurt/Main, 1985), p. 226.

9 Cäcilie Tolksdorf, *John Gays 'Beggar's Opera' und Bert Brechts 'Dreigroschenoper'* (Rheinberg, 1934), p. 74.

10 Ibid., p. 47.

11 Ibid., p. 50.

12 Adorno, 'Zur gesellschaftlichen Lage', p. 123.

13 *Zeitschrift für Musik*, 96 (1929), p. 633.

14 Heinrich Strobel, 'Melosberichte', *Melos*, 7 (1928), p. 498.

15 Ibid.

16 Alban Berg, 'Zu Franz Schuberts 100. Todestag', *Schriften zur Musik*, ed. Frank Schneider (Leipzig, 1981), p. 308.

17 See Thomas O. Brandt, 'Brecht und die Bibel', PMLA, 79 (March 1964); Bernhard F. Dukore, 'The averted crucifixion of Macheath', *Drama Survey*, 4:1 (1965), pp. 51–6; Hannelore Brown, *Brecht: Die Bibel in 'Die*

Dreigroschenoper' (Thesis in partial fulfilment of the 'stud. Kand.', Lunds Universität, Våterminen, 1972).

18 Felix Salten, 'Die Dreigroschenoper', *Neue Freie Presse*, 10 March 1929.

19 Letter dated 10 September 1928 from Weill to Universal Edition.

20 Helen Vendler, 'An Intractable Metal', in *Ariel Ascending*, ed. Paul Alexander (New York, 1985), pp. 10f; originally published in *The New Yorker*, 15 February 1982. It is perhaps worth noting that Vendler's article appeared two years after the offbeat West Coast literary journal *The Threepenny Review* was launched. 'Like Brecht with his *Threepenny Opera*', the journal declared in an attempt to attract subscribers, 'we want to produce something that is both demanding and inexpensive − so that our content, and not our price, will determine our audience.'

21 Werner Hecht, *'Die Dreigroschenoper* und ihr Urbild', in *Brechts Dreigroschenoper* (Frankfurt/Main, 1985), pp. 211, 214.

22 The renowned defence lawyer Erich Frey has related how his friend Harald Paulsen modelled his interpretation of Macheath on a well-known gangster who had died in prison and received a full-scale gangster's funeral shortly before the première at the Theater am Schiffbauerdamm. The gangster in question is 'Matrosen-Willy vom Bülowbogen' who, in January 1923, had been found guilty of robbery with manslaughter and sentenced to five years imprisonment. See Erich Frey, 'Strafverteidiger erinnert', *Quick*, Munich, 7 December 1952, pp. 24ff; Erich Frey, *Ich beantrage Freispruch: Aus den Erinnerungen des Strafverteidigers* (Hamburg, 1959).

23 Werner Hecht, for example, writes of Macheath's speech as the 'unequivocal statement about capitalist relations', *Brechts Dreigroschenoper*, p. 215. Jan Knopf cites the same speech in order to demonstrate 'how far' Brecht goes in 'exposing the real bourgeois face', *Brecht-Handbuch*, vol. 1, Theater (Stuttgart, 1980), p. 59.

24 John Willett, 'Brecht's "The Threepenny Opera" at the Adelaide Festival', *Theatre Quarterly*, 7 (1977), p. 110.

25 Alfred Kerr, 'Letztaufführung', *Berliner Tageblatt*, 12 April 1929; reprinted in Alfred Kerr, *Lesebuch zu Leben und Werk*, ed. Hermann Haarmann *et al.* (Berlin, 1987), pp. 136−8. Christian Bernhard Tauchnitz founded a publishing company in Leipzig in 1837 which became renowned for its pocket-size, soft-cover reprints of, among other things, English literary works, particularly Victorian novels. Kerr's description of *Die Dreigroschenoper* as 'an old Tauchnitz' is clearly meant to belittle both the originality and vitality of Brecht's contribution. The Tauchnitz imprint was finally extinguished in 1955.

26 Elias Canetti, *Die Fackel im Ohr: Lebensgeschichte 1921−1931* (Munich, 1980; Frankfurt, 1985), p. 286.

27 Felix Gilbert, *A European Past* (New York, 1988), p. 88.

28 Axel Eggebrecht, 'Wiedersehen mit einer alten Geliebten', *Norddeutsche Hefte*, 1:7 (1946), pp. 16−19.

29 Axel Eggebrecht and Helmut Rumpf, 'Für Drei Groschen Kritik: ein Streitgespräch über Brechts "Dreigroschen-Oper"', *Volk und Zeit*, 3 (January 1948), p. 23

Bibliography

Some of the titles cited in the endnotes are not included again here.

Adorno, Theodor W., 'Nach einem Vierteljahrhundert', Programme booklet of the Städtische Bühnen Düsseldorf, 1956/56, No. 6, pp. 64−67; reprinted in Theodor W. Adorno, *Musikalische Schriften*, 5, *Gesammelte Schriften*, 18, (Frankfurt/Main, 1984), pp. 548−51

See also Wiesengrund-Adorno, Theodor

Alwens, Ludwig, 'Bert Brechts Dreigroschenoper', *Der Vormarsch*, 2:6 (November 1928).

Aufricht, Ernst Josef, *Erzähle, damit du dein Recht erweist* (West Berlin, 1966); section on *Threepenny Opera* excerpted as 'Die Moritat vom Mackie Messer', *Melos*, 33 (1966), pp. 359−63, 'Die Uraufführung von Brechts "Dreigroschenoper" ', *Neue Zürcher Zeitung*, 31 July 1966, and 'Gesindel zur Uraufführung', *Stuttgarter Zeitung*, 13 Aug. 1966, p. 66

Barbon, Paola, *Il signor B.B.: Wege und Umwege der italienischen Brecht-Rezeption*, Literatur und Reflexion Neue Folge, Vol. 5, ed. Beda Allemann, (Bonn, 1987)

Beckley, Richard J., 'Some Aspects of Brecht's Dramatic Technique in the Light of his Adaptation of English Plays' (MA diss., King's College London, 1961)

Benjamin, Walter, 'L'Opéra de Quat'Sous', unpublished MS; published as 'Nachtrag zu den Brecht-Kommentaren' in Walter Benjamin, *Schriften: Supplementband*, 7, ed. Rolf Tiedemann (Frankfurt/Main, 1989), pp. 347−9; reprinted here in translation as chapter 11

Bentley, Eric, 'A Brecht Commentary', in R. Ley *et al.*, eds., *Perspectives and Personalities: Studies in Modern German Literature* (Heidelberg, 1978), pp. 15−27

'Two Hundred Years of Macheath', in *The Threepenny Opera*, trans. D. Vesey and E. Bentley (New York, 1982)

Bloch, Ernst, 'Lied der Seeräuberjenny in der Dreigroschenoper', *Anbruch*, 11:3 (1929), pp. 125−7

'Zur Dreigroschenoper', *Erbschaft dieser Zeit* (Zurich, 1935; Frankfurt/Main, 1962), pp. 230−2; reprinted here in translation as chapter 9

Briefe: 1903−1975, vol. 2, ed. Karola Bloch *et al.* (Frankfurt/Main, 1985).

Blom, Eric, 'Three-groats Opera', *The Sackbut*, 11 (1931), pp. 211−15; reprinted here as chapter 10

Bohaumilitzky, Walter, 'Caspar Nehers Bühnenbild in den 20er Jahren: Sein Frühwerk' (diss., University of Vienna, 1968)

Brandt, Thomas O., 'Brecht und die Bibel', PMLA, 79 (March 1964)
  Die Vieldeutigkeit Bertolt Brechts (Heidelberg, 1968)

Brecht, Bertolt, '[Über] Die Dreigroschenoper', *Gesammelte Werke*, 17 (Frankfurt/Main, 1967), pp. 989–90; reprinted here in translation as chapter 5

Brown, Hannelore, *Brecht: Die Bibel in 'Die Dreigroschenoper'* (Thesis in partial fulfilment of the 'stud. Kand.', Lunds Universität, Våterminen, 1972)

Butting, Max, *Musikgeschichte, die ich miterlebte* (Berlin, 1955)

Cahn, Geoffrey S., 'Weimar Music in America: its Reception and Impact', *Centennial Review*, 29 (1985), pp. 186–204

Canetti, Elias, *Die Fackel im Ohr: Lebensgeschichte 1921–1931* (Munich, 1980; Frankfurt, 1985)

Casparius, Hans, *In my View: A Pictorial Memoir* (Leamington Spa, 1977)

Casparius, ed. Stiftung Deutsche Kinemathek (Berlin, 1978)

Csampai, Attila, and Dietmar Holland, eds., *Bertolt Brecht/Kurt Weill, Die Dreigroschenoper. Igor Strawinsky, The Rake's Progress: Texte, Materialien, Kommentare* (Reinbek, 1987)

Dahlhaus, Carl, *Musikästhetik* (Cologne, 1967)

Danzi, Michael, *American Musician in Berlin* (Schmitten, 1986)

Drew, David, 'Weill and *Die Dreigroschenoper*', liner note to CBS 02L-257
  Kurt Weill: A Handbook (London, 1987)

Dukore, Bernhard F., 'The averted crucifixion of Macheath', *Drama Survey*, 4:1 (1965), pp. 51–6

Dümling, Albrecht, *Lasst euch nicht verführen: Brecht und die Musik* (Munich, 1985)

Ebbutt, A., '*The Threepenny Opera*: a Berlin Burlesque', *The Times*, 25 September 1928; reprinted here as chapter 7

Eggebrecht, Axel, 'Wiedersehen mit einer alten Geliebten', *Norddeutsche Hefte*, 1:7 (1946), pp. 16–19

Eggebrecht, Axel and Helmut Rumpf, 'Für Drei Groschen Kritik: ein Streitgespräch über Brechts "Dreigroschen-Oper"', *Volk und Zeit*, 3 (January 1948), p. 23

Egk, Werner, *Die Zeit wartet nicht* (Percha am Starnberger See, 1973)

Einem, Gottfried von and Siegfried Melchinger, eds., *Bühne und bildende Kunst im XX. Jahrhundert* (Hanover, 1966)

Einstein, Alfred, 'A German version of "The Beggar's Opera"', *The Radio Times*, 1 February 1935

Engberg, Harald, *Brecht auf Fünen: Exil in Dänemark 1933–39*, translated from Danish by Heinz Kulas (Wuppertal, 1974)

Engel, Erich, 'Neuinszenierung', in *Schriften* (Berlin, 1971), pp. 103–5; reprinted in W. Hecht, ed., *Brechts Dreigroschenoper*, pp. 168–70

Epstein, Peter, 'Dreigroschenoper und Beggar's Opera', *Der Auftakt*, 9:1 (1929), pp. 17–20

F. H. [Fritz Hauenstein], 'Mackie Messer als Kapitalist', *Die Gegenwart*, 5:106 (1 May 1950), pp. 9–10

212   Bibliography

Fetting, Hugo, ed., *Von der Freien Bühne zum Politischen Theater: Drama und Theater im Spiegel der Kritik*, vol. 2, 1919–1933 (Leipzig, 1987)

Fiechtner, Helmut A., 'Dreigroschenoper: Dokumente der Zeit', *Musica Schallplatte*, 2:4 (1959), pp. 80–4

Fischer, Heinrich, 'Die Geburt der Dreigroschenoper über Premiere', *Südwest-Merkur*, Stuttgart, 9 May 1958; reprinted in Kurt Fassmann, *Brecht: eine Bildbiographie* (Munich, 1958)

Fischetti, Renate, 'Gestaltung der Dreigroschenoper in Stück, Roman und Film' (PhD diss., Maryland, 1971)

'Über die Grenzen der List oder Der gescheiterte Dreigroschenfilm: Anmerkungen zu Brechts Exposé "Die Beule"', *Brecht-Jahrbuch* (1976), pp. 43–60

'A Feminist Reading of Brecht's Pirate Jenny', *Communications for the International Brecht Society*, 14 (1985), pp. 29–33

Fleischer, Herbert, 'Romantische und aktuelle Oper: Zur Ideologie der Oper', *Der Scheinwerfer*, 5:18/19 (1932), pp. 9–11

Frey, Daniel, 'Les ballades de François Villon et le Dreigroschenoper', *Etudes des Lettres*, 4 (1961), pp. 114–36

Frey, Erich, 'Strafverteidiger erinnert', *Quick*, Munich, 7 December 1952, pp. 24ff.

Ich beantrage Freispruch: Aus den Erinnerungen des Strafverteidigers (Hamburg, 1959)

Fuegi, John, *Bertolt Brecht: Chaos, According to Plan* (Cambridge, 1987)

Gilbert, Michael John Tyler, 'Bertolt Brecht and Music: A Comprehensive Study' (diss., University of Wisconsin, 1985)

Giles, Steve, 'From Althusser to Brecht: Formalism, Materialism and *The Threepenny Opera*', in: R. Sheppard (ed.), *New Ways in Germanistik* (Berg, 1989), pp. 1–25

'Rewriting Brecht: *Die Dreigroschenoper* 1928–31', *Literaturwissenschaftliches Jahrbuch 1989* (Berlin, 1989), pp. 249–79

Grimm, Reinhold, 'Werk und Wirkung des Übersetzers Karl Klammer', *Neophilogus*, 44 (1960), pp. 20–36

Haas, Willy, 'Was tat sich damals', *Die Welt*, Berlin, 26 January 1957
Bert Brecht, Köpfe des XX. Jahrhunderts, vol. 7 (Berlin, 1958)
Die literarische Welt. Erinnerungen (Munich, 1960)
Zeitgemässes aus der Literarischen Welt (Stuttgart, 1963)

Hadamowsky, Franz, *Caspar Nehers szenisches Werk: Ein Verzeichnis des Bestandes der Theatersammlung der österreichischen Nationalbibliothek* (Vienna, 1972)

Hahnloser-Ingold, Margrit, *Das englische Theater und Bert Brecht: Die Dramen von W. H. Auden, John Osborne, John Arden in ihrer Beziehung zum epischen Theater von Bert Brecht und den gemeinsamen elisabethanischen Quellen*, Schweizer anglistische Arbeiten, vol. 61 (Bern, 1970)

Harper, Anthony J., 'Brecht and Villon: Further Thoughts on some *Dreigroschenoper* songs', *Forum of Modern Language Studies*, 1 (1965), pp. 191–4

Härtling, Peter, *Felix Guttmann* (Darmstadt, 1985)

Hecht, Werner, '*Die Dreigroschenoper* und ihr Urbild', in *Brechts Drei-groschenoper*, pp. 201–24

ed., *Brechts Dreigroschenoper* (Frankfurt/Main, 1985)

Heinsheimer, Hans W., *Menagerie in F#* (New Jersey, 1947)

Best Regards to Aida (New York, 1968)

Hennenberg, Fritz, 'Weill, Brecht und die "Dreigroschenoper": Neue Materialien zur Entstehung und Uraufführung', *Österreichische Musikzeitschrift*, 40 (1985), pp. 281–91

ed., *Brecht-Liederbuch* (Frankfurt/Main, 1985)

'Studien zu Brechts Dreigroschenoper', in Bertolt Brecht, *Die Drei-groschenoper* (Leipzig, 1986), pp. 107–26

Hilliker, Rebecca, 'Brecht's *Gestic* Vision for Opera: Why the Shock of Recognition is more Powerful in *The Rise and Fall of the City of Mahagonny* than in *The Threepenny Opera*', *Text and Presentation*, Comparative Drama Conference Papers, 8 ed. K. Hartigan (Florida, 1988)

Hinton, Stephen, 'The Concept of Epic Opera: Theoretical Anomalies in the Brecht–Weill Partnership', *Festschrift Carl Dahlhaus* (Laaber, 1988), pp. 285–94

Hoffmann, Heinz, 'Gastspiel des Meininger Theaters', *Theater der Zeit*, 14:1 (January 1959), pp. 49–51

Hollaender, Felix, *Lebendiges Theater* (Berlin, 1932)

Hüfner, Agnes, *Brecht in Frankreich: 1930–1963. Verbreitung, Aufnahme, Wirkung*, Germanistische Abhandlungen, 22 (Stuttgart, 1968)

Hunt, Joel, 'Bert Brecht's "Dreigroschenoper" and Villon's "Testament"', *Monatshefte*, 49:5 (1957), pp. 273–8

Jackson, Felix, *Portrait of a Quiet Man: Kurt Weill, His life and times* (unpublished MS)

Jacobs, Nicholas, and Prudence Ohlsen, *Bertolt Brecht in Britain* (London, 1977)

Jarman, Douglas, *Kurt Weill: An Illustrated Biography* (Bloomington, 1982)

Jensen, Walter, 'Die Dreigroschenoper in Amerika, Frankreich und Deutsch-land', *Ford-Revue*, Munich, 6:2 (1955), pp. 15–17

Jhering, Herbert, 'Bemerkungen zu Theater und Film', *Sinn und Form*, 10 (1958), pp. 946–8

Theater in Aktion: Kritiken aus drei Jahrzehnten (Berlin, 1987)

Karsch, Walter, *Was war – was blieb: Berliner Theater 1945–46* (Berlin, 1947)

Kaulla, Guido von, *'Und verbrennen in seinem Herzen': Die Schauspielerin Carola Neher und Klabund* (Freiburg, 1984)

Keller, Hans, 'The Threepenny Opera', *Music Review*, 17 (1956), pp. 153–4; reprinted here as chapter 12

Kerr, Alfred, *Lesebuch zu Leben und Werk*, ed. Hermann Haarmann *et al.* (Berlin, 1987)

Kessler, Harry, *Tagebücher 1918–37*, ed. Wolfgang Pfeiffer-Belli (Frankfurt/ Main, 1961)

Kievitt, Frank David, 'Three Times Three Penny: Brecht's Adaptations of The Beggar's Opera', *Mid-Hudson Language Studies*, 7 (1984), pp. 57–63

Kipling, Rudyard, *Rudyard Kipling's Verse: Definitive Edition* (London, n.d.)

Knopf, Jan, *Brecht-Handbuch*, vol. 1: Theater (Stuttgart, 1980)

Kocks, Klaus, *Brechts Literarische Evolution: Untersuchungen zum ästhetisch-ideologischen Bruch in den Dreigroschen-Bearbeitungen* (Munich, 1981)

Kotschenreuther, Hellmut, *Kurt Weill* (Berlin, 1962)

Kowalke, Kim H., *Kurt Weill in Europe*, Studies in Musicology, 14 (Ann Arbor, 1979)

   ed., *A New Orpheus: Essays on Kurt Weill* (New Haven, 1986)

   'In Trivial [?] Pursuit: Who sings the "Barbarasong"?', *Kurt Weill Newsletter*, 6:2 (1988), pp. 8–11

   'Accounting for Success: Misunderstanding *Die Dreigroschenoper*', *The Opera Quarterly*, 6:3 (1989), pp. 18–38

Kracauer, Siegfried, *From Caligari to Hitler: A Psychological History of the German Film* (London, 1947)

Kraus, Karl, 'Kerrs Enthüllung', *Die Fackel*, 31 (1929), pp. 129–32; reprinted in K. Kraus, *Widerschein der Fackel: Glossen*, *Werke*, ed. Heinrich Fischer, vol. 4 (Munich, 1956), pp. 404–8

Kreilisheim, Eva, *Bertolt Brecht und die Sowjetunion* (diss., University of Vienna, 1969)

Kunert, H., 'Zur Rolle der Songs im Werk von Bertolt Brecht', *Neue deutsche Literatur*, 11 (1963)

Kussmaul, Paul, *Bertolt Brecht und das englische Drama der Renaissance*, Britische und Irische Studien zur deutschen Sprache und Literatur, 2 (Bern, 1974)

Lambert, Constant, *Music Ho! A Study of Music in Decline* (London, 1934)

Lazzari, Arturo, 'Mailänder Inszenierung', *Geist und Zeit: Zweimonatsschrift für Kunst, Literatur und Wissenschaft*, 4 (1957), pp. 39–47

Lenya, Lotte, 'That was a Time!', *Theatre Arts* (May 1956); reprinted as 'August 28, 1928', in *The Threepenny Opera*, trans. Eric Bentley and Desmond Vesey (New York, 1964), pp. v–xiv

Lestiboudis, Herbert, 'Rund um die "Dreigroschenoper"', *Die Gefährten: Monatsschrift für Erkenntnis und Tat*, Lauf/Pegnitz, 11 (March 1947), pp. 92–5

Leuth, Dr, 'Das Vorbild der 3GO', *Sänger-Zeitung*, Chicago, 15:7 (1939), pp. 70–1

Lingen, Theo, *Ich über mich*, Reihe Theater heute, 9 (Velber, 1963)

Linzer, Martin, 'Rostock 1959', *Theater der Zeit*, Berlin, GDR, 14:8 (1959), pp. 51–6

   'Berliner Ensemble 1960', *Theater der Zeit*, 15:6 (1960), pp. 61–5

Lucchesi, Joachim and Ronald K. Shull, *Musik bei Brecht* (Berlin, GDR, 1988)

Lyon, James K., 'Brecht's use of Kipling's Intellectual Property: A new Source of Borrowing', *Monatshefte für den Unterricht*, 61:4 (1969), pp. 376–86

   Bertolt Brecht and Rudyard Kipling (The Hague, 1975)

Melchior, Meik, 'Fernsehinszenierung', *Der Spiegel*, 11, 6 March 1957, p. 54

Mettler, Heinrich, '3GO – Tendenz und Wirkung', *Neue Zürcher Zeitung*, 21 January 1973

Meyer, William Gustav, 'Zur Chemnitzer Uraufführung', *Kunst und Kritik*, 5 (1929), pp. 33–5

Mittenzwei, Werner, *Das Leben des Bertolt Brecht oder Der Umgang mit den Welträtseln*, 2 vols (Berlin, GDR, 1986)

Morley, Michael, *Brecht: A Study* (London, 1977)

Müller, André, 'War das noch Brecht?', *Theater der Zeit*, 12:3 (1957), pp. 53–4

' "Neues vom Tage": Theaterbrief aus Westdeutschland (V)', *Theater der Zeit*, 16:11 (1961), pp. 57–8

'Oberhausen', *Theater der Zeit*, 23:4 (1968), pp. 20–1

Müller, Klaus-Detlef, *Brecht-Kommentar zur erzählenden Prosa* (Munich, 1980)

Bertolt Brecht: Epoche – Werk – Wirkung (Munich, 1985)

Müller, Volker, 'Bukarest', *Theater der Zeit*, 20:4 (1965), pp. 31–2

Natan, Alex, 'The 'Twenties and Berlin', in R.W. Last, ed., *Affinities: Essays in German and English Literature* (London, 1971)

Niessen, Carl, *Brecht auf der Bühne* (Cologne, 1959)

Otto, Teo, 'Die Arbeit mit Georgio Strehler', *Neue Zürcher Zeitung*, 53: 2138, 26 May 1963; reprinted in *Brechts Dreigroschenoper*, ed. W. Hecht (Frankfurt/Main, 1985), pp. 149–54

Meine Szene (Cologne, 1965)

Palm, Kurt, *Vom Boykott zur Anerkennung: Brecht und Österreich* (Vienna, 1983)

Pastorello, Félicie, 'De l'utilité des concepts empruntés à la linguistique pour l'étude d'une métamorphose de texte à travers une traduction', in E. Kushner and R. Struc, eds., *La Littérature comparée aujourd'hui: théorie et pratique*, Actes du VIIe congrès de l'Association Internationale de Littérature Comparée, 2 (Stuttgart, 1979), pp. 375–9

Petersen, Klaus-Dietrich, *Bertolt Brecht: Leben und Werk* (Dortmund, 1966)

Prag–Berlin: Bulletin der Botschaft der Tschechoslowakischen Republik, 12 (December 1956), pp. 13–14

Ramthun, Herta, 'Die "unterdrückte Arie" der Lucy. Ein wenig bekannter Text aus Brechts "Ludenoper" ', *Notate*, 4 (1985), p. 9

Richter, Hans, *Köpfe und Hitzköpfe* (Zurich, 1967)

Rischbieter, Henning, 'Frankfurt', *Stuttgarter Zeitung*, 89, 17 April 1965

'Halle', *Theater heute*, 7:1 (1966), pp. 12–16

Ruf, Wolfgang, *Modernes Musiktheater: Studien zu seiner Geschichte und Typologie* (unpublished Habilitationsschrift, University of Freiburg, 1983)

Salmon, Richard J., 'Two Operas for Beggars: A Political Reading', *Theoria*, 57 (1981), pp. 63–81

Sanders, Ronald, *The Days Grow Short: The Life and Music of Kurt Weill* (London, 1980)

Schebera, Jürgen, *Kurt Weill: Leben und Werk* (Leipzig, 1983)

Schiller, Leon, 'Kampf um "Die Dreigroschenoper" ', *Theaterdienst* (Berlin, GDR), 9:19 (1954), pp. 6–7

Schumacher, Ernst, *Die dramatischen Versuche Bertolt Brechts 1918–33*, Neue Beiträge zur Literaturwissenschaft, 3 (Berlin, GDR, 1954)

Seidel, Gerhard, *Bibliographie Bertolt Brecht* (Berlin, GDR, 1975)

216   *Bibliography*

Seyfarth, Ingrid, 'Karl-Marx-Stadt', *Theater der Zeit*, 21:14 (1966), pp. 31–37
Speirs, Ronald, 'A Note on the First Published Version of *Die Dreigroschenoper* and its relation to the Standard Text', *Forum for Modern Language Studies*, 13 (1977), pp. 25–32
Strehler, Giorgio, *Per un teatro umano* (Milan, 1974)
Strobel Heinrich, 'Melosberichte', *Melos*, 7 (1928), p. 498
  'Mackie Messer in Milano', *Melos*, 26 (January 1959), p. 25
Stuckenschmidt, Hans Heinz, 'Choräle aus dem Schlamm', *Uhu*, 9 (1930), pp. 45–48
Tana, G., 'London', *Theater der Zeit*, 11:4 (1956), pp. 30–2
Taylor, Ronald, 'Opera in Berlin in the 1920s: *Wozzeck* and *The Threepenny Opera*', in Keith Bullivant, ed., *Culture and Society in the Weimar Republic* (Manchester, 1977), pp. 183–9
Tolksdorf, Cäcilie, *John Gays 'Beggar's Opera' und Bert Brechts 'Dreigroschenoper'* (Rheinberg, 1934)
Unseld, Siegfried, ed., *Bertolt Brechts Dreigroschenbuch* (Frankfurt/Main, 1960; 1978)
Victor, Walter, *Freund und Feind: Kritiken aus fünf Jahrzehnten* (Berlin, GDR, 1980)
Völker, Klaus, *Brecht-Kommentar: Zum Dramatischen Werk* (Munich, 1983)
Wagner, Gottfried, *Weill und Brecht: Das musikalische Zeittheater* (Munich, 1977)
Weill, Kurt, 'Korrespondenz über Dreigroschenoper', *Musikblätter des Anbruch*, 11 (1929), pp. 24–5; reprinted here in translation as chapter 6
'Kurt Weill, der Komponist der *Dreigroschenoper*, will den Begriff des Musikdramas zerstören', interview with Kurt Weill, *Wiener Allgemeine Zeitung*, 9 March 1929
Weisenborn, Günther, *Der gespaltene Horizont: Niederschriften eines Aussenseiters* (Munich, 1964)
Weiskopf, F. C., 'Prag', *Neue Deutsche Blätter*, 2:3 (1935), pp. 189–90
Weisstein, Ulrich, 'Brecht's Victorian Version of Gay: Imitation and Originality in the *Dreigroschenoper*', *Comparative Literature Studies*, 7 (1970), pp. 314–35
'Von reitenden Boten und singenden Holzfällern: Bertolt Brecht und die Oper', *Brechts Dramen: neue Interpretationen*, ed. Walter Hinderer (Stuttgart, 1984), pp. 266–99
Werner, Hebert, *Die Stimme der Gemeinde: Monatsschrift der Bekennenden Kirche*, Stuttgart, 1:1 (1949), pp. 14–15
Werner, Jürgen, '"Sehr nett, Polly"', *Sprachpflege: Zeitschrift für gutes Deutsch*, 13:2 (1964), pp. 37–8
Wiegler, Paul, 'Die Dreigroschenoper: Einst und Jetzt', *Musik für alle*, 274 (Berlin, 1929)
Wiesengrund-Adorno, Theodor, 'Zur Dreigroschenoper', *Die Musik*, 22 (1929), pp. 424–8; reprinted here in translation as chapter 8
'Kompositionskritik. Kurt Weill: Kleine Dreigroschenmusik für Blasorchester', *Musikblätter des Anbruch*, 11 (1929), pp. 316–17
Willett, John, *The Theatre of Bertolt Brecht* (London, 1959; 1967)

'Brecht's "The Threepenny Opera" at the Adelaide Festival', *Theatre Quarterly*, 7 (1977), pp. 101–10

Caspar Neher· Brecht's Designer (London, 1986)

Wuthrich, Werner, *Bertolt Brechts Aufnahme in der Schweiz 1923–69* (diss., University of Vienna, 1974)

Wyss, Monika, *Brecht in der Kritik: Rezensionen aller Brecht-Uraufführungen* (Munich, 1977)

Yuill, William Edward, *The Art of Vandalism: Bertolt Brecht and the English Drama* (Inaugural lecture, Bedford College London, 1977)

Zimmermann, Sara, 'The Influence of John Gay, François Villon and Rudyard Kipling on the Songs in Bertolt Brecht's *Dreigroschenoper*' (MA Thesis, Indiana University, 1968)

Discography

STEPHEN HINTON

The following discography is far from complete. It makes no mention, for example, of the countless versions of 'Mac the Knife' recorded by dance bands, jazz crooners and, of late, rock stars.

Section I lists early recordings of vocal excerpts. Of the numerous instrumental arrangements and potpourris, only those relevant to Geoffrey Abbott's chapter on the '*Dreigroschen* sound' are named. An exhaustive catalogue of shellac records, including instrumental arrangements, has been published by Bernd Meyer-Rähnitz in 'Drei Groschen und mehr: Werke von Brecht–Weill auf 78er-Schallplatten', *Fox auf 78*, Autumn 1987, pp. 44–50 and Spring 1988, pp. 24–8. Some recently discovered 78s in Danish, Czech and Hebrew are cited by Jürgen Schebera in 'Neue Entdeckungen auf Schellack', *Notate*, 11:3 (1988), p. 24

Section II lists all 'complete' recordings. Brief but generally judicious comments (by Rodney Milnes) on several of the recordings listed in both sections can be found in *Opera on Record*, ed. Alan Blyth (London, 1984), pp. 329–33.

I Early recordings (Rec. = recorded; Rel. = released; matrix numbers are given in parentheses)

Rec. Nov. 1928
Rel. Jan. 1929
  [instrumental arrangements] 'Kanonensong' (Be 7669) and 'Zuhälterballade' (Be 7674) / Theo Mackeben and the Lewis Ruth Band

                  Odeon 0-2703

Rec. May 1929
Rel. Summer '29
  'Moritat' (A 8473) and 'Ballade von der Unzulänglichkeit' (A 8474) / Bertolt Brecht with orchestra

                  Orchestrola 2131

Rec. May 1929
Rel. Summer '29
  'Barbarasong' (A 8476) and 'Seeräuberjenny' (A 8475) Carola Neher with orchestra

                  Orchestrola 2132

Rec. May 1929
Rel. July 1929
  'Die Songs der Dreigroschenoper': I 'Seeräuberjenny'; II 'Kanonensong'; III 'Liebeslied' (CN 472); IV 'Barbarasong'; V 'Zuhälterballade' [instr.]; VI 'Ballade vom angenehmen Leben'; VII 'Lied von der Unzulänglichkeit'; VIII 'Moritat' (CN 473) / Carola Neher (I, III, IV, VII),

218

Kurt Gerron (II, VI, VIII), Arthur Schröder (III) and the Dreigroschenband

Electrola EH 301

Rec. Aug. 1930 I 'Moritat' (62879) and 'Kanonensong' (62880); II '2.
Rel. Oct. 1930   Finale' (62881) and 'Ballade vom angenehmen Leben' (62882) / Harald Paulsen with Orchestra

Homocord 4-3747 (I)
Homocord 4-3748 (II)

Rec. [?] 1930 'Barbarasong' and 'Seeräuberjenny' / Fritzi Massary, [Theo Mackeben and the Lewis Ruth Band]

Reichsrundfunk-Decelith-Folie C362

Rec. Nov. 1930 I 'Ballade du Tango' (15835) and 'Chant d'amour' (15836)
Rel. Jan. 1931   II 'Ballade de la vie agréable' (15837) and 'Chant des canons' (15838) / [French film cast] Albert Préjean (I, II); Margo Lion (I); Jacques Henley (II); Theo Mackeben and the Lewis Ruth Band

Ultraphon A 717–718

Rec. Dec. 1930 I 'Ouvertüre', 'Moritat' and 'Ballade vom angenehmen
Rel. Jan. 1931   Leben' (15907); II 'Liebeslied (15904); III 'Seeräuber-jenny' (15906); IV '1. Finale' (15908); V 'Barbarasong' and 'Eifersuchtsduett' (15909) VI 'Abschied' and '2. Finale' (15902); VII 'Zuhälterballade' and 'Lied von der Unzulänglichkeit' (15905); VIII 'Moritat' and 'Schluss-choral' (15903) / Gerron (I); Trenk-Trebitsch (I, II, VI, VII); Lenja (III, IV, V, VII, VIII), Helmke (II, IV, V, VI), Ponto (IV, VII)

Telefunken A 752–755
[later re-released as Capitol P-8117 and Telefunken LGM-65028]

II 'Complete' recordings

Streetsinger *S*; Peachum *P*; Mrs Peachum *Mrs P*; Macheath *M*; Polly *Py*; Tiger Brown *TB*; Jenny *J*; Lucy *L*

1954   [Blitzstein version] Price *S*; Wolfson *P*; Rae *Mrs P*; Merrill *M*; Sullivan *Py*; Tyne *TB*; Lenya *J*; Arthur *L* / Theatre de Lys Chorus and Orch., New York / Matlowsky

MGM E3121

1955   Rosvaenge *S*; Jerger *P*; Anday *Mrs P*; Preger *M*; Augustin Py; Guthrie *TB*; Fassler *J*; Felbermayer *L* / Chorus and Chamber Orch. of the Vienna State Opera / Adler

Vanguard VRS-9002

1958   Neuss *S*; Trenk-Trebitsch *P*; Hesterberg *Mrs P*; Schellow *M*; von Koczian *Py*; Gruner *TB*; Lenya *J*; Wolffberg *L* / Günther Arndt Choir – Sender Freies Berlin Orch. / Brückner–Rüggeberg

Columbia 02L-257

1965   Kutschera *P*; Mey *Mrs P*; Korte *M*; Huebner *Py*; Hoermann *TB*;
         Teichmann *J*; Dirichs *L* / Frankfurt Opera Chorus and Orch. /
         Rennert

                                                   Fontana 700 180–1

1968   [re-scored version] Degenhardt *S*; Qualtinger *P*; Drews *Mrs P*;
         Messemer *M*; Baal *Py*; Held *TB*; Wieder *J*; Anders *L* / Last

                                                   Polydor 109 531-3

1970   [French translation by Jean-Claude Hémery] Médine *P*; Thiéry *Mrs
         P*; Barrier *M*; Mestrel *Py*; Santini *TB*; Téphany *J*; Lods *L* / Theatre
         de L'est Parisien Chorus and Orch. / d'Andréa

                                                   Canetti 48838

1976   Brocksmith *S*; Alexander *P*; Wilson *Mrs P*; Julia *M*; Kava *Py*; Sabin
         TB; Greene *J*; Brown *L* / 1976 New York Shakespeare Festival
         Production /Silvermann

                                                   Columbia PS 34326

Index